Coping with the Economic Crisis

In memory of
Ezio Tarantelli

Coping with the Economic Crisis

Alternative Responses to Economic Recession in Advanced Industrial Societies

Edited by
Hans Keman
Heikki Paloheimo
Paul F. Whiteley

Ⓢ SAGE Modern Politics Series Volume 17
Sponsored by the European Consortium for
Political Research/ECPR

Ⓢ SAGE Publications
London • Newbury Park • Beverly Hills • New Delhi

First published 1987

SAGE Publications Ltd
28 Banner Street
London EC1Y 8QE

SAGE Publications Inc
275 South Beverly Drive
Beverly Hills, California 90212

SAGE Publications India Pvt Ltd
C-236 Defence Colony
New Delhi 110 024

SAGE Publications Inc
2111 West Hillcrest Street
Newbury Park, California 91320

British Library Cataloguing in Publication Data
Coping with the economic crisis: alternative
  responses to economic recession in advanced
  industrial societies. — (Sage studies in
  modern politics; 17).
  1. Capitalism — Political aspects
  2. Economic history — 1945-
  I. Keman, Hans   II. Paloheimo, Heikki
  III. Whiteley, Paul F.
  330.9   HB501
  ISBN 0-8039-8118-X
  ISBN 0-8039-8119-8 Pbk

Library of Congress catalog card number 87-062062

Typeset by System 4 Associates, Gerrards Cross, Buckinghamshire
Printed in Great Britain by
J. W. Arrowsmith Ltd, Bristol

Contents

Preface

The contributions to this volume in the ECPR/SAGE Modern Politics Series grew out of a workshop held at the Joint Sessions of the European Consortium of Political Research in Barcelona, Easter 1985. The success of this workshop on 'Styles of Economic Policy-making and Ways out of the Economic Crisis' induced the convenors, Hans Keman and Heikki Paloheimo, together with Paul Whiteley, to publish a number of the papers which were presented.

The motivation behind this book is to try to understand the growing and continuing economic crisis which has overtaken advanced capitalist democracies since the mid-1970s. The main features of this crisis are now well known and consist of decreasing rates of economic growth, increasing inflation and unemployment and slower rates of technological innovation and investment. This has led, amongst other things, to a fiscal crisis in many countries and a changing pattern of economic interdependence. Finally, it appears that this economic crisis increasingly affects the role of the state particularly in the area of social welfare.

This continuing and aggravating situation gives rise to many questions, but the main focus of the book will be on two of these questions. The first is the problem of understanding the magnitude, the causes and the consequences of the crisis. The second concerns governmental responses to the crisis in different industrial countries. These questions break down into a number of subsidiary questions about the options available to governments and the existing constraints on policy-making. In the first part of the book we shall present the state of affairs concerning the available answers to these questions.

In Part II we shall pay attention to the extent to which the weak relationship between policy outputs and economic outcomes is an inherent feature of capitalist societies; and the extent to which the recession is a product of the failure of economic strategies by governments. One of the main factors here are the institutional structures which exist to mediate distributive conflicts in advanced capitalist societies. It has been argued that countries that have developed a strong institutionalized system of concertation between trade unions, employers and the government can cope with shocks to their economies more effectively than countries which lack such institutions. Part of this question concerns also the degree to which the crisis exhibits common features in different countries, and the extent to which performance is worse in some countries than in others, and the factors that explain them. Roland Czada and Franz Lehner will appreciate the process of institutionalization discussing the approaches of

Olson and Katzenstein and assess it by looking at the European experiences. Gøsta Esping-Andersen and Klaus Armingeon expand on these arguments and analyse in more detail the institutional arrangements to enhance policy processes and the consequences of corporatist strategies.

In Part III of the book the responses of governments and related consequences will be focused upon. This is perhaps the most important question of all, and has a number of different aspects. Firstly, there are the economic environments in which countries operate and the extent to which they are integrated into the international economy. Secondly, there are the political and ideological aspects of policy strategies. Different governments have different theoretical ideas about how the economy works and how it can be managed. Finally, there are the outcomes of different economic strategies in terms of public expenditures and societal results. Different strategies produce different outcomes which limit or expand the room to manoeuvre of governments to meet their other political objectives, such as the provision of social welfare. This latter question has explicitly been taken up by Keman and Van Dijk, whereas Andersson and Whiteley focus extensively on the ideas behind the extant economic strategies as well as on their expected effects and actual outcomes. In the final chapter Keman and Whiteley evaluate the answers given in the various chapters to the main questions raised here. We shall indicate what remained unanswered and in what direction further research is necessary. All of the chapters in this book seek to throw light on these matters by making explicit cross-national and inter-temporal comparisons between capitalist democracies.

The fact that this book could be realized is only partly due to the efforts of the editors and owes a lot to a number of other people. Thanks are due first to the participants of the workshop, both those whose papers were included in this volume and those whose papers were not: many of the chapters included in this book have benefited from the comments of those not included. Thanks are due also to the ECPR and its publication committee, in particular Ken Newton and Michael Laver, which sponsored the workshop and encouraged us to follow up with a book. We are also grateful to the positive response of SAGE Publications, particularly David Hill. His assistance surely helped to finish this project. Final thanks are due to the secretarial staff of the various institutes where the editors hold positions or were visiting (i.e. European University Institute in Florence and Virginia Polytechnic and State University in Blacksburg, USA). The secretariat in Leiden carried a particular burden keeping track of the various papers so that a manuscript could be pulled together.

This book is dedicated to the Italian political economist, Luigi Tarantelli, who was assassinated in Rome by the Brigate Rosse during the week that our workshop was held. He had done what we — and all political economists and political scientists for that matter — should do: contribute to the diagnosis of the present economic crisis and try to develop strategies to overcome the crisis. We sincerely hope, therefore, that this volume will mean an advance in this direction and a step forward in developing feasible, alternative responses to economic recession in advanced industrial society.

Hans Keman
Heikki Paloheimo
Paul F. Whiteley
December 1986

I

INTRODUCTION

1

Explanations of the economic crisis and divergent policy responses: an overview

Heikki Paloheimo

After the 1973 oil shock, developed capitalist countries faced severe economic problems. Economic growth declined, terms of trade worsened, and in most countries there were problems of profitability, unemployment and inflation, as well as problems in the balance of payments. When the discipline of the Bretton Woods system collapsed, rates of inflation diverged cross-nationally; rates of unemployment diverged in the same way. In the late 1970s and early 1980s, rates of inflation began to converge again, but levels of unemployment continued to diverge.

The rise of oil prices is not, however, a sufficient explanation of the depth or the longevity of the economic slowdown. In most developed countries, profits and rates of growth of productivity were already falling in the late 1960s. At the same time, rates of inflation and unemployment were slowly increasing. In other words, there were some tendencies towards economic crisis even before the oil shock.

What are the reasons for the contemporary economic slowdown? There are both national and international dimensions that should be taken into account.

1. National dimensions of the economic slowdown

Discussion on the national dimensions of the economic slowdown has mainly focused on the role of wage pressure, and on the expansion of the public sector and the influence of interest groups on the making of economic policy.

In the early 1950s there were unemployed labour reserves in both agriculture and industry, and in some countries net immigration further increased the supply of labour. However, as time went on high economic growth raised industrial employment and reduced the labour reserves in the agriculture sectors of most developed capitalist economies. In this situation the bargaining power of labour became stronger. Wage increases began to surpass productivity increases, and a larger proportion of national income was distributed as wages (Bernabè, 1982; Boltho, 1982).

There are two contrasting views of the way in which an increasing wage share affects economic performance. According to the demand side hypothesis, a large wage share has a positive effect on economic growth. This way of thinking is typically Keynesian; a large wage share is linked to a high aggregate demand, which in turn is linked to high economic growth. This analysis was integral to the prevailing economic doctrine during the golden age of economic growth, especially in the 1960s.

According to the supply side hypothesis a larger wage share in excess of the growth of productivity leaves less room for profits and investment. As a result economic growth declines and unemployment rises. The supply side hypothesis has been intrinsic to contemporary neo-classical economic thought. In recent years the hypothesis has become more widely accepted both in economic theory and in economic policy (Dahmen, 1982 and 1984).

In the following chapters Klaus Armingeon and Gøsta Esping-Andersen will analyse the determinants as well as the economic consequences of wage formation.

Opinions on the role of the public sector have clearly diverged during the last decade. The active role of the Keynesian welfare state was often justified by the theory of market failures. According to this theory there were many instances where the market system did not produce the best possible economic outcome. Therefore, intervention by the government was needed. This intervention took the form of the production of goods — i.e. public goods, merit goods or market goods, and also the form of regulation and redistribution.

However, the implementation of the economic policy interventions may in turn give rise to policy failures. Policy goals may be too ambiguous or policy instruments too unreliable. In the 1970s, policy failures became more salient and many conservatives in particular wanted to give more room to market forces.

The growth of the public sector has always divided opinions in politics, but in the 1970s this cleavage became even stronger. According to basic macroeconomic theory, an increase in taxes can constrain economic growth, whereas an increase in public expenditure can support it, but there is no agreement on the total effects of taxes and expenditures on economic development. In this case, too, we may contrast a demand side hypothesis with the supply side hypothesis.

The demand side hypothesis is based on Keynesian thinking, according to which a balanced growth in public revenues and expenditures is conducive to economic growth. In this view the growth of the public sector increases aggregate demand and this in turn stimulates further economic growth (Johansen, 1971: 34).

The supply side hypothesis is part of the neo-classical critique of the welfare state, based on arguments similar to those advanced in criticism of a larger wage share. As a result of growth in the public sector, the relative contribution of the private sector to the national income declines. Because the wage share has also been rising, profits are undermined. The effect of low profitability is to reduce investments, and bring lower economic growth and rising unemployment (Paloheimo, 1984; OECD, 1985).

Again we have two competing hypotheses. In the golden age of economic growth, studies of fiscal policy in the OECD-countries usually supported the demand side hypothesis (see e.g. Maddison, 1980), but since the passing of the golden age the picture has been more confused. One fact, however, is clear: in the 1970s there was a sharp rise in public expenditure, partly as an automatic consequence of the recession following the oil shock, and partly as a result of a deliberate policy response to the crisis. It is therefore probable that the crowding-out effect of rising public expenditure (OECD, 1985: 189–202) became stronger in this period.

Public administration is often criticized because of its supposed inefficiency. There are many kinds of justification for this: government departments generally have monopoly in their special area of expertise; there is no competition and incentives for efficiency are thus lacking; public goods and merit goods are not sold in the market, and possibilities for measuring efficiency are poorer than in a competitive market system.

Many conservative governments have tried to increase economic efficiency by the privatization of governmental activities. In this area, the Thatcher government has taken the lead (Yarrow, 1986), but almost half of the OECD-countries have privatized some of the activities of the public sector. The easiest form of privatization is to introduce competition between the public and private sectors in the production of welfare services, which seems to be popular even in the social democratic states. In the following chapters Esping-Andersen, Franz Lehner, Hans Keman and Tibert van Dijk will analyse the determinants of the growing public sector as well as its consequences.

The growth of interest organizations is a natural byproduct of capitalist market economies, at least under conditions of stable political democracy. The growth of interest organizations, in its turn, has an effect on the functioning of the market system. It is also possible that the power of interest organizations will become incompatible with the requirements of capitalist production.

In traditional competitive capitalism both wages and prices used to be elastic in demand i.e. responsive to market conditions. With the growth of interest organizations this situation has changed. In organized markets both wages and prices have become rigid downwards (Okun, 1981; Casson, 1981; Olson, 1982). In competitive capitalism, firms arrange their prices according to demand in the market, but in corporate capitalism, firms fix their prices and adjust the quantity sold according to market demand. In the same way, employees in corporate capitalism fix the price of work by collective wage agreements. The amount of labour sold is then adjusted according to the demand in the labour market. Where there is decreasing demand, competitive capitalism adjusts to the situation by lowering prices and reducing wages. In corporate capitalism, a different adjustment is made: firms sell smaller quantities of goods at fixed prices, and buy a smaller amount of labour at fixed wages.

However, there are greatly differing views on the possible effects of interest organizations on economic growth. In chapter two Roland Czada analyses the impact of interest politics on flexible adjustment policies. Czada compares two different theories: one is by Olson (1982) and the other by Katzenstein (1985). Mancur Olson (1982) claims that it is the size of group that is critically significant for determining the effects of group actions. Small groups usually do not need to worry about the social costs of their pressure group policies. Large and encompassing interest groups, on the other hand, are obliged to consider both the redistributive benefits and the social costs of their policies. Large groups cannot externalize the social costs of their pressure policies in the same way as small groups. Therefore, encompassing interest organizations are willing to choose strategies of collective gain, whereas small interest organizations are more likely to choose strategies of redistribution. There are always more potential interests than interest groups, and as time goes on, the number of organized interests increases; as a result, there will be increased institutional 'sclerosis' and greater obstacles to economic growth.

Peter Katzenstein (1985) has a much more positive image of the role of interest organizations. According to Katzenstein the size of the country is a crucial factor in affecting the strategies of interest organizations. Small industrial countries are highly dependent on the international economy. Small states are also forced to increase economic centralization and specialization in order to obtain economies of scale. The interests of the national economy as a whole are very salient in economic policy, and this modifies the strategies of interest organizations. Thus interest group strategies depend on the environment in which the groups operate.

The strategies of interest organizations have profound effects on economic development, but according to Czada, the factors determining these strategies are much more complicated than either Olson or Katzenstein would acknowledge. Institutional arenas and bureaucratic structures of public decision-making have an effect on these strategies. The strategy of interest organizations is dependent on the partisan composition of the government. In addition linguistic and ethnic divisions are also relevant.

2. International dimensions of the economic slowdown

Present-day economic problems are very often analysed as if the problems could be resolved within each nation. It is typical of this way of thinking that the rise of oil prices and dependency on oil have been seen as the main international causes of the contemporary economic slowdown. It is then often argued that each nation must reduce its dependency on imported oil.

This is a very one-sided view of the situation. The first oil shock was merely a single item in a longer causal chain that provoked the crisis. For many years before the oil shock there had been tendencies in the international economy that threatened the Bretton Woods system of fixed currencies. Deficits in the US balance of payments as well as in some other countries were growing all the time. On the other side of the coin, balance-of-payment surpluses were growing in Japan and West Germany. There were also bigger inflationary pressures in some countries compared with others. It was difficult to cope with these problems with the fixed rates of exchange of the Bretton Woods system. As a result, the USA devalued the dollar and the Bretton Woods system collapsed in 1971 (Maddison, 1982: 137–9). The declining value of dollar, in turn, helped to provoke the rise in oil prices.

When we analyse a causal chain of this type in the international economy we find that there were certain important factors which only became really manifest in the 1970s.

One important factor is that in the capitalist world-economy there is no central government to maintain order in international transactions. However, the need for order is just as great in international transactions as in national ones. In the capitalist world-economy there has always been a dominant country as well as follower countries. The dominant country has been the strongest in both technological and economic terms, and is usually the most advanced of all the developed capitalist countries. It has been up to the dominant country to formulate the rules for international transactions (Maddison, 1982: 29–42; Keohane, 1984).

During the nineteenth century, Britain was the leading country in the capitalist world-economy. At the end of the nineteenth century and in the beginning of the present century, the United States displaced Britain and took over as leader. However, the United States did not stabilize her position as leader until the end of the Second World War. Before this stabilization was achieved there was an unstable period in the international monetary system.

Since the late 1960s, the leading position of the United States has been steadily undermined and her technological primacy has weakened. The USA was compelled to abandon the gold standard and to devalue the dollar. Even after some new stabilizing arrangements, such as the European Monetary System (EMS), the system of international monetary transactions is still very unstable. Its stability is further threatened by the big debtor nations in the international monetary system, especially during recessions (Smith and Cuddington, 1984). The collapse of the system of international monetary transactions would have dramatic effects on economic development.

International economic integration was an essential factor in the golden age of economic growth. Between the two World Wars, there was no increase in the size of foreign trade as compared with total production in the developed capitalist countries. After the Second World War the United States initiated a process of freeing international trade. As a result, the volume of foreign trade rose much faster than the volume of production. The liberalization of foreign trade was one of the prime causes of postwar economic growth (Maddison, 1982; 127–8; Olson 1982), but at the same time it undermined the efficacy of national economic policies. In an open economy, there are a number of external influences that cannot be controlled by national policies; and because of economic integration the number of external influences has increased.

In this process the efficacy of national economic policies has declined. In fact, the nation state as a sovereign institution has become oldfashioned in the present world, where national economies are highly dependent on each other. There is more and more a need for co-operation in different policy areas, such as a co-ordination of countercyclical policies, a reduction of pollution and other ecological problems and in the use of scarce national resources.

The international dimensions of the economic slowdown is not the main topic in this book. Our main intention is to make a comparative analysis of economic policy responses to the economic slowdown in developed capitalist countries. This does not mean that we belittle the international dimensions. But space limitations prevent a fuller analysis of this issue (see also chapter nine).

3. Economic policy responses

When the economic crisis emerged in the mid-1970s, governments adopted either stabilizing or expansive countercyclical policies. Essentially governments reacted to the crisis just as they had done in earlier periods. But it soon became evident that the economic situation was no ordinary cyclical crisis. It was much more prolonged than an ordinary cyclical crisis.

When this was realized, a process of learning and innovation began. Governments began to search for new economic policy models. The years 1976–80 were critical years of learning, and in those years, new economic policy ideas and models were presented. The OECD began actively exporting new economic policy ideas to its member countries (e.g. OECD, 1977; OECD, 1979a; OECD, 1979b; OECD, 1981). Political parties began to formulate their economic policy programmes (see e.g. Richardson,

1982; Cox, 1982) and from the late 1970s on, they contested general elections with these new programmes.

The new economic policy programmes developed in three different directions. First, there were policy programmes based on the assumption that the economic crisis is mainly due to problems inherent in the Keynesian model of the welfare state. In this case, it is argued that policy failures are a bigger problem than market failures. These policy programmes are based on revitalized versions of neo-classical economic theory (Budd and Dicks, 1982), supplemented with theories about overloaded government and ungovernability (Brittan, 1977; Rose, 1980). At the prescriptive level these programmes call for more room for the operation of market forces.

Second, there are policy programmes based on the assumption that the economic crisis is the result of the changing dynamics of the market system. In this view failures in themselves are not seen as the main causes of economic problems. The assumption is rather that the economic problems of the market economy are susceptible to a solution. They can be solved by means of an adjustment process by which policy mistakes are corrected. At the core of this, there must be an active, interventionist government.

These policy programmes might be described as 'defensive Keynesianism' or 'post-Keynesianism' (Cornwall, 1983). These have the features of the politics of muddling through (Lindblom, 1959), satisficing decision-making (Simon, 1959) or piecemeal social engineering (Popper, 1945). In this respect there is a clear departure from the global, rationalist and maximizing theories of classical economic theory (van Gunsteren, 1976) prevalent during the golden age of economic growth.

Third, there are policy programmes based on the assumption that all contemporary economic problems are a manifestation of the failures of the capitalist economy. Supporters of this view believe that there is no solution to these problems within the capitalist system. What is needed, they argue, is a transformation of the whole capitalist market economy (Hirsch, 1980; Offe, 1984 and 1985; O'Connor, 1984).

Conservative parties, that were demanding more room for market forces, were generally on the offensive in the political battles of the 1970s and 1980s, while left-wing parties were more inclined to defend the welfare state and Keynesian interventionist policies. During the economic slowdown the popularity of conservative parties increased, and they won general elections and formed right-wing or centre-right governments in one country after the other: in Australia and New Zealand in 1975, in Sweden in 1976, in the Netherlands in 1977, in Britain in 1979, in the USA in 1980, in Belgium and Norway in 1981, in Denmark in 1982, in West Germany in 1982 (government) and 1983 (general election) and in Austria in 1983 (a left-right coalition). Movement to the left has been much more rare and more delayed: France 1981, Sweden 1982, Australia 1983, New Zealand 1984 and Norway 1986.

The economic policy stance of government has clearly changed to a market orientation in the United Kingdom (1979), the United States (1980), Norway (1981), Denmark (1982) and Iceland (1983). There have been modest changes in a market orientated direction in many other countries too. On the other hand, there has been some interventionist tendencies as well, such as the nationalization of banks and industries in France (1981), the strengthening of the corporatist institutions in Ireland in mid-1970s, and the tendencies towards corporatist incomes policy in Australia during the Hawke government after 1983. In some countries, especially in Austria and Finland, there has been a strong continuity in the economic policy model.

A cross-national analysis of economic policies from the mid-1970s indicates clearly divergent tendencies in fiscal, monetary, currency and incomes policies. Governments face problems of both economic and political rationality in their fiscal policy (Tullock, 1976; Keman and Lehner, 1984: 121–30; Lehner and Schubert, 1984). Economic rationality is based on calculations about the efficient utilization of economic resources. Political rationality is based on calculations about the electoral success of the governing party or parties. Keynes's economic theory legitimized the use of deficit budgeting, based on economic rationality. But where deficit budgeting has been legitimized, it has in fact been used as a means of fulfilling political goals. This is because it is politically much more rewarding to deliver public services than to impose new taxes.

Counter-cyclical fiscal policy has never functioned in practice, as it was presented in theory, even in those countries where economic policy has been very Keynesian. During economic recessions, public expenditure has increased, but it has not been politically possible to reduce it during an economic boom (Buchanan and Wagner, 1977). During a period of boom, counter-cyclical measures have generally taken the form of increases in taxation, with the result that the public sector goes on expanding.

After the first oil shock of 1973, budget deficits rose in all developed capitalist countries, partly as an automatic consequence of the recession, and partly as a deliberate policy change to cope with the recession. This was not just a short termed cyclical change. Budget deficits also remained at a higher level in all the developed capitalist countries, with the exception of Norway, Switzerland and the USA. There were big cross-national differences in these deficits, and differences increased even more after the second oil shock of 1979. At the beginning of the 1980s, the public sector borrowing requirement as a percentage of GDP was in double digits in Belgium, Ireland, Italy and Denmark. These kind of deficits were no longer cyclical deficits; they were structural deficits, and this had a detrimental effect on economic performance in these countries. In the early 1980s, deficits were also increasing in Canada, France, the Netherlands, Sweden and the USA. On the other hand, Austria, Japan, Germany and the

United Kingdom did not let their budget deficits increase any more, and Norway and Switzerland were in the lucky situation of having surplus in their public finance (OECD, 1986).

Many governments were worried about the continuous rise in public expenditure, but only a few succeeded in preventing a further rise. After the second oil shock (in 1979), total government expenditure as a percent of GDP declined only in Norway. Austria, Germany and Switzerland stopped further increases, and also in Australia, Finland and Japan increases were small. On the other hand, between the years 1973 and 1983, total expenditures as a percentage of GDP rose 21 percentage points in Sweden, 20 percentage points in Italy and Denmark, and 17 percentage points in Belgium and Ireland. Social security and the production of welfare services have been the main areas of expansion of the public sector. In the Nordic countries and in Austria governments have taken on bigger responsibilities as direct employers. In Denmark the Schlüter government stopped the expansion of employment. However, both in Sweden and Denmark government employment is now almost one-third of the total employment. At the same time, public employment has diminished in the United States, the United Kingdom, the Netherlands, and New Zealand.

Monetary policy has become an essential component of stabilization policy since the mid-1970s. There were many reasons for this development. Inflationary pressures were bigger than before; in many countries fiscal policy had lost its effectiveness as a policy instrument because of the structural budget deficits. According to monetarist doctrine, the growth of money supply is the most important determinant of inflation. Therefore, the control of money supply is a high priority. In the UK, the USA and Iceland (after 1983) the policy of tight money was publicly justified by monetarist doctrines. At the same time Belgium, Australia, Canada, Ireland and Italy raised interest rates without any clear commitment to monetarist doctrines.

In chapter eight Paul Whiteley shows that monetarist stabilization in the UK and the USA has had detrimental effects on economic growth and employment. As a result of high interest rates, productive investment is reduced. At the same time speculative operations in the so-called casino economy flourish. In mid-1980s, these problems have become important political issues, and the popularity of monetarism is declining even among conservative parties.

In currency policy, too, policy styles were diverging from the early 1970s. After the collapse of the Bretton Woods system of fixed exchange rates there have been three different strategies with regard to currency policies. First, by the revaluation of their currencies some countries, especially Austria, West Germany, Japan and Switzerland have tried to prevent foreign inflation from coming into the country. The problem of this strategy is that it threatens the international competitiveness of the domestic industry. Therefore, Belgium, Denmark and Norway, after revaluing their currencies in the 1970s, were compelled to devalue after the second oil shock.

Secondly, some countries, particularly France, Iceland, Ireland, Italy, New Zealand, the United Kingdom, and the United States, devalued their currency. The aim was to try and expand their exports and strengthen their balance of payments. The problem of this strategy is that it imports inflationary pressures from abroad into the domestic economy.

Third, some governments adopted a neutral currency policy by trying to keep the exchange rate at a constant level. These different strategies of currency policy seem to be closely connected to national inflationary pressures. In Austria, Germany, Japan and Switzerland wage increases and inflation has been rather small, and international inflationary pressures have been controlled by the revaluation of the currency. In France, Iceland, Ireland, Italy and New Zealand there has been a spiral of wage and price inflation. This was also the case in Britain during the Labour government of 1974 to 1979. This has undermined the international competitiveness of these economies. Devaluation has been the way to improve competitiveness in the short term, but at a cost of increasing domestic inflationary pressures.

All the policy instruments used for stabilization seem to be highly interconnected. Thus in order to succeed overall, countries have to succeed in all areas of stabilization simultaneously. For example, if there are inflationary pressures in some sectors of the economy these will rapidly spill to other sectors. Incomes policy, for instance, cannot be used if there is not a general confidence that wage inflation can be controlled, and there is such confidence only if all the major sectors of the economy support stabilization. In chapter two, Klaus Armingeon makes a more detailed analysis of the problems of incomes policy in ten West European countries, In chapter six, Hans Keman and Tibert van Dijk show the interconnectedness of policy instruments and relate it to policy performance.

In the same way, the efficacy of monetary policy is dependent on other instruments of economic policy. Governments and central banks can control the official discount rate, but they cannot control the real supply of money in a modern market economy. Therefore, monetary policy as the only instrument of stabilization will be inefficient, since it will have a detrimental effect on economic growth and employment.

4. Determinants of the economic policy models

In a cross-national analysis we may examine features that are common to a larger group of nations, or features that are specific to some nations only. In economic policy each country has some specific features of its own. Many of these reflect long traditions, and they may be very resistant to change. Therefore, it is important to analyse the kind of factors which modify economic policy models.

Differences between national policy models may be due to differences in the economic theories that are dominant at the time. In the golden age of economic growth, for example, classical economic theory was gradually superseded by the Keynesian theories. In this process some nations were pioneers, whereas others accepted the change much later. In the current revitalization of neo-classical theory, some nations have again taken the lead.

The role of economic theory in influencing national economic policy models is constrained by other factors, such as the general economic situation and the power relations of the country concerned. Keynesianism has been rejected in an economic crisis where Keynesian policies had produced unintended effects. But big changes in policy stance have also been made when severe economic pressures did not exist. In Norway, for instance, the Willoch government adopted neo-classical doctrines without such pressures, as Jan Otto Andersson shows in chapter seven.

The power relations of the political forces is another important determinant of national economic policy models. In recent years, several studies on neo-corporatism have stressed the importance of interest organizations in economic policy-making. It has been claimed that the power structures of interest intermediation may be even more important than the political power structures of parliaments and governments.

The divergence in economic policy outcomes may be partly due to a different pattern of interest intermediation and partly the outcome of early Keynesian policies. The way in which national systems of interest intermediation either facilitated or hindered the conduct of Keynesian policies also appear to explain some recent policy innovations.

On the other hand, the policy strategies of interest organizations are dependent on the party system and the policy strategies of the government. In the same way the economic policy strategies of the political parties are dependent on the power structures of interest organizations. In this respect, we may talk about four different types of economic policy regimes. First, there is a situation where trade unions are strong and left-wing parties dominate the government. This situation has been conducive to corporatist interest intermediation. Trade unions are likely to choose strategies of collective gain, that are favourable to economic growth. Governments implement full employment policies and in exchange trade unions respect corporate profits as a way to profitable investments, economic growth and high employment. During the contemporary economic slowdown corporatist mechanisms remained rather stable and they were important in achieving stabilization. Typical examples are Austria, Norway and Sweden.

Second, there are countries where trade unions are strong and left-wing parties are weak or in opposition. Belgium and the Netherlands are typical examples of this, as well as Sweden between 1976 and 1982 and Norway between 1981 and 1985. In this case conflicts between trade unions and government are likely. Trade unions are likely to choose redistributive strategies and governments cannot effectively co-operate with trade unions in the implementation of economic policy. There may be corporatist mechanisms, but they are not as stable as in the first type of regime.

Third, there are countries where trade unions are weak and left-wing parties dominate the government as in Britain from 1974 to 1979, in France from 1981 to 1986, and in New Zealand from 1972 to 1975. Attempts to create corporatist intermediation in, for example, Britain and France have been largely unsuccessful. These governments are likely to prefer Keynesian interventionism compared with neo-classical market-orientated economic policies. Stabilization policies have not been very successful and since there are no institutional preconditions for developing a long-term incomes policy, stagflation has become a real problem. At the same time left-wing governments have been reluctant to implement a tight monetary policy, so inflation has been particularly severe.

Fourth, there are countries where trade unions are weak and conservative parties are in office. Typical examples of this are Canada, France before 1981 and after 1986, Ireland, the United Kingdom after 1979 and the United States. It is just under this type of regime that the revitalization of neo-classical doctrines has been most apparent. Governments have tried to give more room to market forces, and monetary policy has been an important factor in the control of inflation.

There tend also to be some differences in economic outcomes between these four regimes. Under the first regime (strong trade unions and strong left) the level of unemployment tends to be rather low but inflation rises. Under the second (strong trade unions and weak left) and third (weak trade unions and strong left) regimes the level of unemployment tends to be higher compared to the first, but inflation is also a problem. Under the fourth regime (weak trade unions and weak left) the level of unemployment tends to be rather high, and inflation is moderated.

In countries where trade unions are strong a bourgeois government tends to increase inflation. In countries where trade unions are weak it is a left-wing government that tends to increase inflation.

It has also been claimed (see Lange and Garrett, 1985; Paloheimo, 1986) that the conditions for economic growth are better under regimes of the first and last types compared with other regimes. If this is true we can say that there are two different paths to economic growth: a bourgeois, market-oriented way and a social-democratic, corporatist way.

The above four regimes are pure types in that in practice these categories neglect many relevant factors. In reality, there is much variation within each type of regime, because the determinants of economic policy are complex.

Differences in national traditions, especially concerning the role of the state, are also an important determinant of national policy models. The concept of a strong state has historically been more prominent in continental Europe than in Anglo-Saxon countries. To describe these differences, Kenneth Dyson (1980) used the terms 'state society' and 'stateless society'. In the 1980s, it seems to be clear that the revival of neo-classical economics has been more pronounced in 'stateless societies'. In chapter seven Jan Otto Andersson analyses national traditions in the Nordic countries, a group of 'state societies'. In comparative analysis people very often talk about the Scandinavian model or the Nordic model. However, a closer examination reveals that there are great differences between the individual countries.

National policy models may be influenced by the institutional structure of the state. Economic policy instruments are rather different in unitary states compared with federal states. In federal states, it may be more difficult to use fiscal policy as an instrument of economic policy, because of the highly decentralized and fragmented structure of the public economy (Scharpf, 1984). Similarly sectionalization of public administration may have great effects on the policy strategies of interest groups.

National economic policy models are highly dependent on the economic situation of the national economy. National economies differ in size, structure-cyclical situation, and also in their position in the world market. All these things have an effect on national policy models. Small national economies, for example, are more exposed to the world market and the interests of the export industry are then highly respected. In small national economies, the development of export industry has important effects on the national economy as a whole. Therefore, the interests of export industry are often seen as general national interests. Centralized corporatist mechanisms are highly developed especially in some small states. In reality, the whole question of centralization is a different matter in small states compared with large ones.

In small exporting countries economic policy has generally been more supply-orientated than in big countries. In these countries economic policy has always been used to support export industry. In the 1970s, there was an increased emphasis on the supply side in economic policy. In this situation, the need for a reorientation was smaller in those countries where economic policy was already supply-side orientated. This explains the continuity in the Austrian, Finnish and Swedish policy models.

Most of the above mentioned factors are national determinants of economic policy models. But there are also important international determinants. Economic policy in the USA greatly affects the economic policies of other developed capitalist countries (Story, 1984); and economic policies in bigger countries influence economic policies in smaller neighbouring countries. The European Community has tried to integrate economic policies in the member countries (Antola, 1980; Davenport, 1982; Lodge, 1983). Similarly OECD is an important exporter of new economic policy ideas. In the late 1970s it exported ideas on monetary policy and the related question of controlling the growth of the public sector.

5. Problems of implementation

The implementation of economic policy is a complex and difficult task. In some cases, there are too many institutional constraints on the proposed economic policy. The goals of political decision-making are often confused or obscure (Lane, 1985). The decision makers themselves very often have conflicting goals, and the decisions that are finally taken are usually the result of a compromise. Different authorities within the state also often have conflicting goals. Departments of Labour, for example, may have a policy of increasing employment in areas where large numbers of unemployed people live. At the same time, Departments of Industry may try to encourage migration to those areas where the demand for labour is high.

The mechanisms of political decision-making are also uncertain (Lane, 1985). We have a very limited knowledge of the causal mechanisms at work in society. The use of any policy instrument usually has many different kinds of effects. Some of these effects may have been intended, but there will almost certainly be other, unintended, effects. It is even possible that the actual effects of a policy will turn out to be quite the opposite of what was intended (Elster, 1978: 106–20; Giddens, 1979: 139–41). In a market economy there are many factors that can undermine the efficiency of economic policies (Friedman, 1962). For instance, progressive taxation may be used as a tool to equalize incomes in society. But since people are aware of the tax schedules they may try to compensate for their impact by tax avoidance schemes of all types (van Arnhem and Schotsman, 1982: 323; Dahmen, 1984: 35). As a result gross incomes may become even more unequal.

There are many international constraints on the implementation of economic policy. The French experience of Keynesian expansive policy in 1981 clearly shows the limitations of demand management policies in the developed capitalist countries. The French attempted to expand aggregate demand at a time when other countries were implementing restrictive policies and as a result failed because of pressures on the franc. In the late 1970s, the international competitiveness of national economies and balanced foreign trade became more important issues. This made most countries implement rather restrictive economic policies. This kind of situation has been clearly detrimental to economic growth and employment. There is a deflationary bias in the contemporary capitalist world economy, reinforcing restrictive policies and discouraging expansive ones. There are two different directions that countries can choose in order to avoid the negative effects of this bias: governments may try to increase their economic independence by imposing import and export controls. Alternatively, they may co-ordinate their macroeconomic policies more closely and reflate together at the international level (Stewart, 1983).

The implementation of a market-orientated policy model may lead to a number of problems. In chapter eight, Paul Whiteley analyses the monetarist experiments conducted by the Thatcher government in Britain and the Reagan administration in the USA. According to Whiteley, the basic propositions of monetarism are (1) that supply of money is the main cause of fluctuations in money incomes; (2) the money supply does not directly influence the real economy; (3) that market mechanisms when left to themselves are an effective means of steering the economy.

Using econometric models, Whiteley shows that there is a reciprocal relationship between money supply and money incomes, but that the effect of money supply on money incomes is much smaller than monetarists believe.

The Thatcher government produced a fiscally induced recession in the real economy, which diminished growth and investments as well as dramatically increased unemployment. By contrast, in the United States the economic policy seemed to have been more successful.

A policy programme which aims to isolate interest organizations and to reduce their power involves both theoretical and practical problems. In neo-classical economic theory, it is claimed that perfect competition in atomized markets is a sufficient condition for an efficient allocation of resources. The laissez-faire policy model, however, suggests that perfect competition in non-organized markets is a necessary condition for an optimal allocation of resources. But this is true only under some highly restrictive conditions.

There are also practical problems in reducing the power of interest organizations. A market orientated change in economic policy does not automatically reduce the power of interest organizations. Decisive governmental intervention is needed if the power of interest organizations is to be reduced, and thus a move towards a market orientated approach requires more intervention not less. A policy of this type will inevitably meet strong resistance, especially among organized labour (Gregory, 1984). A reduction of the power of interest organizations can also change power relations in society in favour of capital. In a capitalist economy it is the role of enterprises to hire labour and to make investments. If there are no interest organizations, economic power remains clearly in the hands of the owners and managers of enterprises (Offe, 1984).

According to the neo-classical model, the need for a market orientated policy is greatest in those countries where the public sector is large; where interest organizations are strong; and where redistributive policies are highly egalitarian. But from the following chapters it becomes clear that the market-orientated policy change has been greatest in those countries where the public sector is not very large, where interest organizations are not very strong and where redistributive policies have not been very egalitarian.

It is possible that a laissez-faire policy model may become an ideological mask for a new kind of corporate capitalist class rule. The dismantling of the welfare state may bring about even greater inequalities. A policy which purports to aim for competition may in fact be a mask for reducing the power of organized labour in society. Passivity in demand management may bring about continuous mass unemployment. Class divisions in society may be increased and class conflict may thus be aggravated. In such a situation, the traditional law and order functions of the government receive new prominence. However, in societies with fragmented interest organizations and weak labour parties, a market orientated economic policy seems to be the probable way of resolving problems of profitability and growth.

The implementation of an interventionist economic policy is not without problems. Incomes policy seems to be the critical core of the interventionist policy model. However, the establishment and maintenance of an incomes policy is difficult. There seems to be no possibility of enforcing an efficient incomes policy in countries with highly fragmented interest organizations, and in those countries where incomes policies have been established, the maintenance of these gives rise to many problems. Such a policy functions only on condition that it is not overloaded by sectional interests.

In the case of centralized incomes policy, decision-making becomes highly technocratic. Parties and pressure groups become more and more legitimizers of the 'system rationality' that is adopted. As a result, there will be growing tension between the decision-making elite and their reference groups. Society will be divided horizontally into two sub-cultures (Helander and Anckar, 1983: 145–67). The decision-makers live in their own world of 'system rationality', whereas other citizens live in a 'Lebenswelt' of their own.

The horizontal division of society does not eliminate the traditional functional division between capital and labour. In an organized economy there is a continuous struggle for economic power. It is possible that the quiescence of labour must be purchased by expanding public expenditure, or by giving more economic power to labour organizations, for example, in the form of workers councils and wage earner funds. In such a situation, it is possible that the owners of capital will break down the post-Keynesian consensus. In any event, the high levels of public expenditure in highly corporatized countries begins to threaten the functioning of the market system and gives rise to new problems.

Conclusion

The implementation of economic policy is a complex task. The degree of control over the economy is rather modest. However, in some countries there is more control than in others. We know quite a lot about the 'virtuous circles' and 'vicious circles' in economic life. Both virtuous and vicious circles have complex social preconditions, and these preconditions are often quite resistant to change. But still, the more we know, the better we will be able to cope with economic crisis.

In the mid-1980s, there seems to be a new round of learning going on. Economic policy responses implemented during the late 1970s and early 1980s are now under critical consideration. The high tide of monetarism seems to be over, and Keynesian approaches to the politics of expansion seem to be on the agenda again. Thus it is possible that the recent divergence in economic policy is now coming to an end; but, as yet, future prospects for the world economy remain obscure.

References

Antola, E. (1980) 'Political Harmonization of Economic Integration. Competition Policy as an Indicator of Political Integration in the EEC in 1958–1972', *University of Turku, Department of Sociology and Political Science, Studies on Political Science*, No. 7.

Bernabè, F. (1982) 'The Labour Market and Unemployment', in A. Boltho (ed.), *The European Economy. Growth and Crisis*. Oxford: Oxford University Press.

Boltho, A. (ed.) (1982) *The European Economy. Growth and Crisis*. Oxford: Oxford University Press.

Brittan, S. (1977) *The Economic Consequences of Democracy*. London: Temple Smith.

Buchanan, J. and R. M. Wagner (1977) *Democracy in Deficit: The Political Legacy of Lord Keynes*. New York: Academic Press.

Budd, A. and G. Dicks (1982) 'Inflation — A Monetarist Interpretation', in A. Boltho (ed.), *The European Economy. Growth and Crisis*. Oxford: Oxford University Press.

Casson, M. (1981) *Unemployment. A Disequilibrium Approach*. Oxford: Martin Robertson.

Cornwall, J. (1983) *The Conditions for Economic Recovery. A Post-Keynesian Analysis*. Oxford: Martin Robertson.

Cox, A. (ed.) (1982) *Politics, Policy and the European Recession*. London/Basingstoke: Macmillan.

Dahmen, E. (1982) 'Does the Mixed Economy Have a Future?', in B. Ryden and V. Bergström (eds), *Sweden: Choices for Economic and Social Policy in the 1980s*. London/Boston/Sydney: George Allen & Unwin.

Dahmen, E. (1984) 'Taloudellinen kehitys ja muutospaineet. Kokemuksia Suomesta ja muualta', *Suomen Pankin julkaisuja, Sarja C: 7b*, Helsinki.

Davenport, M. (1982) 'The Economic Impact of the EEC', in A. Boltho (ed.), *The European Economy. Growth and Crisis*. Oxford: Oxford University Press.

Dyson, K. (1980) *State Tradition in Western Europe*. Oxford: Martin Robertson.

Elster, J. (1978) *Logic and Society. Contradictions and Possible Worlds*. Chichester/New York/Brisbane/Toronto: John Wiley & Sons.

Friedman, M. (1962) *Capitalism and Freedom*. Chicago: Chicago University Press.

Giddens, A. (1979) *Central Problems in Social Theory. Action, Structure and Contradiction in Social Analysis*. London/Basingstoke: Macmillan.

Gregory, R. (1984) *Trade Unions, the Law and Economic Recovery in the United Kingdom: a Preliminary Sketch*. ECPR Joint Session of Workshops, Salzburg, 13–18 April.

Helander, V. and D. Anckar (1983) 'Consultation and Political Culture. Essays on the Case of Finland', *Commentationes Scientiarum Socialium*, 19. Tammisaari: The Finnish Society of Sciences and Letters.

Hirsch, J. (1980) *Der Sicherheitsstaat: Das 'Modell Deutschland'. Seine Krise und die neuen sozialen Bewegungen.* Frankfurt a.M.: Europeische Verlagsanstalt.

Johansen, L. (1971) *Public Economics.* Amsterdam/London: North-Holland Publishing Company.

Katzenstein, P. J. (1985) *Small States in World Markets. Industrial Policy in Europe.* Ithaca and London: Cornell University Press.

Keman, H. and F. Lehner (1984) 'Economic Crisis and Political Management: an Introduction to the Problems of Political Economic Interdependence', *European Journal of Political Research*, 12(2): 121–30.

Keohane, R. O. (1984) 'The World Political Economy and the Crisis of Embedded Liberalism', in J. H. Goldthorpe (ed.), *Order and Conflict in Contemporary Capitalism.* Oxford: Clarendon Press.

Lane, J.-E. (1985) 'Introduction: Public Policy or Markets? The Demarcation Problem', in J.-E. Lane (ed.), *State and Market. The Politics of the Public and the Private.* London/Beverly Hills/New Delhi: Sage.

Lange, P. and G. Garrett (1985) 'The Politics of Growth: Strategic Interaction and Economic Performance in Advanced Industrial Democracies', *The Journal of Politics* 47(3): 792–827.

Lauber, V. (1984) *Changing Assumptions in French Economic Policy.* ECPR Joint Session of Workshops, Salzburg, 13–18 April.

Lehner, F. and K. Schubert (1984) 'Party Government and the Political Control of Public Policy', *European Journal of Political Research*, 12(2): 131–46.

Lindblom, C. (1959) 'The Science of "Muddling Through"', *Public Administration Review*, 19: 79–88.

Lodge, J. (ed.) (1983) *Institutions and Policies of the European Community.* London: Frances Pinter.

Maddison, A. (1980) 'Western Economic Performance in the 1970s: A Perspective and Assessment', *Banca Nationale Del Lavoro Quarterly Review*: 247–90.

Maddison, A. (1982) *Phases of Capitalist Development.* Oxford/New York: Oxford University Press.

O'Connor, J. (1984) *Accumulation Crisis.* Oxford/New York: Basil Blackwell.

OECD (1977) *Towards Full Employment and Price Stability.* Paris: OECD.

OECD (1979a) *Monetary Targets and Inflation Control.* Paris: OECD.

OECD (1979b) *Facing the Future: Mastering the Probable and Managing the Unpredictable.* Paris: OECD.

OECD (1981) *The Welfare State in Crisis.* Paris: OECD.

OECD (1985) The Role of the Public Sector. Special Issue of the *OECD Economic Studies*, 4, 1985.

OECD (1986) *Economic Outlook. Historical Statistics 1960–84.* Paris: OECD.

Offe, C. (1984) *Contradictions of the Welfare State.* London/Sydney/Melbourne/Auckland/Johannesburg: Hutchinson & Co.

Offe, C. (1985) *Disorganized Capitalism.* Cambridge/Oxford/New York: Polity Press.

Okun, A. M. (1981) *Prices and Quantities: A Macroeconomic Analysis.* Oxford: Basil Blackwell.

Olson, M. (1982) *The Rise and Decline of Nations. Economic Growth, Stagflation, and Social Rigidities.* New Haven/London: Yale University Press.

Paloheimo, H. (1984) 'Distributive Struggle, Corporatist Power Structures and Economic Policy of the 1970s in Developed Capitalist Countries', in H. Paloheimo (ed.), *Politics in the Era of Corporatism and Planning.* Tampere/Ilmajoki: The Finnish Political Science Association.

Paloheimo, H. (1986) *The Effect of Trade Unions and Governments on Economic Growth*. ECPR Joint Session of Workshops. Gothenburg, 1–6 April.

Popper, K. (1945) *The Open Society and Its Enemies*, I. London: George Routledge and Sons.

Richardson, J. (ed.) (1982) *Policy Styles in Western Europe*. London/Boston/Sydney: George Allen & Unwin.

Rose, R. (ed.) (1980) *Challenge to Governance. Studies in Overloaded Politics*. Beverly Hills/London: Sage.

Scharpf, F. W. (1984) 'Economic and Institutional Constraints on Full-Employment Strategies: Sweden, Austria, and West-Germany, 1973–1982', in J. H. Goldthorpe (ed.), *Order and Conflict in Contemporary Capitalism. Studies in the Political Economy of Western European Nations*. Oxford: Clarendon Press.

Simon, H. (1959) *Administrative Behaviour. A Study of Decisionmaking processes in Administrative Organization*. 2 ed., 7 pr. New York: Macmillan.

Smith, G. W. and J. Cuddington (eds) (1984) *International Debt and the Developing Countries*. Washington: World Bank.

Stewart, M. (1983) *Controlling the Economic Future. Policy Dilemmas in a Shrinking World*. Thetford, Norfolk: Wheatsheaf Books.

Story, J. (1984) *Western European Politics and the Dollar: National Dependency Versus Regional Autonomy*. ECPR Joint Session of Workshops, Salzburg, 13–18 April.

Tullock, G. (1976) *The Vote Motive*. London: Institute of Economic Affairs.

van Arnhem, J. C. M. and G. J. Schotsman (1982) 'Do Parties Affect the Distribution of Incomes? The Case of Advanced Capitalist Democracies', in F. G. Castles (ed.), *The Impact of Parties. Politics and Policies in Democratic Capitalist States*. London/Beverly Hills: Sage.

van Gunsteren, H. R. (1976) *The Quest for Control. A Critique of the Rational-central-rule Approach in Public Affairs*. London/New York/Sydney/Toronto: John Wiley & Sons.

Yarrow, G. (1986) 'Privatization in Theory and Practice', *Economic Policy. A European Forum*, 1(2): 324–64.

II

POLICY PROCESS, INSTITUTIONAL STRUCTURES AND STRATEGIES

2

The impact of interest politics on flexible adjustment policies

Roland Czada

Coping with crisis means to adjust to change. In the following chapter I will argue that the relations between governments and organized interests are highly significant with regard to a country's adaptive capacities. The argument is based on a discussion of two recent publications (Olson, 1982; Katzenstein, 1985) and empirically supported by a comparative analysis of structures of interest politics and adjustment policies of sixteen western industrialized countries.

'The distinctive strategy by which small European states adjust to change derives from corporatist domestic structures that have their origins in the 1930s and 1940s.' This conclusion of Katzenstein's (1985: 210) empirical investigations assigns highly adaptive capacities to small countries where strong interest groups participate in economic policy-making. Small domestic markets result in economic openness and dependence. These factors create a compelling need for consensus, that achieves a continuous sequence of political bargains and enhances the flexibility of societal organizations (p. 32ff.). This contrasts with Olson's (1982) findings according to which 'special-interest organizations and collusions reduce efficiency and aggregate income in the societies in which they operate and make political life more divisive' (p. 47). Olson's theoretical argument is based on the assumption that — on balance — interest groups have little or no incentive to make any significant sacrifices for the society as a whole. Instead they protect their members sectional interests by collusive action. In the long run emerging distributional coalitions will 'slow down a society's capacity to adopt new technologies and to reallocate resources in response to changing conditions, and thereby reduce the rate of economic growth' (Olson, 1982: 65).

According to Katzenstein, interest organizations promote industrial adaption and economic growth. Olson claims they produce institutional sclerosis and economic decline. In contrast to this I will argue that political exchange relationships given by historical traditions, ideological affiliations, political institutions and patterns of state-group linkages determine organizational action. Hence the impact of group politics on flexible adjustment policies depends widely on factors outside the organizational domain of interest groups. In the next sections I will discuss Olson's and Katzenstein's approaches and challenge their findings with empirical data. Subsequently I will present variables which modify their explanations of collective action.

1. Policy innovations and political theory

Until the 1960s it was widely accepted that interest groups not only supported democracy but also promoted social and political innovativeness and economic wealth. From David Truman's *The Governmental Process* (1951) to Charles Lindblom's *The Intelligence of Democracy* (1965) the tenet was that pluralist politics produced favourable outcomes. Analogous to economic markets, politics was described as a process of mutual adjustment among a multitude of power holders. The competition of interests effectively balanced the various claims on the national product and yielded the desired supply of political goods. There was broad agreement within the 'group school' that pluralist politics positively correlated with flexibility and innovativeness and therefore resulted in outstanding problem solving capacities.

The classical pluralist conception came under pressure from an individualist rational-choice perspective offered in Mancur Olson's *Logic of Collective Action* (1965), and from an institutionalist or even statist point of view given by several contributions on the New Corporatism (Schmitter, 1974; Lehmbruch, 1977). In 'The Logic' Olson demonstrates that the conditions for organizing interests vary by group size. There is little incentive to join a large interest-organization, because one can hardly be excluded from the results of its collective actions. Large organizations act independently of an individual's contribution, whereas in small groups individual membership might decide upon the supply of collective goods. As small homogeneous groups provide for goods that are exclusive to their members it is more attractive to join them. With these arguments, the pluralist belief in symmetrical organization and representation was refuted. The pluralist system appeared to be biased in favour of small distributive coalitions at the expense of more general interests.

The corporatist critique of the pluralist paradigm started from empirical observations (e.g. Lehmbruch, 1977; Schmitter, 1974; Katzenstein, 1984, 1985). It also contained a thrust against the 'Logic' of Mancur Olson. In several European countries societal organizations not only successfully organized large heterogeneous groups, but also participated in public policy-making. Instead of pluralist 'pressure politics' and lobbying, these organizations acted as integral parts of comprehensive policy-networks. They were often incorporated into national politics.

Corporatists refuted the pluralist approach because it understood policy-making as a one-way process of pressure and influence. Instead they conceived of it as a process of organized exchange within policy networks. Interest groups were no longer seen as autonomous entities but as inter-twined with each other and with governments and administrations. So far, the corporatist critique of pluralism differs fundamentally from the Olsonian one. Olson's methodological individualism neglects institutional interlocking and governmental policies. In this respect Olson remains deeply rooted in the American 'group-school'.[1]

Olson's (1982) theoretical argument is based on the assumption that — on balance — interest groups have little or no incentive to make any significant sacrifices in favour of general purposes, but are looking for maximum pay-offs for their members. This has the effect of leading to social rigidity and economic decline. Only if interest-organizations encompass large segments of a society must they regard the overall consequences of their actions.[2] But in the long run, Olson expects associational systems to be dominated by distributive coalitions. As a result, social rigidities, in particular 'sticky wages', will disturb markets and restrict governmental policies of flexible adjustment.

2. On the limits of organizational approaches

Olson's theory intersects with corporatist approaches in one respect. It provides also for an explanation of interest group policies that are not harmful to overall societal goals of economic growth, stability and high employment. Corporatists explain this by institutional interlocking, exchange and concertation of organizational with governmental policies (e.g. Lehmbruch, 1984), whereas Olson confines the explanation to internal organizational attributes.

> If an organization represents, say, a third of the income producing capacity of a country, its members will, on average, obtain about a third of the benefit of any effort to make the society more productive. The organization will therefore have an incentive to make sacrifices up to a point for policies and activities that are sufficiently rewarding for the society as a whole. (Olson, 1982; 46)

Olson's underlying concept of 'encompassing organizations' appears somewhat problematic. As an example, the German union of Metal Workers (IGM), one of the largest unions in the western world, has about 2.5 million members. Hence it represents not more than 4 percent of the population or about 6 percent of the labour force. But the IGM is affiliated with sixteen other unions within the German Confederation of Unions (DGB) that covers more than 30 percent of the labour force. And despite the absence of coercive powers on the DGB's side, wage demands as well as bargaining strategies appear to be considerably co-ordinated. Even those unions which are located outside the DGB follow the policies espoused by its biggest member unions. The representativeness of the latter appear to be much higher than indicated by organizational size. Thus it is rather difficult to comprehend an organization's scope only by structural attributes. Informal linkages and the size of potential groups are important as well. For instance Farmer's associations could not be 'encompassing' with respect to society as a whole, because their potential membership is too low nowadays. But as an approximation one might say that if the potential group size is very large as in the case of labour unions, overall membership density and organizational centralization decide on how 'encompassing' unions are. Olson's explaining variable appears to be '*relative size*', determined by the proportion of actual organizational size and potential group size to the society as a whole. Additionally one has to take account of organizational centralization and co-ordination.

According to Olson, downward 'stickiness' of wages is a major restriction to economic adaptation. Hence 'encompassing' unions would have an incentive to restrict their wage demands in favour of economic adjustments. This means that large group size, centralization and high membership density of organizations should be related to socially responsive political action. Labour unions for instance, to which this characterization applies, should support economic adjustment policies. Fortunately this correlation can be tested empirically. Comparisons of data on wage-restraint, economic adjustment, inflation, real growth, unionization and centralization of unions in liberal democracies (Table 1) do not fully support Olson's hypothesis.[3]

Following Olson's argument we would expect responsible wage policies in countries with 'encompassing' organizations of labour. Such organizations have no incentive to hurt themselves by wage-demands which exceed the distributive margins of an economy. Therefore wage increases (at least in relation to real growth) and inflation should be lower and economic adjustment higher in such countries relative to the others. Now, correlations of the policy-variables mentioned above with membership density and centralization of unions produce coefficients of -0.57 (union centralization and inflation), 0.49 (union centralization and economic adjustment) and -0.36 (unionization and economic growth) at the best. These results do not fully support an organizational hypothesis because the variance (r^2) of policy outcomes explained by organizational variables is barely 25 percent. Moreover high membership density and centralization of unions are of opposite impacts on inflation, but both increase economic adjustments and reduce economic growth. Hence some correlations are contrary to Olson's hypothesis, especially when economic growth is concerned (see Table 1). Even if one employed multiple regression techniques and simultaneously treated membership density and organizational centralization as

TABLE 1

Unions' organizational structures and economic policy outcomes

	Unionization (percent)	Centralization	Real growth[1] (percent)	Inflation[1] (percent)	Economic adjustment[2]	Real wages[1] (percent)	Economic openness[3]
Australia	50	2	2.60	11.90	4	2.90	29
Austria	60	9	2.90	6.30	6	3.50	61
Belgium	75	7	1.90	8.20	14	4.30	84
Canada	30	1	3.20	9.30	3	3.00	44
Denmark	50	5	2.70	11.00	8	3.70	58
Finland	65	6	2.10	12.60	10	0.90	55
France	25	2	3.00	11.10	7	4.50	33
FR Germany	35	4	2.80	4.80	11	2.70	42
Ireland	55	1	3.60	15.50	12	4.10	76
Italy	40	1	2.30	17.10	n.a.	5.70	41
Japan	35	1	4.30	9.90	n.a.	0.70	19
Netherlands	33	8	2.20	7.10	13	2.70	89
New Zealand	55	1	0.60	14.30	n.a.	0.50	50
Norway	45	7	5.00	9.00	9	4.90	78
Sweden	85	7	1.40	10.30	5	1.40	47
Switzerland	30	3	−0.80	4.00	n.a.	1.40	66
United Kingdom	50	1	1.80	16.00	1	0.80	44
USA	25	1	3.30	9.30	2	0.60	12

[1] 1973–78, annual average

[2] see Appendix, Economic Adjustment is a measure for the 'Modernization of an Economy' given by structural adjustments and increases in industrial productivity

[3] imports and exports as a share of GNP (1971–73)

TABLE 1 continued

	V081 Union-centr.[1]	V079 Unionization	Correlation coefficients V071 Real wages	V026 Inflation	V020 Real growth	V067 Economic adjustment[1]	V034 Foreign trade
V081	1.0000						
V079	0.2780	1.0000					
V071	0.2689	-0.0197	1.0000				
V026	-0.5739	0.2644	0.0742	1.0000			
V020	-0.1695	-0.3648	0.3729	0.0827	1.0000		
V067	0.4917[2]	0.2564	0.4466	-0.3344	-0.0110	1.0000	
V034	0.6187	0.3504	0.3831	-0.1986	-0.1585	0.7063	1.0000

[1] r_s
[2] r_τ, others r

Sources: V081, V079: Wilensky, 1976; Schmitter, 1981; Korpi and Shalev, 1979; V071: German Fed. Bureau of Statistics; V067: see Appendix; V026, V020, V043: OECD – Economic Surveys.

independent variables, the variance explained would not exceed 30 percent. Empirically this results from several outliers: Belgium and Denmark with high unionization do not coincide with Olson's model as far as wages are concerned, whereas Sweden and Austria diverge with respect to industrial productivity.[4] Of the countries with corporatist or 'encompassing' organizations only Austria's inflation record fits the argument. Low real wage growth in Japan, the USA, Canada, UK, Ireland, Australia and New Zealand is due to high inflation or even stagflation, as figures in Table 1 indicate. Simultaneously, most of these countries with heterogeneous industrial relations-systems show the smallest economic adjustments during the 1970s. Interestingly, in the Netherlands and Germany, with relatively low membership density but politically incorporated labour unions, low wage pressures and outstanding economic adjustments are to be found. Summing up, high unionization and centralization do not always result in responsive bargaining, while low unionization and less centralized union structures may lead to low real-wage growth.

Olson's hypotheses rest on two basic assumptions, which appear to be doubtful in the light of empirical investigation. The one assumption is that various organizational properties — size, internal structures, membership characteristics and external relations — could be concentrated in one-dimensional concepts, like those of 'encompassing' organizations or 'distributive coalitions'. The other assumption refers to the impact of organizational properties on policy-making. Here too Olson treats policy outcomes as characteristically interwoven: for him, low wages result in low inflation and flexible adjustments of industrial structures and thereby promote economic growth. Factually, the various impacts of wages on economic developments would depend on given industrial structures, patterns of state intervention, world-market integration and factor-intensities, e.g. the share of labour costs in certain industries (cf. Meidner, 1980). Hence it is not amazing at all that empirical analysis shows rather complex patterns of economic policy-making in western industrialized countries.

As far as political institutions are concerned, these findings support von Beyme's (1984: 217) comment: 'The organizational explanation has its merits, but the minimization of factors like historical tradition, ideology, alternative organizational models, or the symbiosis of left parties and unions, would take revenge on those who compare systems of interest inter-mediation cross-nationally.' It is certainly not only the problem of empirical analysis mentioned here. But more likely these factors will exercise a systematic influence on organizational incentive structures which goes beyond that of size and scope. Hence we should ask for theoretical objections against the 'political mechanics' suggested by Olson's theory and then try to explain our empirical data in detail.

Offe (1984: 242f.) refers to size as having an ambiguous impact on organizational behaviour. Societal responsibility of organizations is not fully determined by size and membership density, 'relative size' as we call it. This holds true only if associational monopolization reduces those sectors of a society, against which adversary behaviour will positively pay off for large encompassing groups. But those 'exploitable' sectors can expand due to reasons other than organizational ones. For instance, growing state revenues following from economic growth and progressive tax systems, or from natural resources as in the case of North-sea oil, will change incentive structures and organizational action. According to Schwerin (1980) the highly centralized Norwegian labour unions and business organizations met in a 'robber's coalition' against the state, whereby unions fought for social services and business-associations for industrial subsidies. This behaviour was rational for the unions, since alternative tax cuts would have hurt their redistributive aims and existing wage structures. It was also rational for employers, since increasing social wages was seen as a prerequisite for the union's wage restraint in collective bargaining.

Apart from economic reasons, changing political forces may also alter incentive structures. The emergence of Swedish 'Wage Earners Funds' indicates that individualist rational choice criteria might become rather fluid, in particular if conflicting policy objectives like economic growth, stability and full employment are concerned. Centralized unions with high membership density as in Sweden can hardly sacrifice full-employment interests in favour of a more productive society, economic rationalization and low inflation. Instead they found strategies like the devaluation of the Krona, 'Wage Earners Funds' or 'Active Labour Market Policies' more attractive to protect their organizational and membership interests.[5] Now those strategies cannot be put into effect by unions but depend on governmental policies. Hence they rest on certain political prerequisites, such as exchange relationships between government and union policies. In particular these interorganizational relations should be added to sheer group size and membership density as explanatory variables. As an example, real wage cuts in Sweden during the eighties rested on the organizational ability of politically incorporated unions to obtain the implementation of 'Wage Earners Funds' in return for moderate wage policies.

German industrial relations provide an illustrative example of 'encompassing' behaviour without an 'encompassing' structure. Centralization and membership density of unions are rather low,[6] nevertheless they pursue moderate wage policies. Here too we find political and institutional factors which modify the impact of organizational attributes. Among these are historically rooted commitments to social partnership. The ideology of social partnership in Germany rests on fatal experiences with class conflict during the Weimar Republic and the resulting Fascism. It was reinforced by the division of the country and the cold war, which transformed class conflicts into a competition of political systems and hence strengthened capitalist values in West Germany. Additionally, the social partnership was strengthened by the union's belief in a crisis-free management of the economy. The German Social Democratic party also provided a 'social memory' in favour of limited class struggle. And social democratic policies were able to support solidarity norms within the workers movement during the Keynesian expansionist period of the seventies. This became evident with the practice of 'Lohnführerschaft' (wage leadership), which means that certain national unions or even regional subsections opened collective bargaining, and other regions and unions followed their settlements. This happened even though organizational structures and unionization were far away from what Olson would qualify as 'encompassing'. It is interesting to note that the practice of wage-leadership came under pressure during the subsequent regime of neoconservative economic policies. The bourgeois coalition governments strove for flexible wage structures by changing the federal Employment Act in 1985. Thereafter, temporary unemployment indirectly caused by industrial conflict was no longer covered by the national unemployment scheme, if demands were the same in regions and industrial branches with actual industrial conflict and in those regions and firms indirectly afflicted by strikes and lock outs. In this way union's incentives to adopt differentiated wage demands changed without any change of organizational structures.

Obviously there are more factors than organizational attributes which affect collective action. Olson's model turns out to be too simple to grasp some of the really important variables, in particular those which link interest groups to party politics and government policies both on an institutional and ideological level. The question remains to be answered whether Katzenstein provides for a more comprehensive analytical framework.

3. Small states in world markets

Katzenstein (1984, 1985) elaborates the argument that economic problem configurations, problem perceptions and patterns of interest-intermediation have one explanatory variable in common, which determines a country's economic policy. According to his analysis in *Small States in World Markets* (1985) the most decisive factor was sheer size — not of organiz-ed interests as in Olson's model but of national states; and his argument is theoretically just as convincing as Olson's.

Small industrial countries appear to be highly sensitive to world economic developments. Hence they try to protect their economies against unforeseeable impacts from outside. Simultaneously small states are forced to economic centralization and specialization by the rationale of economies of scale. In addition to problems originating in foreign trade, small markets do not provide for stochastic compensations between declining and growing industries. Since, for example, the Belgian economy was highly specialized in steel and textile industries, it was particularly hit by the economic crisis of the 1980s which was in fact a crisis of exactly those industries.

For obvious reasons, small countries should seek some political protection from world economic disturbances. That is where corporatism comes in. In Katzenstein's view corporatism in small countries results from a perception of a common fate and the spread of common fears. But this 'idea of a community of the vulnerable (yielding in) a general commitment to share equitably the burdens of adapting social institutions to a continuously changing world' (Sabel, 1983, cited in Katzenstein, 1985: 199) is far from Olson's argument. Olson follows an individualistic utilitarian path of explanation — collective action is fully determined by sectional interests of single organizations and their members. Katzenstein starts from a common interest formulated in comprehensive bargaining systems and forced by fear and the idea of a common fate.

Katzenstein argues in a much more complex manner than Olson. Nevertheless he does not attach importance to party politics as an explaining variable of associational behaviour:

> Corporatism. . . is not strongly associated with the domination of a particular party and ideology. Data on working-class mobilization (as measured by the percentage of workers unionized and of the electoral strength of leftist parties) show that working-class mobilization is too high for Britain's weak corporatism, too low for the Netherland's and Switzerland's strong corporatism. Corporatism is thus not strongly associated with the mobilization of the working class. (Katzenstein, 1985: 97)

Katzenstein refers to Cameron's (1978) and Wilensky's (1981) analyses. Cameron argued that openness of economies was a better predictor of public spending than socialist incumbency. And Wilensky emphasizes the impact of catholic parties on welfare state policies. It is true that in Belgium, the Netherlands and France welfare spending is as high as in countries dominated by Social Democrats during the postwar era. But there are differences in the structure of welfare spending: paternalist policies of Christian Democratic parties rely heavily on transfer payments, whereas Social Democrats are in favour of social services.[7] There are also differences in labour market and industrial policies, which Katzenstein refers to as liberal corporatist and social corporatist strategies. I shall come back to these policies in the next section. Here I suggest that both Olson and Katzenstein do not attach importance to party politics.

Now, do our data support Katzenstein's hypothesis? The correlations of real wage growth, economic growth and inflation with economic openness (Table 2) do not significantly differ from those with organizational variables. But economic adjustment, measured by structural change and gains in industrial productivity, is highly correlated with a country's dependence on world markets ($r_s = 0.71$). Thus Katzenstein's general hypothesis is strongly supported. Additionally there are some interrelations between a country's smallness and associational structures (population correlates with centralization of unions: $r_s = 0.55$). Small countries are often characterized by thoroughly organized systems of interest intermediation. Except for Switzerland and Ireland, centralization of unions in small countries is high and except for the Netherlands and Switzerland membership density is high as well. This means that the arguments of Olson and Katzenstein do not contradict each other empirically, for 'encompassing' organizations appear to be a special feature of small countries.[8] But still 'relative size' of unions and size of countries will not explain wage policies or industrial adjustments, and there is 50 percent of the variation left which could not be explained by economic openness.[9] Moreover, the differences of policy outcomes and underlying economic strategies between small countries like Sweden and Austria on the one hand, Belgium and the Netherlands on the other, are too big to satisfy such a general explanation. How should we approach this problem? In the following sections patterns of adjustment policies will be analysed and confronted with structural variables.

4. Strategies of economic adjustment

In the context of Olson's *The Rise and Decline of Nations*, economic adjustment means to increase a country's competitive position in world markets. There are several ways to positively adjust economies in times of crisis. A country's international competitiveness rests on two factors: industrial productivity and economic structure. Productivity is a formula which means output per person employed during a certain time unit, whereas economic structure designates qualitative properties (availability and specialization of products) as well as the goodness of fit between a country's supply of industrial products and international demand structures. An important structural attribute is the ability to shift productive factors — labour and capital — to new expanding industries.[10] Productivity gains and structural adjustments result in modern industries and increase a country's position on world markets. There is, however, a third way to cope with adaptive pressures: cheapening of labour. Whereas capital markets are highly internationalized and,. hence, difficult to control politically in some countries, labour markets are still useful for adjusting cost pressures by real wage cuts. Another argument is that flexible wages will promote labour mobility and thereby lead to structural adjustments. In our context it is interesting to note that — according to Olson — 'encompassing' unions would have an incentive to help modernize the economy, but would hardly have an incentive to accept real wage cuts, since this would probably cause a drop in membership and undermine organizational stability. Obviously there is a trap of rationality associated with the thesis of 'encompassing' organizations. Apparently 'encompassing' unions should act against their members' immediate interests in high wages to support economic modernization. This could hardly be explained by an individualistic logic of collective action. Instead one should think of an exchange relationship in which governmental goals, organizational and membership-interests are to be balanced. And such an exchange is probably shaped by power-relations between the actors involved. Hence Olson's argument, that structure provides for definite rational choice criteria and thereby influences organizational behaviour, appears to be a half-truth. Structural properties of organizations might cause a dilemma which can be solved only by external political intervention. This argument will be illustrated below with reference to empirical data.

Theoretical considerations and empirical findings result in three initial approaches to solve politically the problems of economic adjustment: (1) to make wages more flexible, a strategy suggested by Olson; (2) to increase productivity within a given industrial structure, which means to generally stimulate industrial investments; (3) to structurally adjust industries and labour markets, which means to selectively support skills, industrial products, firms or sectors. It is true that these methods are interconnected with each other, but adjustment strategies usually start from one of these initial choices. So we can find labour substituting policies of rationalization on the one hand, which were often influenced by governmental incentives: subsidies, special interest rates, low taxes on investments etc. On the other hand, there are market strategies which basically rest on flexible wages. Their advocates reject industrial subsidies and macro-economic structural intervention. Both strategies affect the micro-economic level, whereas structural adjustment is left to market forces. The third approach rests on macro-economic considerations. It tries to advance economic structures by strategic intervention into capital and labour markets. Austrian and Swedish economic policies are outstanding examples of such policies (cf. Czada, 1986).

Which of these strategies are to be found in the countries analysed here? Table 2 shows the variables — structures of employment, industrial productivity, real wages — that changed most dramatically in favour of economic adjustment during the 1970s.

One can observe four patterns of flexible adjustment policies:
1. Cheapening of labour: *Market-policy.*
2. Substitution of labour: *Economization.*
3. Shifting of labour: *Structural policy.*
4. Mixing the strategies: *Concerted policies.*

Apparently cheapening of labour as an isolated measure results in low gains of industrial productivity, whereas economization obviously widens the distributive margins for unions' wage policies (see Table 1). Both patterns, however, met with mass unemployment in the 1980s. In contrast the politics of concertation resulted in real-wage cuts and low productivity gains, but showed considerably high structural adjustments and low unemployment in the 1980s.[11]

TABLE 2
Strategies for coping with crisis[1]

	Shifting of labour	Substitution of labour	Cheapening of labour
Austria	X		X
Canada			X
Belgium		X	
Denmark		X	
Finland	X	X	
France		X	
FR Germany	X	X	
Ireland	X		
Italy	X		
Japan	X	X	
Netherlands		X	X
Norway	X		X
Sweden	X		X
Switzerland	X		X
United Kingdom			X
USA			X

[1] That ranks of countries in the variables 'Structural Adjustment', 'Productivity' and 'Real Wages' (data: see Table I and Appendix) have been compared. If one variable was higher ranked than others, that indicates this variable to be a 'strategic' one. If two variables were ranked within a range of two ranks, that indicates a 'policy-mix' of two approaches, say shifting of labour by active labour market policies, and cheapening of wages by moderate wage policies.

Note: This table does not contain any information about the success of policies, but only about the relative weight of structural adjustments, gains in productivity and real-wage cuts as strategies for coping with crisis.

Obviously the adjustment strategies shown in Table 2 correlate with systems of interest intermediation. Market policy is attributed to countries with pluralist labour market organizations. Policies of economization are to be found in countries where strong industrial unions participate in public policy-making sectorally. Belgium and Denmark are outstanding examples of sectoral interpenetration of unions and state bureaucracies. Similar structures can be found in West Germany where unions have participated in social policy-making since the beginning of Bismark's social security schemes. Besides they are represented in the labour market administration, on the board of the 'Kreditanstalt für Wiederaufbau' (which gives special loans to industry), and in a host of advisory councils at the parliamentary and administrative level (Menzel, 1980; Süllow, 1981). Apart from their sectoral scope, tripartist institutions in Germany are characterized by advisory functions and do not include executive rights as in Sweden or Austria.

A special variant of 'selective' corporatism emerged with union incorporation into the management of the German Sarre-steel crisis (Esser, et al., 1983). The unions had to answer for dismissals and early retirement schemes which they had agreed upon with employers and government. This pattern resulted in ostracism against the weakest — low qualified foreign and female workers — and is far removed from the Swedish style of a more symmetrical corporatism that is dominated by 'solidaristic' norms. German labour market policies rest on a compensatory strategy of welfarism; actually they consist of social policies.[12] This might stem from paternalist traditions and is related to the union's sectoral participation in social policy. In contrast labour market policies in Sweden, and to a certain extent in Austria, are based on industrial policies. Corporatist intermediation does not rest on sectoral tripartist cartels but relies on a much broader trans-sectoral incorporation of unions into overall economic policy.

German unions actively supported economic adjustments, and they did so at the expense of marginal groups of the labour force. Swedish unions supported economic adjustments as well, but they relied on active industrial policies of the type espoused by the corporatist Labour Market Board. The German strategy was successful, as figures of structural change and productivity indicate. Swedish policies were also successful, despite low unemployment and medium rankings in adjustment and productivity. The question here is: which unions are 'encompassing' in Olson's sense? Could 'encompassing' behaviour mean excluding parts of the potential membership in favour of industrial adjustments or does it mean to balance between organizational integration and adjustment policies?

Membership density in Swedish unions is so high (about 90 percent) that a selection of 'crises-losers', non-organized marginal groups, would be impossible. What about Belgium and Denmark, however, which still have high membership densities of 75 and 50 percent respectively, but which encounter mass unemployment? There is some interunion rivalry in Denmark which probably amplifies the selective impacts of crises on industrial sectors and parts of the labour force on the one hand, and supports rationalization strategies on the other. A similar setting is found in Belgium which shows the highest rates of productivity growth in the seventies. Here the rivalry is between the French-speaking Walonian unions representing the old steel and textile industries and the Flemish unions sited in the rising coast regions. What we can see is that linguistic conflicts and industrial structures additionally modify Olson's organizational approach.

The analysis of economic adjustment policies made clear that organizational size will not determine organizational action. That is because politically incorporated or otherwise powerful producer groups have to submit themselves to the conflicting aims of economic policy. If they do so, they must act against those groups in society or parts of their membership which will actually suffer from rapid economic adjustments; if not, they slow down productivity and economic adjustment to the disadvantage of all. So Olson's argument on 'encompassing' organizations seems also true the other way around. Large organizations have an incentive to hurt the interests, at least in part, of their membership and by so doing they serve their own organizational purposes as well as the overall concerns of the society in which they operate. Policies of economic adjustment exemplify the ambiguous character of organizational size. How organized groups will act in real situations depends on factors which are located within a broader political spectrum. In the next sections I will identify some of the most important of these factors.

5. A political explanation of collective action

There are considerable differences of policy outcomes within Katzenstein's sample of small European states. Productivity gains in industry during the seventies were lowest in Norway and Sweden and highest in Belgium and the Netherlands. For Norway and Sweden this follows from a dualistic economic policy. Productivity is accelerated in export branches for reasons of international competitiveness and moderated in the sheltered sector for reasons of high employment (cf. Edgren et al., 1973; Lundberg, 1985). This coincides with our findings which show relatively high structural adjustments in Norway and Sweden without respective gains in overall industrial productivity.

In these countries economic policy navigates between conflicting aims of industrial adjustment and full employment. Within a sample of sixteen countries Sweden, Norway and Austria endorsed a middle way of economic modernization and achieved the lowest rates of unemployment. Simultaneously, labour unions are the most centralized with highest membership density and thoroughly incorporated into politics in these countries. Such 'encompassing' unions have a strong incentive to help modernize the economy and to protect their members' jobs. But they can do this only with the support of government policies. To achieve structural adjustments without negative side effects on labour markets and unions' organizational capacities requires government involvement in industrial and labour market policies. These policies provide for elements of political exchange and thereby decide on incentives of organizational actions. As illustrated by the Swedish record, the unions moderated their wage claims before the central confederation LO achieved control of its member-unions' wage policies. They did so to secure social-democratic governance, which had previously restored their bargaining power through Keynesian policies (Martin, 1984: 197ff.; cf. Korpi, 1978: 80ff.). Thus the political exchange between a governing party and affiliated unions gave birth to the 'Swedish Model'. The unions' option did not result from organizational structures. Unionization and organizational centralization were relatively low in the thirties, and Sweden was the country with extremely high strike activities during the first decades of the twentieth century (Korpi and Shalev, 1979). On the other hand, this political exchange was due to a Keynesian economic strategy which rested on the interventionist abilities of a small country. Of the states which applied Keynesian policies during the thirties, Sweden had by far the most powerful central administration and governmental direction, as was shown by comparisons of Swedish policies with the New Deal in the USA (Weir and Skocpol, 1985). Even in Nazi-Germany the economic expansion of the thirties, in particular new employment schemes and industrial reconstruction plans, suffered from departmentalization and lacked coordination (Mommsen, 1985).

Small states favour economic interventionism for many reasons. One of them is that of economic vulnerability and common fears which support the *formulation* of consensual policies as described by Peter Katzenstein. In addition, high regional and ownership concentrations of industries provide for an increase in the flow of information and facilitate the *administration* of selective economic policies. As an example, the Austrian Chancellor keeps in close contact with all major private and public business leaders and the Swedish government has its agents on the boards of large companies — based on informal agreements or as official representatives (for instance in the financial sector).[13] Hence, a country's smallness affects policies not only via dominant ideologies and characteristic incentive structures. Of course, the latter will influence the process of policy formulation, but policy outcomes — so important for political exchanges — depend on the process of implementation as well. Only if governments and interest organizations are able to 'deliver' both consensual and technical support will corporatist strategies succeed. The importance of organizations as agents of implementation was rather underestimated by Olson and many researchers on corporatist arrangements. Unions that are incorporated into the administration of industrial and labour market policies[14] appear to be both special interest groups and agents of governmental policy. Thus technical aspects of organizational co-ordination influence the success of political strategies, which in turn motivates organizational action and neocorporatist exchange.[15] Now, organizational incentive structures have come to be increasingly complex when institutional interlocking and mixed policies emerge. How unions collectively act then depends heavily on incentives provided by public policies and interventionist capabilities of governments.

Correlations of smallness of countries, world market dependency, industrial ownership-concentration, corporatism and social democratic governance (Table 3), indicate a causal setting that goes beyond that of Olson's and partly of Katzenstein's arguments. One could rank these attributes to look for the operating mechanisms behind them. With the aid of a simple Guttman scale,[16] we are able to ascertain the decisive meaning of party government for organizational development.

TABLE 3
The prerequisites of corporatist political exchanges

Guttman scale (corporatism) using

V061	Trans-sectoral corporatism	Division point = 3.00
V003	Postwar dominance of social democracy	Division point = 3.00
V081	Centralization of unions	Division point = 6.00
V079	Unionization	Division point = 45.00
V075	Concentration of economic ownership	Division point = 3.00
V034	External economic dependency	Division point = 45.00
V036	Smallness of domestic markets	Division point = 1.00

RESP = 1 for values equal to division point and above

ITEM RESP	V061 0	V061 1	V003 0	V003 1	V081 0	V081 1	V075 0	V075 1	V079 0	V079 1	V034 0	V034 1	V036 0	V036 1	TOTAL	
7	0	3 (ERR)	0	3	0	3	0	3	0	3	0	3	0	3	3	Austria / Sweden / Norway
6	1	0	0	1 (ERR)	0	1	0	1	0	1	0	1	0	1	1	Finland
5	2	0	1	1	1	1 (ERR)	0	2	0	2	0	2	0	2	2	Belgium / Denmark
4	2	1	3	0	2	1	1	2 (ERR)	1	2	0	3	0	3	3	Netherlands / Ireland / New Zealand
3	1	0	1	0	1	0	0	1	1	0 (ERR)	0	1	0	1	1	Switzerland
2	2	0	1	1	2	0	2	0	0	2	2	0 (ERR)	1	1	2	Great Britain / Australia

											Canada Italy
1	2	2	2	2	2	0	2	2	2	2	2	Germany (FR) Japan, France USA
						ERR						
0	0	0	0	0	0	2	0	0	0	0	0	2
	4	4	4	4	4	0	4	4	4	4	4	4
												18
												14

Sums	14	4	12	6	9	9	8	10	8	10	5	13
Percents	78	22	67	33	50	50	44	56	44	56	28	72
Errors	0	1	0	2	1	1	2	0	2	0	1	0

18 cases were processed   0 (or 0.0 percent) were missing

Statistics
Coefficient of reproducibility = 0.8889
Minimum marginal reproducibility = 0.6349
Percent improvement = 0.2540
Coefficient of scalability = 0.6957

	V061 Corporatism[1]	SOZDEM Social Democrats dominant	V081 Union-centralization	Correlation coefficients V079 Unionization[1]	V075 Industry concentration	V034 World-market integr.	V036 Smallness of countries (GDP)
V061	1.0000						
SOZDEM	0.6382**[2]	1.0000					
V081	0.7036**	0.5118*	1.0000				
V079	0.3134	0.6028	0.3709	1.0000			
V075	0.3200[2]	0.4029	0.4264*	0.6461*	1.0000		
V034	0.6402*	0.4576	0.6187*	0.3504	0.7470*	1.0000	
V036	0.2991	0.2843	0.3952	0.4795	0.7845**	0.6373*	1.0000

* Significant at 0.01   ** Significant at 0.001
1 Pearson corr
2 Kendalls tau; others r_s
Sources: SOZDEM: Schmidt, 1982; V034: Pryor, 1972; V061: Czada, 1986; others: see Table 1.

The rankings of variables and countries give some insights into the structured relationships of political 'input-factors' discussed here. Generally the scale supports the hypothesis that the smallness of countries results in a high degree of world market integration. Moreover, most of the small countries are highly unionized and have extremely concentrated industrial structures. Additionally, six of the small countries have highly concentrated labour unions, and out of these, five experienced social democratic governance in more than half of the years between 1945 and 1980. Only Sweden, Austria, Norway and Finland combine all these attributes simultaneously, whereby three of them are known as corporatist countries (compare the ranking in Franz Lehner's contribution in this book). In the first instance, the scale shows that corporatism has many prerequisites, which indeed originate in smallness and economic openness of countries. Below I will explain why some countries 'climbed up' towards 'trans-sectoral' corporatism, and others stayed on the lower ranks of the scale.

Unfortunately, we cannot correlate policy outcomes with this 'scale of corporatism'. Obviously each ranking tells its own story. This is especially true for those countries which are not easily placed on the scale. These are Great Britain, Switzerland, the Netherlands and Belgium. On the whole, correlations with policy outcomes would yield a somewhat curvilinear relationship. For instance, cautious wage policies of unions are a feature of countries placed at both ends of the scale (see real wages, Table 1). Simultaneously these countries experienced much lower gains of industrial productivity during the seventies than those on the middle ranks of the scale.

Probably we should take the scaling procedure as a heuristic device. One could get some insights by an analysis of outliers — countries which do not fulfil the ordering principles of the scale. There is no problem with the corporatist cases. Sweden, Austria, Norway are small countries with strong unions, concentrated and centralized industrial structures and the longest social democratic incumbency. Unions are incorporated across the fields of industrial and labour market policies (Czada, 1986). Japan, France and Germany, on the other hand, are economically large countries, less dependent on foreign trade and with diversified and regionally more scattered industries. Social democratic governance in the postwar era was much lower than in Sweden, Britain, Austria, Norway and Denmark. Nevertheless, labour unions were incorporated on the firm-level (Japan), controlled by paternalist regulation (France)[17] or ideologically integrated for historical reasons and organizationally by industrial 'Mitbestimmung' and politically incorporated through participation on several boards and advisory councils (e.g. Germany). Beside these countries of corporatism without labour, which means that labour unions are of only marginal significance when overall economic strategies are concerned, we find countries with pluralist systems of industrial relations. These are also placed on the lower ranks of the scale. But what about the countries in between these clusters of corporatist and pluralist systems of interest intermediation? Here smallness does not necessarily lead to high unionization (Netherlands, Switzerland), and politically incorporated unions are not always related to moderate wage policies (Belgium, Denmark). These appear to be those countries which are covered by neither Katzenstein's nor Olson's generalizations. Whereas Katzenstein describes the most important mechanisms of corporatist integration and Olson explains the logic of pluralist 'distributive-coalitions', both neglect those cases where pluralist segmentation and corporatist participation interfere with each other. As a hypothesis, the political structure of such countries might be characterized by extremely complex societal cleavages. Hence, the resulting conflicts call for political institutions which one cannot put on a level with pluralist or corporatist settings. To analyse those deviant cases in more detail would probably fill the explanation gap left by the theories of Olson and Katzenstein.

6. The impact of party politics and bureaucratic structures

Britain is a big country with relatively low dependency on foreign trade and low monopolization of industries.[18] Normally this results in low unionization, but in fact more than 50 percent of total civilian employment is organized within an extremely decentralized system of craft unions.[19] Moreover, social democratic governance in Britain was as high as in Austria or Norway during the postwar era.

As a rather terse explanation one could think of union security arrangements (closed shops) and of conservative corporatist attempts which may have fostered unionization during and after wartime economies but did not support organizational hierarchies. A more general approach which coincides with our arguments above focuses on the fragmentation of capitalist interests and shortcomings of the British state and administration. In some instances British governments tried to integrate unions and organized businesses into industrial and labour market policies. The first national tripartite governmental agency with union membership and representatives of the newly merged Confederation of British Industries (CBI), the 'National Board for Prices and Incomes' (NBPI), was set up in 1965 by the Labour government, and abolished in 1971 by the newly elected Conservative government. The board's tasks were to be imbedded in a comprehensive programme of policies called 'The National Plan' concerning the labour market, macro-economic development and budgetary planning. In fact, integration of these policies failed. In particular, extensions of the NBPI's functions became frustrated as a result of deficient departmental co-ordination, unbalanced and changing relationships between government, unions and the employers, problems of the Trade Union

Congress (TUC) with its affiliates and tensions within the governing Labour party and its trade union base. The board had been working neither in close detailed liaison, nor in close co-ordination with the conduct of monetary and fiscal policy (Corina, 1975). Of course, there were some restrictive factors within the interest organizations involved, but even if they agreed upon certain measures, these have been thwarted by counter-active government policies. British governments could not deliver 'Swedish' policies in exchange for the unions' incorporation.

Until the 1960s, British economic policy followed a pattern known as 'stop — go' policy. Most often consensual expansionist policies were accompanied by the need to devalue the pound sterling. It was 'the basic primitive instinct of governments faced with deteriorating balance of payments' (Balogh, 1978: 128) which usually turned them back to a restrictive course. These problems had been institutionalized in permanent conflicts between the Department of Economic Affairs and the Treasury, with which both Labour and Conservative governments had to contend. There is a host of literature in respect to British planning which shows the crucial importance of interventionist capabilities on the side of governments and administration. Leruez (1978) argues that the absence of state administrators in industrial politics led to a sectoral instrumentalization of public funds. Keith Middlemas (1979) and Tom Nairn (1977) give an account of bureaucratic fragmentation in British politics, and in a comparison of Keynesian policies in Sweden, USA and Britain, M. Weir and Th. Scocpol (1985) demonstrate the importance of state structures for the conduct of interventionist policies.[20]

Doubtless there was a lack of concertation in British politics. But problems in the process of economic policy formation did not at first result from decentralized unions. Although Britain was less dependent on foreign trade than other European countries, its economic problems were due to world market developments and resulting adaptive pressures. Policies of industrial adjustment suffered from volatile economic strategies caused by changes of government and conflicting aims of industrial growth on the one hand, and a strong currency on the other. Furthermore, it suffered from bureaucratic fragmentation, in particular after 1964 when the newly elected Labour government tried to actively support industrial adjustment. This does not mean that the British state apparatus was fragmented with respect to the administration of day to day problems, but incapable of getting coherent solutions on the most conflicting fields of economic policy-making. Certainly societal cleavages played a prominent role in this respect. In particular, the conflict of financial and industrial interests within the capitalist class was an unique and decisive feature of British capitalism (cf. Zysman, 1983). Moreover, British industrial capitalists were organized in a pullulate variety of small interest-groups. In contrast to Olson's theory, the multitude and pluralist isolation of economic interests did not strengthen economic markets or the state's interventionist capacities. Hence the incentives for industrial progress were not embodied within appropriate institutions of interest intermediation and political intervention. To solve the problems of industrial decline the British state was overloaded in a structural sense. It did not suffer from lack of resources of legitimation but from institutional barriers within its internal organization.

The Netherlands pose a somewhat difficult problem, fitting least with the Guttman scale. Small, highly dependent on foreign trade but with relatively low industrial concentration ratios,[21] the Netherlands are poorly unionized (33 percent), but, nevertheless, have highly centralized labour unions which did not lead to Social Democratic dominance.

Here again we should refer to some characteristics of governments and bureaucratic structures. Shifting coalitions and complex mechanisms of coalition building restricted the political exchange of governments with societal groups. Certainly the Dutch unions have been incorporated into politics, but political strategies were based on intricate coalition agreements which determined the political debate — in particular when fiscal and economic policies were concerned. Thus the political role of the Dutch unions was far from that of their Swedish or Austrian counterparts. On the other hand a traditionally strong bureaucracy increased its autonomy in the conduct of industrial and social policy. Mokken and Stokman (1978) give an account of prominent links between bureaucratic resorts and interest groups that are often shielded against party politics and the parliamentary arena. The sectorally strong bureaucracy feels bound to technocratic norms and liberal orientations.

Dutch corporatism remained institutionally strong but lost its significance for economic strategy formation during the seventies. This was due to a shift of emphasis from incomes policies to industrial and labour market policies. The Dutch corporatism could not develop beyond cyclical incomes policies, which followed from universal principles (e.g. competitive unit labour costs) and were regulated by law and technocratic expertise. Thus they were characterized by bureaucratic procedures and varying measures of government direction.[22] A bureaucracy's ability to settle more complex distributive conflicts in the field of employment and industrial policies appears to be rather limited. It was probably for that reason that in the intricate and highly conflicting field of industrial policy consensual interventionist strategies did not work in the same way as with incomes policy. The breakdown of corporatist institutions in the field of industrial policy like the NEHEM (Nederlandse Hertsructuringsmaatschapij) and the 'Beleidscommissie Sheepsbouw' illustrates the problems of selective intervention (Zimmermann, 1986).

Party politics provided another distinguishing feature of the Netherlands. Despite the unions' political incorporation which generally leads to lower unemployment, the Netherlands has the second highest rates of unemployment during the 1980s in the countries reviewed here. Simultaneously, the highest welfare spending is also to be found in that country. That coincides with industrial minimum-intervention by coalition governments of Christian Democrats and right-wing Liberals since 1978. Christian Democratic parties often combine social interventionism with industrial market policies. This strategy reflects internal 'cross-pressures' of 'catch–all-parties' which have to balance between a strong conservative clientele, working-class support and agrarian partisans. Hence redistributive policies of Christian parties rest on industrial market strategies and concentrate on income maintenance programmes and subsidies. Only those allow for selectively rewarding certain constituencies and generally do not interfere with markets and individual consumerism, as is true of a public service economy often preferred by Social Democrats.

Dietmar Braun and Hans Keman emphasized four attributes of Dutch policy-making — the sectoralization of interest politics, high institutional stability, state dominated bargaining, and highly volatile policy strategies during the postwar era (Braun and Keman, 1986). Now, how can institutional stability result in volatile policies, which range from corporatist to neoliberal strategies? Their analysis suggests that sectoralism has fostered 'cyclical' shifts in policy-making. But sectoralism can lead to distributive coalitions and political stalemate as well. Probably one should point to the dominant role of bureaucracy and technocratic political expertise again and combine these with the special problems given by economic openness.

World market integration of the Netherlands is one of the highest of all western industrialized countries. That has favoured compensatory welfare policies and working-class integration. But why then are there no active labour market policies and high unemployment? The answer is to be found in the very same variable: if external economic dependency, measured by the sum of exports and imports as a share of GNP, approaches 100 percent, the effectiveness of national industrial policies necessarily declines. National measures will then no longer suffice for interventionist structural adjustment policies, and governments will have to rely on market mechanisms instead. Hence they could no longer serve as guarantors of corporatist exchanges. There is hardly a linear relationship between economic openness and policies of industrial adjustment as Katzenstein and Cameron suggest. Certainly, economic openness favours the politics of compromise, but there is a turning point beyond which the implementation of national policies becomes thwarted by excessive world market dependencies. Apart from reasons of logic, peculiarities of labour market and industrial policies of the Netherlands and Belgium in relation to other small countries do support such considerations. These countries have the highest foreign trade ratios and are strongest interpenetrated with multinational enterprises, and simultaneously combine the highest rates of unemployment and increases of industrial productivity with top-rankings in welfarism.[23] The ever increasing world-market dependency, and the subsequent external vulnerability obviously restricts interventionist industrial strategies in such a way that there are no other alternatives to cope with crisis than compensatory social policies. Apparently this was also true for British politics during the sixties, when the external vulnerability of the pound sterling paralysed economic policy-making. Balogh (1982: 129) states with respect to the conflicts between the efforts to maintain high interest rates on the one hand, and expansionist industrial strategies on the other: 'unfortunately, one could generalize...and say that when you *could* plan, you don't and when you *do* plan, you can't'. Similarly Maldagué (1982: 152) interprets Belgian experiences, which will be discussed below.

In sum, Dutch policy-making shows again that a country's size, economic openness and associational structures are highly ambiguous with respect to organizational incentives and collective action. Coping with crises by a compensatory strategy which combined paternalist welfare policies and industrial market strategies resulted from Christian orientations, interventionist limitations caused by excessive world market integration and sectoral corporatism. Not the least, Dutch policy-making was characterized by the strong representation of religious cleavages. The confessional pillarization of society resulted in a highly centralized system of interest intermediation, but, nevertheless, created complex policy networks. Thus organizational size serves no longer as a major determinant of incentive structures. As an example, the Dutch welfare organizations are strongly interconnected with labour unions. The union's persistence on issues of public welfare, for example, their demand for an indexation of social wages, might result from such historical networks.

There are some parallels between the Netherlands and Belgium. The latter is characterized by dominant Christian parties, the highest foreign trade quotas, politically incorporated unions, high rates of unemployment and extensive welfare policies.[24] With regard to the Guttman scale it appears to be an outlier as well. Scalability is especially disturbed by factors such as union centralization and social democratic governance. Considering her smallness, high dependence on foreign trade, high industrial concentration and high unionization of 75 percent, Belgium should have had some social democratic governments. The reason why Belgium does not fit the scale might above all result from linguistic diversity and conflict. As already mentioned, these factors make industrial policies difficult to formulate when regional crises are concerned. Of course, Belgian union-federations are highly incorporated into policy-making but, as in the Netherlands, elite consensus rests on a formal rather than a substantial basis. Procedural rules are central, whereas the Swedish politics of compromise primarily revolves around material strategies. In Switzerland,[25] Belgium and the Netherlands linguistic or religious diversity resulted in consociational politics, but it was Keynesian policy which led to the Saltsjöbaden agreement in Sweden.

In the field of linguistic or religious conflicts traditional values super-imposed themselves on organizational incentives. How organizations behave depends less on actual assessments but more on historical circum-stances. Although organizations act as 'social memories', this aspect of collective action is entirely absent from Olson's perspective of rational choice theory. It is probably for that reason that the Netherlands, Belgium and Switzerland fit least with his argument. But even Katzenstein underestimates the role of Christian and Social Democratic parties and of non-class societal cleavages which are of importance for the explanation of different policies of industrial adjustment.

Although membership density was more than twice as high as in the Netherlands,[26] Belgian unions were much more strike prone and struggled for the highest real wage gains during economic crisis. Despite weak social democratic governance and highly centralized unions, a difference was to be found in the union's autonomy. There were no governmental controls of union activities in Belgium. As in Britain, industrial relations were not regulated by law (Lecher, 1981). On the other hand, unions were incorporated into national and sectoral tripartist institutions and did effec-tively control firm-level bargaining. But effective political participation was limited to labour market and wage policies, which were formulated by the 'National Labour Council'. As in the Netherlands, overall economic strategies rested on compensatory social policies, whereas economic adjustment was left to market forces. Unemployment as well as industrial productivity gains were the highest in Belgium of the western industrialized countries.

Belgium was particularly hit by crises in the steel and textile sectors, which were the major industries in that country. Industrial reconstructions, closures and regional shifts of industries increased unemployment at the end of the seventies. Despite the highest economic openness in Europe, internal strains of dominant Christian parties and strong distributive conflicts between Flemish and Walonian regions, interventionist industrial policies have had little success. Hence the unions' incentive was to translate their corporatist properties into high wages and compensatory social policies for the unemployed.

7. Conclusion

Labour unions act in a political environment which is characterized by a rather complex web of institutional linkages and ideological affiliations. These interrelationships affect perceptions of problems and strategic choices of organizational actors. The incentive structures that emerge from a continuous sequence of political bargains derive not only from internal organizational attributes as put forward by Olson, or from problem configurations given by a country's smallness and world market integration as suggested by Katzenstein.

It is true that a country's smallness results in economic dependency and thus often supports industrial concentration and organizational growth, but smallness is hardly associated with complexions of party government and patterns of economic strategies. In particular, there are different styles of political exchange under Social Democratic and Christian Democratic governments. The first call for interventionist strategies not only in the field of social policy but also in industrial and labour market policies, whereas the latter rely on market forces to achieve economic adjustments. Christian Democratic parties are often affiliated with confessional unions and business associations, and thus exchange relationships are restricted to compensatory social policies.

Apart from party systems and governments, bureaucratic structures influence the shape and content of state-group-linkages. At first the degree of sectionalism found in systems of interest intermediation depends on bureaucratic structures. As an example, 'encompassing' unions can be linked with sectoral administrations as in West Germany, Belgium and, to a certain degree, in the Netherlands, or participate in overall policy-making as in Austria, Sweden and Norway. Secondly, bureaucratic styles and capacities determine the elements of exchange — single policy measures — which can be implemented successfully.

The politics of exchange does not follow a voluntaristic concept but rests on certain institutional prerequisites. Industrial and organizational central-ization are some of them, but in particular, governments have to guarantee the adherence of contractual policies. They must be able to conduct their own part of an agreement and to control the 'contractual fidelity' of other participants. This is particularly important to labour unions, since they can hardly sanction private firms which do not follow pre-agreed strategies of concerted policies. Administrative prerequisites are lowest with incomes and social policies, whereas industrial interventionist policies call for strong and effective bureaucracies. It was probably for this reason that contractual incomes policies often could not spill over to industrial and labour market policies.

Governments and bureaucracies modify organizational incentives. This is especially true for large and centralized labour unions in the fields of industrial and labour market policies. 'Encompassing' unions can hardly obtain rational choice criteria from inside their organizations. If they help modernize the economy they risk dismissals and hurt their members' immediate interests; if not, they slow-down the economy and thereby infringe on the long-term interests of their membership and of the society as a whole. This dilemma can only be solved with the aid of governments. If they support unions by implementing active labour market policies or by introducing union-based forms of codetermination, governmental policies relieve unions from some negative results of increased industrial rationalization and structural changes.

In sum, the impact of interest organizations on policies of economic adjustment should not be isolated from party politics, in particular party-group linkages, governmental strategies and national bureaucratic styles. For these factors are strongly and, as I tried to show, systematically related to organizational incentives; in particular if organizations encompass large groups of a society. Additionally, broader cleavage structures of religious or linguistic conflicts will probably affect organizational settings as well as reactions to adaptive pressures from world markets. And not least, a strong impact of policy characteristics on organizational incentives was discovered. The possibilities of political exchange do not only vary with factors mentioned above, but also with policy fields. On the one hand, this results from sector specific organizational participation — say in social policy, labour market, or industrial policy. On the other hand, these policies contain peculiar conflict structures. Industrial policy, as it intervenes into the productive structure of an economy, meets the nerve-centres of a capitalist system, whereas incomes policy is geared to solve distributive conflicts on the basis of macro-economic considerations.

Appendix

Economic modernization was measured by two indicators: structural adjustment and increases of industrial productivity. Structural adjustment indicates the shifts of employment towards growing industries within a sample of seven industrial sectors (Figure A1). The concept of productivity means output per person employed during a certain time unit. Thus productivity gains (Table A1) mean an increase in the output/employment ratio at a given working time. This is based either upon raising outputs in growing industries, or drops in employment in crisis industries. As shown in Table A1, indicators of structural adjustment and changes of industrial productivity are independent from each other during the 1970s. The reason is to be found in heterogeneous industrial structures, whereby a productivity slowdown in crisis industries or politically sheltered sectors is compensated by productivity growth in competitive sectors. Additionally, output and employment in a certain industrial sector can grow without respective gains in productivity as a result of specialization and changing demand structures. As an example, there is only one country — Denmark — in which increasing employment in leather and shoe-producing sectors (Figure A1) is to be found. The success of Danish handicraft leather products does not rest on rationalization. Nevertheless it means structural change.

The data was processed from figures collected by the United Nations (*UN — Industrial Statistics*) and covers the period from 1970 to 1977. It is not suited for use in econometrics for several reasons, but should give a sufficient indication of a country's rank in cross-national comparisons of industrial modernization.

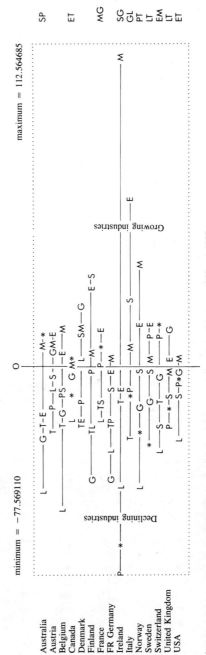

FIGURE A1
Shifts of employment[1]

Textile   plotted with (T)
Leather & prod. plotted with (L)
Paper & prod.   plotted with (P)
Glass & prod.   plotted with (G)
Iron and Steel   plotted with (S)
Machinery   plotted with (M)
Electr. Machinery plotted with (E)

Points exceeding the scale of the graph and points where two or more variables have the same value will be plotted with (*). The variable concerned will be indicated on the far right hand side of the graph.

[1] The graph shows shares of employment in seven industrial sectors as they changed between 1970 and 1977.
Source: UN — Industrial Statistics (1980 edn), New York: UN-Publications.

TABLE A1
Structural adjustment and productivity

	Structural adjustment[1]	Productivity[2]	Modernization[3]
Australia	62	3.8	11
Austria	67	4.8	9
Belgium	128	9.4	1
Canada	18	4.1	12
Denmark	−6	7.3	7
Finland	90	7.1	5
France	58	5.8	8
FR Germany	118	3.9	4
Ireland	368	6.1	3
Italy	n.a.	5.3	n.a.
Japan	n.a.	9.1	n.a.
Netherlands	n.a.	8.3	2
Norway	161	2.1	6
Sweden	77	3.1	10
United Kingdom	50	2.4	14
USA	46	3.0	13

[1] Increase of the growing industries' share of industrial employment plus the losses of the declining industries' share of industrial employment (1970–77, in percent)
[2] Average of annual changes 1970–77
[3] Rank order of countries, given by the combined ranks in variables structural adjustment and industrial productivity (see text).
Sources: *UN — Industrial Statistics*, see Figure A1, Neef and Capdevielle (1980)

TABLE A2
Real wages in industry (1975 = 100)

	1976	1977	1978	1979	1980	1981	1982
Austria	102	105	107	109	110	110	110
Belgium	102	104	107	110	112	115	112
Denmark	104	105	108	112	113	113	114
Finland	101	98	97	101	102	102	n.a.
France	104	107	111	113	115	116	119
FR Germany	102	106	108	110	110	110	109
Ireland	99	101	107	110	112	108	n.a.
Italy	104	111	115	118	119	124	125
Japan	101	103	105	108	108	109	111
Netherlands	100	101	102	102	100	97	97
Norway	107	108	108	106	105	102	102
Sweden	107	103	101	101	97	95	95
Switzerland	100	100	103	101	102	101	102
United Kingdom	101	96	101	103	102	103	106
USA	103	105	106	103	99	98	98

Source: International Labour Organization, 1984: *World Labour Report*, Geneva

Notes

1. Lehmbruch (1986) points out parallels of pluralist and Olsonian thinking. Both approaches concentrate on organizations which are rather isolated against each other, neglect governmental interventions and favour a mechanistic idea of political action.

2. This part of the argument was added to the 'Logic' in a second book, *The Rise and Decline of Nations* (Olson, 1982).

3. Olson himself refers to labour unions to illustrate his argument. In his eyes unions cause downward 'sticky' wages, which end up in stagflation and economic decline. Organizational size, representativity and the scope of bargaining decide — via incentive structures — on the detailed mechanisms of this interrelation. Data on unionization and centralization of unions should suffice for an empirical framework, since unions' potential membership usually represents a huge share of a nation's population. Data on economic adjustment are processed in a technical appendix.

4. Sweden and Austria record considerably strong employment shifts during the seventies, but Sweden especially suffers from a productivity-slowdown which reaches that of the USA. Detailed data are to be found in the appendix.

5. cf. Esping-Andersen's contribution in this book.

6. Unionization in Germany is 33 percent, whereas in Sweden 85 percent of the labour force are unionized. Headey (1970), Wilensky (1976), Schmitter (1981) and Korpi and Shalev (1979) qualify Germany's organizational centralization as low.

7. Christian Democratic parties often combine social interventionism with industrial market policies. This strategy reflects internal 'cross-pressures' of those 'catch–all–parties' which have to balance between a strong bourgeois clientele, working-class supports and agrarian partisans. Moreover such parties appear to be organizationally fragmented along industrial, labour and agrarian factions. Links of Christian Democratic governments with societal interest groups are often influenced by 'confederate' party structures, which provide for complex networks of party affiliated groups. Thus strategies of social paternalism, sectoral participation and industrial market policies might arise from organizational attributes of Christian Democratic parties. I wish to thank Josef Schmid, who will elaborate this argument in a doctoral thesis on the German Christian Democratic Party (CDU).

8. Nevertheless correlations are only medium because there are some outliers among the large countries. The United Kingdom and Italy have unionization rates as high as the average of small countries.

9. Unfortunately, one cannot make use of multivariate statistical methods because of the small number of cases and multicollinearity between independent variables. But the correlation-matrix indicates that the variance in economic adjustment explained by organizational variables and economic openness will probably fall short of 60 percent.

10. Hardes (1981) employs indicators of economic change, e.g. employment shifts between economic sectors, to measure structural adjustment. Esser et al. (1983) emphasized labour substituting effects within economic branches. The splitting-up of factors of economic competitiveness used here was inspired by articles of J. David Richardson (1971) and Klaus Henkner (1981). I am indebted to Gerd Gierszewski who called my attention to their analysis. In the following economic modernization has a two-dimensional meaning covering structural adjustments and gains in industrial productivity.

11. Unemployment rates in 1983 were: Australia (9.9), Austria (4.1), Belgium (13.9), Canada (11.8), Denmark (10.5), Finland (6.6), France (8.3), Federal Republic of Germany (8.0), Italy (9.8), Japan (2.6), Netherlands (13.7), Norway (3.3), Sweden (3.5), Switzerland (0.9), United Kingdom (12.6), USA (9.5). Sources: OECD, *Labour Force Statistics*; OECD, *Economic Outlook* 38, December 1985.

12. Swedish and German labour market policies are compared in Johanesson and Schmid (1980).

13. I am indebted to Professor Dahrendorf, who gave me some information about close personal contacts and informal networks between business leaders and leading politicians in Austria and Sweden.

14. We cannot go into the institutional settings of Swedish and Austrian policy-making, but refer to Marin (1982) about Techno-corporatism in Austria, and to several contributions of the International Institute of Management, Berlin, on Swedish labour market and industrial policy, e.g. Hanf et al. (1977). See also Ruin (1974).

15. In a comparison of Swedish, Austrian and German labour market policies, Scharpf (1984) could demonstrate that exchange relationships between governments, national banks and unions are in fact networks of implementation.

16. A Guttman scale works like a multiple riddle screen, which becomes closer meshed step by step. It scales variables and cases according to certain conditions. Here the least difficult condition appears to be smallness of countries followed by economic openness, unionization, industrial centralization, unions' centralization, Social Democratic governance and trans-sectoral political incorporation of unions. Apparently trans-sectoral political incorporation rests on all other attributes mentioned before: Social Democratic dominance, union centralization, etc.

17. Pluralism in French labour relations is a product of state interventionist strategies which should restrain communist predominance. Several laws and ad hoc interventions provided for protections of minorities and rules of representation. Peter Jansen (1985) worked out this etatist (in labour relations) and paternalist (in social policy) relations historically.

18. According to Pryor (1972: 133) overall concentration ratios differ significantly between France, Italy, Great Britain, West Germany, USA and Japan with lower levels of industrial concentration, and Sweden, Canada and Belgium with higher levels. Following Stephens (1979) Austria and Switzerland belong to the countries with higher levels. Overall economic concentration appears to be rather unchanged over time. Dunning and Pearce (1985) report a minor decline of overall industrial concentration in all western capitalist countries during the sixties, whereas from 1973 on concentration increases again. But this is caused by specific developments of industrial sectors and therefore does not change the ranking of countries. Small states with small national markets usually have higher concentrated industries than large countries.

19. Forty-five percent of unionization appeared to be the division point above which conditions become stipulating for corporatist integration as well as for social democratic governments and high union centralization.

20. I wish to thank Edgar Grande who called my attention to this discussion. He transferred the hypotheses developed with British Keynesianism to the analysis of monetarist and neo-liberal policies. Apparently coherent state structures seem to be of such an importance that weakly or even 'negative' interventionist approaches depend on them as well as Keynesian interventionist policies.

21. Concentration ratios were computed by Pryor (1972), who discovered the Netherlands to be an outlier with respect to high correlations between a country's smallness and economic monopolization. Additionally he found little variation of overall industrial concentration over time.

22. The Dutch system of incomes politics rested on a meticulously balanced interplay of three bodies: the self-regulated 'Foundation of Labour', the 'Social-Economic-Council' based on public-law, and the 'Board of Mediators' directed by governments. This system of incomes policy showed remarkable institutional stability considering highly volatile policy strategies during the seventies.

23. The Netherlands and Belgium are among the countries with highest social transfer payments to private households. The Netherlands come to 28.4 percent as a share of GNP,

Belgium to 21.4 percent, whereas Sweden — dependent upon its emphasis on public social services — achieves 'only' 18.6 percent (all figures of 1979, source: OECD, 'National Accounts Statistics', Czada 1986). Even if one takes overall social security spending, Belgium ranks among the four countries with the highest quotas (Netherlands, Sweden, France, Belgium).

24. Belgium's economic openness varies between 84 percent exports and imports as a share of GNP 1972 and 107 percent 1979.

25. As Switzerland is not discussed in detail here, I refer to Franz Lehner's analysis 'Pressure Politics and Economic Growth: Olson's Theory and the Swiss Experience', in Mueller (ed.) (1983).

26. In Belgium unionization comes to 80 percent (Lecher, 1981: 35). The union confederations CSC (Christian, Flemish) and FCTB (socialist, Walonian) concentrate on certain industries and regions. Thus factual concentration of decision-making is similar to that of the Netherlands.

References

Balogh, T. (1978) 'Britain's Planning Problems', pp. 121–36 in S. Holland (ed.) *Beyond Capitalist Planning*. Oxford: Basil Blackwell.

Braun, D. and J. E. Keman (1986) 'Politikstrategien und Konfliktregulierung in den Niederlanden', *Politische Vierteljahresschrift* (PVS), 27: 78–99.

Cameron, D. (1978) 'The Expansion of the Public Economy', *American Political Science Review*, 72(1): 243–61.

Corina, J. (1975) 'Planning and the British Labour Market: Incomes and Manpower Policy 1965–70', pp. 177–201 in J. Hayward and M. Watson (eds) *Planning, Politics and Public Policy. The British, French and Italian Experience*. Cambridge: Cambridge University Press.

Czada, R. (1986) 'Zwischen Arbeitsplatzinteresse und Modernisierungszwang', doctoral dissertation. Konstanz: University of Konstanz.

Dunning, J. and D. Pearce (1985) *The World's Largest Industrial Enterprises*. New York: St. Martin's Press.

Edgren, G., K. O. Faxén and C.-E. Odhner (1973) *Wage Formation and the Economy*. London: Allen & Unwin.

Esser, J., W. Fach and W. Väth (1983) *Krisenregulierung*. Frankfurt am M.: Suhrkamp.

Hanf, K., B. Hjern and O. Porter (1977) *Implementation of Manpower Training: Local Administrative Networks in the Federal Republic of Germany and Sweden*. International Institute of Management and Administration (IIM-dp 77–112) Wissenschaftszentrum Berlin.

Hardes, H. D. (1981) *Arbeitsmarktpolitik, Arbeitsmarktstrukturen und Beschäftigungsprobleme im internationalen Vergleich*. Tübingen: Mohr.

Headey, B. (1970) 'Trade Unions and National Wage Policies', *Journal of Politics*, 32: 407–39.

Henkner, K. (1981) 'Zur Stellung der Bundesrepublik im internationalen Handel', *DIW Vierteljahreshefte*, 2/3: 166–98.

Jansen, P. (1985) 'Verrechtlichung der französischen Gewerkschaftspolitik? Gewerkschaftliche Handlungsbedingungen im historischen Wandel', doctoral dissertation, Berlin: Free University.

Johanesson, L. and G. Schmid (1980) 'The Development of Labour Market Policy in Sweden and in Germany. Competing or Convergent Models to Combat Unemployment?', *European Journal for Political Research*, 8: 387–406.

Katzenstein, P. (1984) *Corporatism and Change: Austria, Switzerland and the Politics of Industry*. Ithaca/London: Cornell University Press.

Katzenstein, P. (1985) *Small States in World Markets. Industrial Policy in Europe*. Ithaca/London: Cornell University Press.

Korpi, W. (1978) *The Working Class in Welfare Capitalism: Work Unions and Politics in Sweden*. London: Routledge.

Korpi, W. and M. Shalev (1979) 'Strikes, Industrial Relations and Class Conflict in Capitalist Societies', *British Journal of Sociology*, 30: 164–87.

Lecher, W. (1981) *Gewerkschaften im Europa der Krise*. Köln: Bund Verlag.

Lehmbruch, G. (1977) 'Liberal Corporatism and Party Government', *Comparative Political Studies*, 10: 91–126.

Lehmbruch, G. (1984) 'Concertation and the Structure of Corporatist Networks', pp. 60–80 in J. H. Goldthorpe (ed.) *Order and Conflict in Contemporary Capitalism*. Oxford: Oxford University Press.

Lehmbruch, G. (1986) 'Interest Groups Government, and the Politics of Protectionism', *Aussenwirtschaft*, 41 (2,3): 273–302.

Lehner, F. (1983) 'Pressure Politics and Economic Growth: Olson's Theory and the Swiss Experience', pp. 203–14 in D. C. Mueller (ed.) *The Political Economy of Growth*. New Haven: Yale University Press.

Leruez, J. (1978) 'Macro Economic Planning in Mixed Economics. The French and British Experience', pp. 26–52 in J. Hayward and O. A. Narkiewicz (eds) *Planning in Europe*. New York: St. Martin's Press.

Lindblom, Ch. E. (1965) *The Intelligence of Democracy — Decision Making through Mutual Adjustment*. New York: The Free Press.

Lundberg, E. (1985) 'The Rise and Fall of the Swedish Model', *Journal of Economic Literature*, 23: 1–36.

Maldagué, R. (1982) 'Die Herausforderungen der staatlichen Planung', *Annalen der Gemeinwirtschaft*, 51: 145–60.

Marin, B. (1982) *Die Paritätische Kommission. Aufgeklärter Techno-Korporatismus in Österreich*. Wien: Internationale Pubilkationen.

Martin, A. (1984) 'Trade Unions in Sweden: Strategic Response to Change and Crisis', pp. 190–348 in P. Gourevitch et al. (eds) *Unions and Economic Crisis: Britain, West Germany and Sweden*. London: Allen & Unwin.

Meidner, R. (1980) *Zur Problematik einer nationalen Lohnpolitik. Grenzen lohnpolitischer Nivellierungsbestrebungen in Schweden*. Berlin: International Institute of Management, dp 80–14.

Menzel, H.-J. (1980) *Legitimation staatlicher Herrswchaft durch die Partizipation Privater?* Berlin: Duncker & Humblot.

Middlemas, K. (1979) *Politics in Industrial Society*. London: André Deutsch.

Mokken, R. S. and F. Stokman et al. (1975) *Graven naar macht*. Amsterdam: Van Gennep.

Mommsen, H. (1985) 'Der Nationalsozialismus und die Auflösung des normativen Staatsgefüges. Paper presented at the Otto Kirchheimer Symposium, Berlin (13–15 November). To be published in W. Luthardt and A. Söllner (eds) *Verfassungsstaat, Souveränität, Pluralismus*. Otto Kirchheimer zum Gedächtnis, Opladen: Westdeutscher Verlag.

Mueller, D. C. (ed.) (1983) *The Political Economy of Growth*. New Haven: Yale University Press.

Nairn, T. (1977) 'The Twilight of the British State', *New Left Review*, 101–2: 13–61.

Neef, A. and P. Capdevielle (1980) 'International Comparisons of Productivity and Labour Costs', *Monthly Labour Review*, 103: 32–39.

Offe, C. (1984) 'Korporatismus als System nichtstaatlicher Makrosteuerung', *Geschichte und Gesellschaft*, 10: 234–56.

Olson, M. (1965) *The Logic of Collective Action*. Cambridge Mass.: Harvard University Press.

Olson, M. (1982) *The Rise and Decline of Nations*. New Haven: Yale University Press.

Przeworski, A. (1980) 'Social Democracy as a Historical Phenomenon', *New Left Review*, 122, July–August.

Pryor, F. L. (1972) 'An International Comparison of Concentration Ratios', *The Review of Economics and Statistics*, 54: 130–40.

Richardson, J. D. (1971) 'Constant Market Share Analysis of Export Growth', *Journal of International Economics*, 1: 227–39.

Ruin, O. (1974) 'Participatory Democracy and Corporatism: The Case of Sweden', *Scandinavian Political Studies*, 9: 171–86.

Sabel, Ch. F. (1983) 'From Austro-Keynesianism to Flexible Specialization: The Political Preconditions of Industrial Redeployment in an "Astgemeinschaft"', ms, Vienna: Österreichische Nationalbank.

Scharpf, F. W. (1984) 'Economic and Institutional Constraints of Full-Employment Strategies: Sweden, Austria and West Germany 1973–1982', pp. 257–90 in J. H. Goldthorpe (ed.) *Order and Conflict in Contemporary Capitalism*. Oxford: Oxford University Press.

Schmidt, M. G. (1982) *Wohlfahrtsstaatliche Politik unter bürgerlichen und sozialdemokratischen Regierungen*. Frankfurt a.M./New York: Campus.

Schmitter, Ph. (1974) 'Still the Century of Corporatism?', *The Review of Politics*, 10: 85–131.

Schmitter, Ph. (1981) 'Interest Intermediation and Regime Governability in Contemporary Western Europe', pp. 287–330 in S. Berger (ed.) *Organizing Interests in Western Europe: Pluralism, Corporatism and the Transformation of Politics*. Cambridge: Cambridge University Press.

Schwerin, D. (1980) 'The Limits of Organization as a Response to Wage-Price Problems', pp. 71–106 in R. Rose (ed.) *Challenge to Governance*. London/Beverly Hills: Sage.

Stephens, J. D. (1979) *The Transition from Capitalism to Socialism*. London: Macmillan.

Süllow, B. (1981) 'Die gewerkschaftliche Repräsentation in öffentlichen Gremien. Ein Beispiel für institutionalisierte korporative Interessenvermittlung', *Soziale Welt*, 32: 39–56.

Truman, D. B. (1951) *The Governmental Process*. New York: Knopf.

United Nations (various years) *UN — Industrial Statistics*. New York: UN Publications.

van Putten, J. (1984) 'Policy Styles in the Netherlands: Negotiation and Conflict', pp. 168–96 in R. Richardson (ed.) *Policy Styles in Western Europe*. London: Allen & Unwin.

von Beyme, K. (1984) 'Der Neokorporatismus — Neuer Wein in alten Schläuchen', *Geschichte und Gesellschaft*, 10: 211–33.

Weir, M. and Th. Skocpol (1985) 'State Structures and the Possibilities for "Keynesian" Responses to the Great Depression in Sweden, Britain and the United States', pp. 107–65 in P. D. Evans, D. Rueschemeyer and Th. Skocpol (eds) *Bringing the State Back In*. Cambridge NJ: Cambridge University Press.

Wilensky, H. (1976) *The New Corporatism. Centralisation and the Welfare State*. London/Beverly Hills: Sage.

Wilensky, H. (1981) 'Leftism, Catholicism and Democratic Corporatism. The Role of Political Parties in Recent Welfare State Development', pp. 345–82 in P. Flora and A. Heidenheimer (eds) *The Development of Welfare States in Europe and America*. New Brunswick/London: Transaction Books.

Zimmermann, E. (1986) *Neokorporatistische Politikformen in den Niederlanden. Industriepolitik, kollektive Arbeitsbeziehungen und hegemoniale Strukturen seit 1918*. Frankfurt a.M./New York: Campus.

Zysman, J. (1983) *Governments, Markets and Growth. Financial Systems and the Politics of Industrial Change*. Ithaca/London: Cornell University Press.

3
Interest intermediation, institutional structures and public policy

Franz Lehner

Introduction
In his well-known book *The Rise and Decline of Nations*, Mancur Olson (1982) argues that in the modern pluralist democracies special interest groups have a disproportionate amount of power. Contrary to the assumptions of the traditional pluralist theory of democracy (e.g. Dahl, 1971), Olson argues that interest intermediation in modern democracy is characterized by a high degree of organization of special interests, whereas the distribution of organizational capacities and influence of general interests usually is fairly low. In Olson's view, this reduces the capacity of a society to adopt new technologies and to reallocate resources in response to changing conditions.

Moreover, such special interests also inhibit competition in the private sector. Consequently, government intervention which is based on the influence of special interest organizations reduces the rate of economic growth and the level of aggregate income in a society, as well as the overall efficiency of the economy. Special interest groups are also likely to create a condition of stagflation with high 'natural' rate of unemployment.

In Olson's view much of the incapacity of governments to cope with economic crisis may be assigned to the deficiencies of pluralist interest intermediation. Not only that, pluralist interest intermediation is a major cause of economic crisis.

Olson's argument is consistent with several studies which argue that pluralist interest intermediation has a negative impact on the political-economic development of advanced capitalist societies. In these studies, such interest intermediation is considered a major cause of ungovernability in general. It produces both inefficient and disputed policies. Even worse: it enhances government interventions which create problems of market failure rather than solving them (see, for example, Beer, 1966; Buchanan, 1975; Ionescou, 1975; Lehmbruch, 1977; Lehner, 1979; Lehner and Widmaier, 1983; Offe, 1972; Rokkan, 1966; Schmitter, 1981; Wilensky, 1976). This type of argument offers an interesting approach to the understanding of governments' capacities to cope with economic crisis. However, it contains considerable theoretical and empirical weaknesses.

Olson's argument, for example, neglects institutional structures. It analyses politics and political economy in terms of distributive conflicts, but neglects the institutional arrangements within which distributive conflicts are eventually accommodated. Other studies, in particular the so-called 'liberal corporatism' ones, concern themselves with different institutional structures, but unlike Olson they do not offer a comprehensive theoretical framework. The logic as well as the empirical support is rather weak.

In this article, Olson's theory is assessed in relation to the impact of different political structures on public policy-making, economic performance and governments' capabilities.

1. Institutional structure, pressure politics and public policy
Olson's theory includes two different sets of assumptions. The first set contains a general theoretical argument concerning the behaviour of interest organizations in the process of *policy-making*. Based on his *Logic of Collective Action* (Olson, 1965), he argues that this behaviour strongly depends upon the size of interest organizations.

For small interest groups strong incentives exist to advance special interests without considering the costs which their activities impose on the economy and society as a whole. They tend to maximize special interests at the expense of efficiency, productivity, innovation and growth, and to form distributional coalitions which are narrow in scope. This often results in particularistic and inefficient public policies.

Contrary to this, for large and thus more encompassing organizations, strong incentives exist to take account of the costs which their activities impose on the economy and society. They tend, therefore, to avoid the negative impacts of their activities on efficiency, productivity, innovation and growth, and support efficient public policies. This argument implies that economic efficiency, productivity, innovation and growth in democratic societies is lower if policy-making is influenced and determined by small special interest organizations of a pluralist nature.

The second set of assumptions concerns the formation of small and specialized interest groups. As Olson demonstrates in *The Logic of Collective Action*, small and specialized interest groups are more easily organized than large and encompassing ones. This implies that democracies tend to increase the number of small special interest organizations over time, which leads to a situation, in which public policies are increasingly dominated by such groups.

This argument is theoretically well developed and is plausible. It seems to overestimate the relevance of organizational capacities for the efficacy of interest politics and seems to underestimate the competition among interest groups (see Colby, 1983; Dean, 1983; Schubert, 1987). Nevertheless, it points at potentially very important deficiencies in pluralist interest intermediation.

It does not, however, consider structural solutions to these deficiencies. Rather, Olson, assumes a general and uniform tendency towards an increasingly pluralist interest intermediation. Olson indeed argues that the longer the time period of democratic politics the more public policy is determined by small and specialized interest organizations, and the lower is efficiency, productivity, innovation and growth.

In my view, this argument is wrong, since it neglects the ways in which interest groups interact among themselves and with government. This process takes place within institutional settings and structural arrangements which are not uniform across the advanced democracies. They do not only vary considerably across countries, but also within countries across policy areas.

In some policy areas we find weak structures and rather dispersed interactions of a large number of interest groups, parties and governmental agencies. Other policy areas are characterized by integrated structures and the interaction of a few vested interest groups as well as a central government. In some policy areas, the accommodation of conflict takes place within highly bureaucratic structures; in others rather informal bargaining may exist. In some countries, one type or another may be dominant; in others there may be considerable variation across policy areas.

The different types of policy networks within and across countries shape the interaction of government and other relevant actors. They restrict or enhance the power of interest organizations to varying degrees, and allow for more or less particularism or facilitate a more or less encompassing degree of interest intermediation. Different policy networks shape the structure of interest intermediation as well as the ways in which interest groups interact among themselves and with the political-administrative system (cf. Lehner, 1986; Lehner and Keman, 1984; Lehner, et al., 1983).

In a growing political science literature, it has been argued that the deficiencies of pluralist interest intermediation can be overcome by the establishment of highly centralized and monopolistic bargaining between government and vested interest groups. Often it is suggested that such bargaining fundamentally changes interest intermediation — 'liberal corporatism' is said to replace pluralism. It has further been conjectured that such a change is associated with an increase in policy performance, namely in higher political stability and economic efficiency (cf. Lehmbruch, 1977; Panitch, 1977; Schmitter, 1977, 1981; Wilensky, 1976; see also Lehmbruch and Schmitter, 1982; Schmitter and Lehmbruch, 1981).

The theory of liberal corporatism is similar to Olson's argument: it assumes that public policy is more efficient the more comprehensive is the scope of interest intermediation (cf. Schmitter, 1981). In contrast to Olson's analysis, the theory of liberal corporatism takes account of the variety of different structural arrangements that may serve to mediate interests (cf. Czada, 1983; Lehmbruch, 1984).

However, the theory of liberal corporatism remains a set of vague hypotheses, rather than a systematically developed theory. Nevertheless, it opens interesting research perspectives concerning the relationship between structural arrangements and public policy. These have been taken up in a number of recent policy studies investigating the structural determinants of public policy and economic performance (e.g. Keman, 1984; Paloheimo, 1984a, 1984b, 1984c; Scharpf, 1981; Schmidt, 1982a, 1984; see also OECD, 1982).

Studies emerging from this theory open an interesting avenue for a deeper investigation of the relationship between organized interest intermediation, pressure group politics and the efficiency of public policy. They consider the impact of different structural arrangements or modes of organized interest intermediation on the efficacy of particular interests and the balance of interest aggregation.

They suggest a hypothesis which is simple in its content but rich in its potential consequences. The hypothesis is that in advanced democracies the management of distributive conflict and economic performance is better if their institutional structures can integrate interest intermediation and, therefore, constrain the disproportional influence of special interests on public policy. This hypothesis is consistent with the logic of Olson's theory.

2. The institutional control of pressure politics: some empirical evidence

For a crude test of this hypothesis, we use an ordinal scale of different modes of interest intermediation. Such a typology has recently been developed by Lehmbruch (1984) and Czada (1983). In another article (Lehner, 1986) I have modified this typology. In the following I will use this modified typology which is shown in Figure 1. The typology describes different modes of organized interest intermediation with a high or low degree of institutional integration. Institutional integration increases from the first to fifth mode. Using this typology, we will test a number of hypotheses deriving from our basic hypothesis.

Our basic hypothesis assumes that the capacity of democratic systems to manage distributive conflict is the higher the more integrated organized interest intermediation. The first hypothesis is:

Hypothesis 1:
The higher the institutional integration of interest intermediation in modern democratic societies, the lower the amount of distributive struggle in these societies.

A useful indicator for the amount of distributive struggle in democratic societies is strike activity. Figure 2, which is taken from Lehner (1986), shows the relationship between strike activity and the integration of interest intermediation. Figure 2 certainly lends some support to Hypothesis 1.

FIGURE 1
A scale of interactions of private and public sector

1. Pluralism	fragmented and segmented interest intermediation	USA Canada France
2. Weak corporatism	institutionalized participation of organized labour in certain areas; narrow scope of collective bargaining	UK Italy
3. Medium corporatism	sectoral participation; but broad scope of collective bargaining	Ireland Belgium Germany Denmark Finland Australia
4. Strong corporatism	tripartite concertation with broad scope; encompassing co-ordination of income policies	Austria Sweden Norway Netherlands
5. Concordance	encompassing co-ordination of the interactions of the private and the public sector	Japan Switzerland

Source: Czada (1983); Lehmbruch (1984), with some modification and extension.

In general, those countries with a more integrative mode of interest inter-mediation tend to have less strike activity than those with a weak integration. However, both the pluralism and the concordance countries deviate considerably from the expected linear relationship. Moreover, there is obviously no significant difference between pluralism and weak corporatism.

This indicates that the relationship is not very strong. Indeed, if we calculate the relevant rank correlation, we obtain a value, $r = -0.43$. Obviously, the sign is in the expected direction, but the value of the coefficient is rather low. If we exclude pluralist countries, the value increases to $r = -0.54$. Hence, the data shown in Figure 2 point at some relevance of institutional integration.

Our basic hypothesis also postulates that institutional integration of interest intermediation results in a better economic performance. Major aspects of economic performance are the variations in unemployment and inflation. Concerning this, the following hypotheses derive from our basic hypothesis:

FIGURE 2
Strike activity and integration of interest intermediation
in OECD-countries, 1960–79
(rank ordering positions, relating to strike activity 1960–9 and 1970–9)

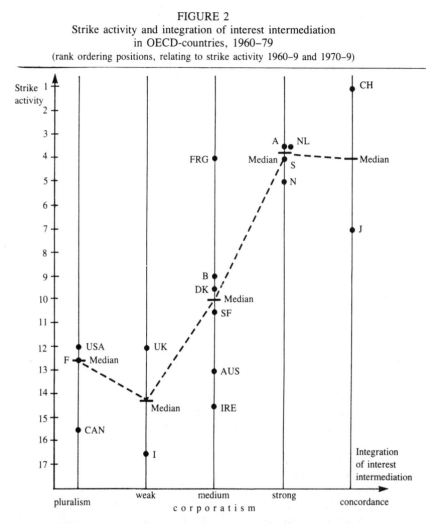

Source: Lehner (1986).

Hypothesis 2:
The higher the institutional integration of organized interest intermediation in democratic societies, the better the performance in terms
of unemployment and inflation.
Hypothesis 3:
The higher the institutional integration of organized interest intermediation, the better the performance of democratic societies with
respect to the relationship between unemployment and inflation.
Hypothesis 3 concerns the well-known Phillips-curve. It assumes that

countries with a high integration are likely to deviate from the Phillips-curve in the form of a low unemployment and low inflation, whereas countries with low integration are likely to deviate from the Phillips-curve in the form of high unemployment and inflation.

The relevant information for an empirical discussion of these two hypotheses is shown in Figure 3. Looking at the inflation rates indicated in Figure 3, we can easily see that our data do not support Hypothesis 2. There is only a very weak tendency in the predicted direction. Moreover, there is much variation within each category. We must, therefore, conclude that the impact of different modes of interest intermediation on inflation seems to be rather low. We also should note that again the pluralist countries perform considerably better than is theoretically expected.

A similar situation exists with respect to unemployment. Again the data generally do not provide strong support for Hypothesis 2 although there exists some qualified support for the proposition. As is the case with inflation, there is a considerable variation within the different categories, but we should, however, note that the countries with a high degree of institutional integration ('strong corporatism' and 'concordance') tend to perform considerably better than most other countries. As far as unemployment concerned then, institutional integration seems to have a somewhat stronger impact on outcomes.

Interestingly enough, the picture becomes much clearer when we consider inflation and unemployment together in the Phillips-curve relationship. As Figure 3 shows, there are remarkable differences between categories. Clearly, Figure 3 supports Hypothesis 3 although again this support is not very strong.

Altogether, our rather crude analysis of the relationship between the institutional integration of interest intermediation and inflation and unemployment suggests considerable ambiguities in the relationship. This ambiguity also exists with respect to economic performance and fiscal expansion. In this respect, our theoretical argument suggests:

Hypothesis 4:
   The higher the institutional integration of interest intermediation in democratic societies, the better their economic performance and the lower their fiscal expansion.

Both economic performance and fiscal expansion are not precisely defined in a generally accepted way. They need, therefore, an operational definition. Here, economic performance is defined in terms of (1) growth of GDP, 1969–80; (2) GDP per capita, 1980; (3) control of inflation, 1960/66–1974/80; and (4) control of unemployment, 1960/66–1974/80. Overall economic performance is measured as the median of each country's ranking on these four variables.

Similarly, fiscal expansion is defined in terms of (1) growth of outlays, 1960–80; (2) level of outlays in percentage of GDP, 1980; (3) increase in

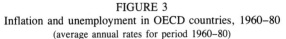

FIGURE 3
Inflation and unemployment in OECD countries, 1960–80
(average annual rates for period 1960–80)

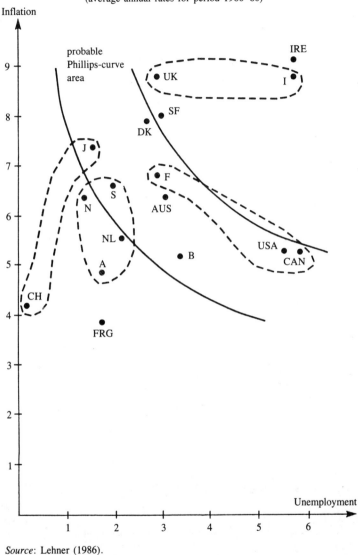

Source: Lehner (1986).

taxation, 1960–80; (4) level of taxation in percentage GDP, 1980, and
(5) public debts in percentage of GDP, 1977–81. Again, overall expansion
is measured as the median of each country's ranking on these variables.

While the relevant data are not shown here (see Lehner, 1986), Figure 4 contains the information on the overall ranking of the relevant countries in terms of their economic performance and fiscal expansion. Note that a low number on economic performance indicates a better performance while a low number on fiscal expansion indicates high expansion, that is a low fiscal performance.

FIGURE 4
Institutional structure, economic performance, and fiscal expansion
in OECD countries, 1960–80
(overall ranking as described in text)

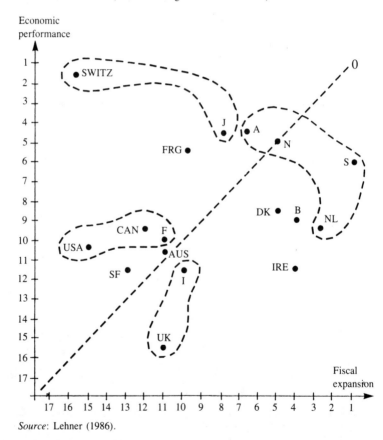

Source: Lehner (1986).

As Figure 4 shows quite clearly, the more integrated countries ('strong corporatism' and 'concordance') tend to perform better than less integrated ('weak corporatism' and 'pluralism').

If we look at the data underlying Figure 4, we could, however, see that the generally better performance of the integrated countries is not uniform. Switzerland, for example, has moderate growth only but ranks high on GDP per capita and performs well on rates of unemployment and inflation. Similarly the relatively high overall performance of Sweden is accounted for primarily by a high GDP per capita and a low unemployment rate. Similarly, among the low performers, only the United Kingdom ranks low on all four variables, whereas Italy, for example, performs relatively well with respect to GDP growth and unemployment.

The evidence in Figure 4 certainly provides considerable support for Hypothesis 4 as far as economic performance is concerned. The situation is quite different when we consider fiscal expansion. In this respect, the 'strong corporatism' countries perform much worse than predicted, whereas the 'pluralism' countries are much better. The 'concordance' countries behave not uniformly — whereas Switzerland performs well, Japan is rather mediocre.

The relationship between economy performance and fiscal expansion gives us some indication of the relative economic efficiency of public policy. We may define high efficiency as a combination of high economic performance and low fiscal expansion while a high fiscal expansion and a low economic performance may indicate inefficiency. Defined in this way, the efficient countries are those to upper left on the dashed line 0 in Figure 4; the inefficient ones are those to the lower right of that line. But as far as efficiency is concerned, the data in Figure 4 do not support Hypothesis 4.

3. Interest intermediation, institutional structures and public policy: the relationship revisited

In the previous discussion we have examined the relationship between institutional structures and public policy performance. The underlying hypothesis was that countries with integrated interest intermediation would have a higher capacity to manage conflict and perform economically better than the others.

This hypothesis received considerable support with respect to the management of distributive conflict, weaker support with respect to economic performance and little or no support with respect to fiscal performance. Moreover, the empirical evidence pointed to a considerable ambiguity in the relationships. This requires further theoretical investigation.

We accept that we have used only a crude procedure in empirically investigating the relevant relationship. We did not, for example, control for intervening economic variables. While this is true, we ought to acknowledge that even a crude test should show better results if the relevant relationship is as clear as theoretically postulated. The deviation from our theoretical expectation, therefore, needs to be explained. There are, in most cases, particular factors which explain deviation from theoretical expectation. The Federal Republic of Germany, for example, often deviates in performance from other 'medium corporatism' countries. An ad hoc explanation could refer to the existence of strong elements of concertation between labour and capital.

Such an explanation, however, does not improve the explanatory power of our hypothesis concerning the relationship between institutional structures and policy performance — unless it can be generalized in terms of a systematic redefinition of the meaning of institutional structures. So far, our argument has basically been concerned with institutionally determined capacities to integrate interest intermediation and to provide for an encompassing interest aggregation. We have, however, neglected the transaction costs involved in interest intermediation and aggregation. We have, in other words, neglected the fact that capacities have their price.

An interesting approach to these problems is offered by Buchanan and Tullock (1962), who argue that in collective decision-making the externalities of decisions decrease as the inclusiveness of decision-making increases. At the same time, transaction costs increase as well. In other words: the less inclusive the level of participation, the more that the costs of public goods and services are externalized to individuals and groups receiving little or no benefits from those goods and services, and the lower is, accordingly, the efficiency of provision.

Political decisions with high externalities create, as Buchanan (1975) points out, ongoing distributive conflict and changing distributive coalitions. They provoke, in other words, the type of situation Olson (1982) describes. Thus, the less integrated interest intermediation the lower the capacity of the political system to manage distributive conflict. This hypothesis is supported by the data shown in Figure 2.

In order to increase efficiency, we have to increase participation which, however, also increases transaction costs in terms of time, organizations and other efforts. Thus, the more integrated interest intermediation, the higher the transaction costs. This lowers the capacity of a political system to adjust timely and flexibly to economic change. Moreover, transaction costs resulting from interest intermediation will be imposed upon government and will increase public spending. This explains some of the features shown in Figure 4.

Following this line of argument, it may be suggested that different types of structural arrangements of the interactions between government and private sector are associated with different positive *and* negative policy-making potentials. On the positive side, they may offer different capacities to manage distributive conflicts and economic policy; on the negative side, they tend to create different types of deficiencies (Lehner and Keman, 1984; Lehner et al., 1983).

In a simplified and abstract manner this situation is described in Figure 5 which is taken from Lehner et al. (1983). In this figure different types of positive and negative policy-making potential is associated with each type of structural arrangement. Corporatist interactions, for example, allow on the one hand for cooperative policy-making, but may also result in much inflexibility and immobilism. By contrast, strongly fragmented interactions and a high amount of particularism may often be associated with uncontrolled interest aggregation and policy-making, but may also enhance spontaneous policy-making with a considerable effectiveness and efficiency. The argument illustrated in Figure 5 certainly needs to be developed further and brought into a more concrete and precise format. Basically, however, it provides a means by which we can more systematically explain the ambivalence of institutional structures which we have observed in the previous section.

FIGURE 5

Positive and negative policy-making potentials of institutional networks

		Political administrative decision structure	
		integrated	fragmented
Organized interest intermediation	integrated	Co-operative policy-making Immobilism Inflexibility	Private bargaining Sectoralization
	fragmented	Authoritative allocation Overregulation Routinization of problem-solving	Spontaneous policy-making Uncontrolled developments Randomization of problem-solving

If we look into the working of different institutional structures, we often find that it is associated with a specific type or set of policies. Corporatism, for example, heavily relies on a tripartite concertation of income policies and, thus, on successful attempts to reduce income inequality. This strategy is, obviously, effective with respect to the settlement of distributive conflict and, more specifically, the avoidance of labour disputes. It is alsosuccessful in reducing unemployment. At the same time it, however, enhances fiscal expansion because it involves considerable public spending on income policies and on active labour market policies.

A somewhat different case exists in Switzerland. There, consociational democracy provides for a broad scope of interest aggregation. Like Sweden, Switzerland has a good performance in accommodating distributive conflicts. Switzerland also performs well with respect to inflation and unemployment, because of her capacity to concert labour and capital. The encompassing scope of interest aggregation is capable of creating a stable accommodation of distributive conflicts and provides a stable political context of economic activity. The price for this, however, is a considerable immobility in the policy-making process which restricts active interventions of the Keynesian type. This explains much of the modest growth in Switzerland throughout the 1960s and 1970s (cf. Lehner, 1983b).

Yet another case exists in a pluralist system, such as that of the United States of America. Much of economic policy in the United States is based on particular interest politics, and logrolling among organized interest groups. Co-ordination of policies and concertation of labour, capital and government is hard to achieve. This does not allow for a consistent economic policy but enhances considerably the influences of special interest groups creating the type of problems Olson describes.

However, within a pluralist structure, externalities that result from policy choices may be compensated through a change of coalitions. As James Buchanan (1975) argues, pluralist structures enhance this process. While this creates considerable problems of government growth and policy failure (cf. Lehner and Widmaier, 1983) a broad, diversified and heterogeneous set of policies concurrently offered by government may also provide various incentives for the private sector. In addition pluralist structures may enhance flexible adjustment as a response to different policies of needs in the private sector.

Moreover, since under these conditions, public policy is not able to steer economic development in a systematic fashion, market forces may oppose public policy. In addition, actors in the private sector may gain a considerable leeway in response to economic policy. Given a strong government pluralist interest intermediation will not only produce those negative impacts on the economy which Olson predicts. Rather, the weaknesses in public policy formation may hinder effective government intervention and, thus, leave much of economic development to the market.

Generalizing these cases, we may assume that certain institutional structures enhance certain policy strategies and restrict others. For any given institutional structure there exists a larger or smaller set of policy strategies which can be effectively performed within this structure. In other words, we may assume that policy-choices are, with narrower or wider limits, determined by institutional structures.

Assuming that for any given institutional structure there exists a set of policy strategies that can be performed, this implies that institutional structures account for the different strategies used to solve the relevant problems. This in turn implies that institutional structures only partially determine economic performance. Different strategies may be available to cope effectively and efficiently with particular economic problems. It does not imply, however, that the relationship between structures and performance is undetermined and open. It is quite obvious that not every strategy available to a political system is capable of solving its problems. Rather, we may assume that for any given type of problem there only exists a limited set of policies which are capable of effectively solving it. In other words, we may assume that the range of potentially effective policies is more or less narrowly determined by the properties of the problems.

When we analyse the relationship between institutional structures, policy-strategies and economic performance, we are, thus, talking about two different sets of available policies. The first set is the set of policies which can be performed in a given institutional structure. The second set is the set of policies which are potentially effective and efficient. The intersection between the two sets marks the political system's capacities to effectively and efficiently solve economic problems. These capabilities in turn determine economic performance. This is shown in Figure 6.

FIGURE 6
Determinants of policy capacities

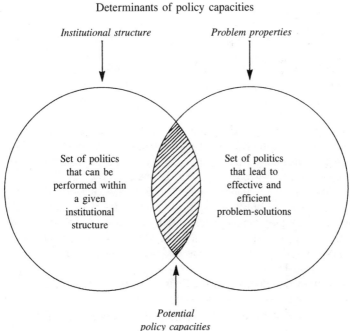

The approach outlined opens interesting avenues for further theoretical and empirical investigation of the complex relationship between institutional structures, policy strategies and economic performance. In the following, this relationship is further discussed with the example of technological modernization.

4. Institutional capacities and industrial policy

In modern industrial society, most governments have assumed an important role in promoting the technological modernization of industry. They intervene more or less heavily in the development, application and use of technology. With the remarkable exception of Switzerland and Japan, governments in OECD-countries finance, as Table 1 shows in more detail, roughly half of the gross expenditures for research and development. In Switzerland, government only covers about 20 percent of these expenditures and in Japan about 25 percent. However, the Japanese government nevertheless intervenes heavily into technological development while in Switzerland government interventions in this area are limited.

As we have pointed out before, the encompassing interest intermediation in Switzerland constitutes a favourable condition for the accommodation of distributive conflict and for the provision of stable political conditions for the economy. At the same time, it constitutes an unfavourable condition for active interventionistic policies. In Switzerland, therefore, economic policy is for the most part confined to the provision of infrastructures and the safeguarding of political-economic stability. Technological and economic development remains in the realm of the market (cf. Germann, 1975; Katzenstein, 1984; Kriesi, 1982; Lehner, 1984, 1985; Schmidt, 1985).

Switzerland is not capable of actively engaging in special technology policies. Financial incentive programmes for the development and application of new technologies or massive government procurement programmes supporting technological modernization are hardly feasible within the restrictions of the Swiss system. The only way in which research and development can be supported by government is through the education system and by aiding academic research. However, even this faces financial restrictions (cf. Katzenstein, 1985; Lehner, 1986).

Considering this situation, we may characterize Switzerland as a typical (and perhaps the only) example of liberal state with a comparatively low level of government intervention in technological and economic development. Much of this can be attributed to the encompassing and non-competitive pattern of interest intermediation which marks the consociational systems.

An interesting contrast to the Swiss case is Japan. Like Switzerland, Japan has an integrated non-competitive pattern of interest intermediation. Unlike Switzerland, however, interest intermediation in Japan does not

TABLE 1

Gross national R&D expenditure: public funded as a percentage of total GERD in selected OECD countries

	1970	1971	1972	1973	1974	1975	1976	1977	1978	1979	1980	1981	1982
USA	59.8	—	58.5	56.5	54.4	54.8	54.1	53.9	52.7	51.8	50.1	49.2	48.7
Japan	—	28.9	28.7	28.3	28.8	29.7	29.4	29.5	30.1	29.4	27.9	26.9	25.5
FR Germany	45.4	46.5	49.4	49.7	50.0	47.4	46.9	44.2	44.7	42.5	—	41.6	42.1
France	59.6	58.7	57.9	56.9	55.8	54.2	51.8	51.8	—	50.3	—	52.8	—
UK	—	—	48.6	—	—	51.9	—	—	47.0	—	—	47.7	—
Italy	42.7	41.1	41.7	45.1	41.6	43.1	45.6	47.8	48.3	43.9	45.3	47.2	48.5
Canada	—	62.8	64.6	64.5	62.6	61.9	62.6	62.6	60.2	55.9	53.7	51.5	53.1
Netherlands	44.4	44.5	44.4	44.6	43.3	44.9	45.6	47.0	47.6	48.8	47.8	47.2	48.4
Switzerland	13.9	14.2	14.9	15.5	14.7	17.4	18.0	21.1	23.0	23.8	—	21.4	—
Norway	59.4	—	63.6	—	61.7	59.1	—	61.7	62.7	59.8	58.6	57.2	—
Finland	—	44.3	—	48.8	—	48.4	—	46.8	—	45.4	—	43.6	—

Data partly estimated.
Source: OECD (1985).

have a pluralist but rather a monopolistic structure. Labour as well as small business are excluded and the established co-operation is confined to government and big enterprises. Unlike Switzerland, Japan is certainly not an example of a liberal state, but rather has to be considered as a strongly interventionist state.

Throughout the postwar period, the Japanese government has been involved in strong attempts to promote industrial modernization. Unlike most other OECD-countries, industrial policy in Japan does not primarily rely on direct subsidies for research and development (see Table 1). Rather, it utilizes a broad set of different instruments including taxation, the regulation of financial markets, tariffs and non-monetary restrictions on imports, the regulation of foreign investments, and the provision of information and advice.

These instruments are integrated in a comprehensive strategy based on the concerted planning of government and industry. Japanese industrial policy attempts to facilitate the financing of research, development and innovation, to maintain domestic competition and to protect Japanese industry against competition from outside (cf. Alten, 1981; Keno, 1980; Okita, 1980; Rothwell and Zegveld, 1981; Zysman, 1983).

In comparison to other OECD-countries, Japan has a remarkably well-coordinated economic and industrial policy. It has managed to avoid policy fragmentation and to integrate all relevant policies into a strategy of industrial modernization.

The comparatively high integration of economic and industrial policy in Japan is the result of the monopolistic structure of interest intermediation. The strong interlocking of government and big industry, as well as the exclusion of labour and small business from the relevant decisions allows for a concentrated effort to modernize industry. Other interests and conflicting goals do not enter the policy-making process in a systematic manner. In particular, the exclusion of labour, which is not strongly organized in Japan, avoids distributive problems in economic and industrial policy.

The avoidance of distributive conflicts in Japan derives from the social policies of the large enterprises. These enterprises provide sufficient social security for most of their workers. The workforce in small companies by contrast are much less secure, but they do not constitute a strong labour movement (cf. Lecher and Welsch, 1983; Pempel and Tsunekawa, 1979; Tokunaga, 1983).

The Japanese system obviously relies on the capacities of the large enterprises to accommodate distributive conflict within their own labour relation system. To the extent to which the large enterprises successfully do this, government does not need a high capacity to accommodate distributive conflicts. Quite clearly, the political system with its monopolistic interest intermediation has a rather low capacity to accommodate distributive conflicts. A significant increase in such conflicts would most likely exceed the relevant capacities of government. This may be a potential deficiency of the Japanese political economy.

A second potentially relevant deficiency is the concentration of the co-operative interactions of government and the private sector in the large enterprises. As a result of this, the Japanese system has a structurally low capacity to deal with the interests and problems of small and medium firms, and the relevant sector of the economy. Consequently, modernization and innovation in the Japanese economy is, for the most part, concentrated in the large enterprises. The research and development spending of the Japanese manufacturing sector, as percentage of the over-all surplus, is still low in comparison with the United States, Germany, the United Kingdom and Sweden (cf. OECD, 1986: 36).

Considering this, we may assume that Japan has a structurally determined tendency to enhance economic concentration. Government policy is unlikely to support the developing of a differentiated and flexible economic structure which allows for effective adjustment through the market. Rather, the further technical and economic development of Japan seems to derive mostly from the effective planning of government and big industry.

Altogether, we may conclude that Japanese political-economic structures have a high capacity to effectively pursue a concentrated modernization policy due to a rather monopolistic interest intermediation. On the other hand, the systems' capacity to manage distributive conflicts and to secure a differentiated economic structure may be rather low.

At this point we should note that Japan and Switzerland both have a high degree of institutional integration of interest intermediation, but differ strongly with respect to the scope integration. While Switzerland integrates a broad and pluralistic interest structure, Japan only includes big business. Accordingly, structural capacities concerning public policy formation differ considerably. Switzerland has a high capacity to accommodate distributive conflicts, but a low capacity to actively intervene in technical and economic development. Japan has a high capacity to do the latter, but a lower one with respect to managing distributive conflicts.

This difference in capacities may explain some of the different empirical findings for the two countries reported in the third section of this article. Moreover, it suggests that the hypothesis on which our empirical investigation was based is inadequate. In order to further discuss this issue we will briefly look at industrial policy in two countries with a low degree of institutional integration of interest intermediation, namely the United States and the United Kingdom.

In the United States, industrial policy has both a strong military and civilian component. These two components are related to each other. In the military area, government strongly intervenes in technological development

in order to secure the country's military strength. The major instruments
are military procurement and the financing of research and development
projects. The military area plays an important role in technological
innovation and the modernization of American industry.

In the civilian area, government intervenes primarily in order to advance
the international competitiveness of American industry and to maintain
and reinforce innovation in industry. Much of the intervention takes the
form of regulation on domestic competition, and the maintenance of high
technological standards in oligopolistic or monopolistic industries.
Moreover, government regulations restrict international transfer of
advanced technology. Finally, both on the federal and the state levels
various programmes exist to advance the domestic transfer of advanced
knowledge, to establish and to maintain advanced research, to increase
innovation in small and medium firms and to facilitate the financing of
research and development (cf. Edmonds, 1983; Herbert and Hoar, 1982;
Rothwell and Zegveld, 1981; Wachter and Wachter, 1983; Zysman, 1983).

In the civilian area, industrial policy operates with a wide range of
different instruments. This includes regulation, governmental or quasi-
governmental research and development, subsidies, taxation, tariffs,
government procurement, the provision of risk capital and joint ventures
of government and the private sector. A larger number of federal and state
agencies are involved in these programmes.

Considering the scope of industrial policy, its financial volume and the
number of different programmes it becomes clear that the United States
is not much less interventionist than Japan when it comes to promoting
industrial modernization. The relevant difference between these countries
lies not in the volume and the intensity of government intervention in
industrial modernization, but rather in styles, strategies and operating
conditions of industrial policy.

In Japan, industrial policy is integrated into a comprehensive strategy
with mutually co-ordinated instruments and is based on a strong co-
operation between government and big industry. In the United States there
exists a variety of different programmes of Federal and State agencies
which are barely integrated. There is no comprehensive strategy, but rather
a wide set of segmented policies.

Japanese industrial policy attempts a planned steering of government
and private sector activities. Contrary to that, industrial policy relies much
more on the provision of positive and negative incentives rather than on
the direct steering of private sector activities. Japanese industrial policy
is an active policy, in the United States, a pluralist interest intermediation
with a comparatively low level of institutional integration hardly allows
any systematic industrial policy. Industrial policy involves competing
interests and a larger number of different government agencies. This means
there is no encompassing co-ordination of interest intermediation.

At this point it is interesting to compare the United States and Switzerland. Both countries have pluralist structures of interest intermediation. In Switzerland, however, consociational decision-making provides for a high level of integration whereas in the United States institutional integration is low. Thus the policy capacities with respect to industrial modernization differ considerably.

In Switzerland, the highly integrated but nevertheless pluralist structures strongly inhibit government intervention into technical and economic development, and make an active industrial policy almost impossible. In the United States too, an active industrial policy is beyond the structurally determined capacities of the political-economic system. Nevertheless, there is much government intervention in technical and economic development. The relevant policy pattern, however, fits quite well to that described in Olson's theory.

This points clearly to the importance of institutional integration of interest intermediation. Due to a high degree of institutional integration and in spite of a pluralistic interest structure, Switzerland avoids the problems of pluralist interest intermediation described by Olson, and remains liberal with respect to industrial modernization. In contrast to that, the United States is rather interventionistic. This is also the case for the United Kingdom.

In the United Kingdom we observe a similar situation concerning industrial policy as in the United States. There exists a larger number of different policies and programmes which are barely co-ordinated. In both countries, there is a considerable influence of special interests on industrial policy and related problems of effectiveness and efficiency. In the United Kingdom, however, distributive problems strongly influence industrial policy whereas there is little such interference in the United States (cf. Hayward, 1976; Grant, 1982; Rothwell and Zegveld, 1981; Wilks, 1983).

In spite of similar patterns of industrial policy, the United Kingdom performs much less well than the United States. As Figure 7 demonstrates, the United Kingdom has a low performance both with respect to average annual rate of growth of output and of expenditures whereas the United States perform somewhat better with respect to R&D expenditures, and much better with respect to output. Both countries perform less well than Japan.

The policy performance of the United States in comparison with the United Kingdom may be the product of a different economic context. In spite of some decline industry in the United States has still a high level of modernization and competitiveness. In the United Kingdom, this level is still considerably below that of the United States, even if there has been some catch-up in recent years (cf. OECD, 1986: 48ff.). This marks an important difference in the operational conditions of industrial policy.

In the United States, industrial policy need not be very effective in order to maintain a relatively high performance. In the United Kingdom, industrial

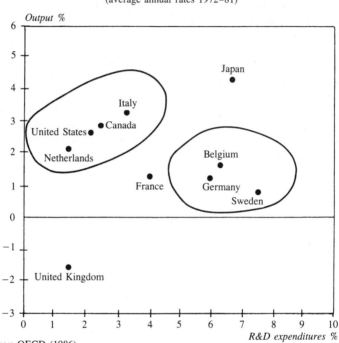

FIGURE 7
Growth in manufacturing output and R&D expenditure
(average annual rates 1972–81)

Source: OECD (1986).

policy not only needs to reinforce innovation in industry but it also needs to compensate for deficiencies in industrial modernization in order to reach a similar performance as the United States. The task of industrial policy is, thus, more difficult to achieve in the United Kingdom than in the United States.

Our brief comparison to the United States and the United Kingdom points again to the inadequacy of our basic hypothesis. In industrial policy, both countries have similar structures of interest intermediation and similar policies, but they differ considerably in performance.

5. Conclusions: interest intermediation and the management of economic policy

In view of Olson's theory, the relationship between the structure of interest intermediation and economic performance can be described by two simple hypotheses:

  1. The more pluralist interest intermediation and the smaller the scope of distributional coalitions, the lower the economic performance in a democratic society.

2. The longer the period of unlimited democracy in a society, the more pluralist the interest intermediation and the more distributional coalitions accumulate.

The first hypothesis contains a structural argument, the second a historistic argument. Let us consider the second hypothesis first.

Olson's second hypothesis implies that economic performance declines over time in a democratic society. It is something like a general historical law for democratic societies — a law which attempts to explain the (economic) rise and decline of nations. However, as Popper (1960) points out, such explanations involve serious methodological problems which we will not further discuss here. Instead, we will discuss the empirical validity of this hypothesis. My contention is, that Olson's historical argument is simply false. Among the democratic industrial nations, there are some which clearly contradict the argument. Two relevant examples of this are Switzerland and Sweden. Moreover, even the Japanese case does not fully fit into Olson's argument.

Compared to other OECD countries, Switzerland has indisputably experienced a long period of unlimited democracy. It has also developed pluralist structures of interest intermediation. Yet, Switzerland performs relatively well economically. Among the OECD countries, it has about the highest GDP per capita and it ranks low on inflation and unemployment. More importantly, Switzerland is still a good example of a liberal government which intervenes relatively little in the economy (cf. Lehner, 1983b; Schmidt, 1985). The major reason why Switzerland contradicts Olson's hypothesis is that in spite of a pluralistically organized society, there is no accumulation of distributional coalitions. Rather, the institutional structures of the Swiss political system force organized interests to attempt to form broad and encompassing coalitions. To be clear, we are not speaking of substantial consensus among organized interests, but about procedures and rules for enhancing or even enforcing a broad aggregation or diverging and conflicting interests (cf. Lehner, 1984; Lehner and Homann, 1987).

A similar point can be made about Sweden. In the same way as Switzerland, Sweden has experienced a comparatively long period of democracy but it also has a strongly integrated interest intermediation. After the Second World War, a corporatist network developed which integrates the major interest groups and provides for an encompassing interest aggregation. Contrary to Olson's scenario of historical development, Sweden has developed from pluralist interest intermediation to corporatism. This is also true of other countries like Norway and the Netherlands. In these cases, institutional regulations have been imposed on pluralist interest structures and this has changed the pattern of interest intermediation (cf. Czada, 1983; Lehmbruch and Schmitter, 1982; Panitch, 1977; Schmitter and Lehmbruch, 1981).

While the Swiss and the Swedish cases obviously contradict the Olson hypothesis, the Japanese one at a first glance seems to accord with the hypothesis. Japan has a relatively short period of unlimited democracy and it performs well as far as growth and innovation is concerned. However, it still ranks only tenth among the OECD countries with respect to GDP per capita (OECD, 1985). Nevertheless, we may consider Japan as a very successful country.

As far as the structure of organized interests is concerned, Japan again seems to fit Olson's theory well. However, economic policy in Japan contains most of the features which Olson (1982: 36ff.) assigns to a developed pluralist country. Economic development in Japan is rarely left to the spontaneous co-ordination of the market but is rather subject to massive government interventions — Japan is anything but a liberal state. These interventions involve highly complex regulations and a strong degree of protectionism (Alten, 1981; Keno, 1980; Rothwell and Zegveld, 1981). Moreover, economic policy in Japan is not based on an encompassing interest aggregation or on distributional coalitions with a broad scope. Rather, it is dominated by one particular interest group, i.e. big enterprise and the technologically advanced industries. Small business, the low-technology industries, and labour are not systematically included in the decision-making process. Thus interest intermediation is monopolistic rather than encompassing (cf. Lehmbruch, 1984; Pempel and Tsunekawa, 1979; Sato, 1980; Tokunaga, 1983).

Considering all this, we may conclude that Japan does not fit Olson's theory once we look into the details of the Japanese case. In other words, Olson's theory does not explain either the Japanese pattern of economic policy, or the relationship between this and the Japanese interest structure.

The examples of Switzerland and Sweden demonstrate that there is no uniform historical tendency toward an accumulation of narrow distributional coalitions and the domination of economic policies by such coalitions. The Japanese case shows that there is no strict correspondence between historically developed interest structures and patterns of economic policy. All the three cases demonstrate in different ways that Olson's historical argument is weak, if not false — there is no clear historical tendency for democratic nations to avoid or to be a victim of economic crises.

This relates to an important argument which James Buchanan makes in his well-known book *The Limits of Liberty* (Buchanan, 1975). As Buchanan shows, the type of development which Olson describes results from significant deviations from consensus in society, and a process of changing coalitions resulting from this development. This occurs if and only if the rules of public choice allow for the effective formation of distributional coalitions with a narrow scope. Thus, we are not talking about a general historical tendency but rather a matter of institutional regulation. This means that Olson's theory and his argument concerning the relationship between structure of interest intermediation and economic performance offers a fruitful approach for the analysis of the impact of institutional regulation. However, the empirical investigation presented in this article has shown that the structure of interest intermediation can only partially explain economic performance. Olson's theory needs to be modified and enlarged. Institutionally imposed rules and regulations enhance or restrict the power of special interest groups and the formation of narrow or broad distributional coalitions. We may, however, apply the logic of Olson's theory to the institutional structure of interest intermediation and consider the degree to which different institutional structures enhance or restrict encompassing interest intermediation.

Two different aspects of interest intermediation are of relevance here; first, the inclusiveness/exclusiveness and second, the integration/fragmentation of interest intermediation. The first aspect relates to the degree to which organized interests participate in policy-making; the second to the degree to which interest intermediation is co-ordinated. Both aspects may vary independently. Switzerland, for example, has an inclusive and Japan an exclusive intermediation. In both countries, interest intermediation is integrated. The two aspects determine the power of organized interests and shape the formation of distributional coalitions.

An interest intermediation which is both inclusive and integrated restricts the power of distributional coalitions with a broad scope. Switzerland is a good example for this case. If, however, interest intermediation is inclusive, but fragmented, special interested groups gain a potentially high amount of power within a process of changing distributional coalitions which are narrow in scope. The United States may be considered an example of this case. In the case of an exclusive, but integrated system of interest intermediation we may expect a polarized structure of power with those included having high power and those excluded low power within a stable, but narrow distributional coalition. Japan, and to lesser degree the corporatist countries, may illustrate this case. Finally an exclusive and fragmented intermediation again enhances a polarized power structure, but produces unstable and narrow distributional coalitions. The United Kingdom may fall into this category. Due to the electoral system, governments in Britain usually operate on a narrow interest base. The resulting distributive conflicts produce a potentially high degree of instability when government changes.

The two aspects are also important with respect to policy choices. Olson's argument implies a strong correspondence between the structure of interest intermediation and policy choices. Our analysis of this relationship suggests that the structure of interest intermediation restricts possible policy choices but does not fully determine them. Regardless of the specific content of policies, we may, however, associate different policy types with different types of institutional structure.

In the case of an inclusive and integrated interest intermediation, capacities for active interventionistic policies are low. Consequently, the overall amount of government intervention in the economy tends to be comparatively low. Economic policy tends to concentrate on the provision of infrastructures and the maintenance of stability. Again, we may refer to the example of Switzerland.

In the case of exclusive and integrated interest intermediation, capacities for active interventionistic policies are high. We may, as is the case in Japan, expect a heavy involvement of government in the planning and steering of economic development. In the case of inclusive, but fragmented interest intermediation, as in the United States, the government's propensity to intervene is high, but its capacities for active interventionist policies is low. We may, therefore, expect that government quite heavily intervenes in the economy with a large variety of different policies. At the same time, we may expect a low co-ordination of the different policies and a low control of government over the economic impact of these policies.

Finally, in the case of a both exclusive and fragmented interest intermediation we may expect a considerable government intervention. This intervention may be more concentrated, but not more co-ordinated. Ongoing distributive conflicts tend to create an unstable and even cyclical production of public policy; such features can be observed in the United Kingdom.

Building up on the argument briefly sketched out here, we may gain a better theoretical understanding of the relationship between interest intermediation and economic policy-making. This is necessary in order to further advance our knowledge of governments' capacities to avoid or to cope with economic crisis. Yet, we have to consider that our analysis suggests that given policy choices have different impacts on different aspects of the economy. Moreover, it suggests that the impacts of policies on the economy are influenced by economic conditions. Olson's theory neglects these problems of policy impact. A better theoretical understanding of governments' capacities to cope with the economy would also have to incorporate systematic hypothesis on policy impacts.

References

Alten, G. C. (1981) 'Industrial Policy and Innovation in Japan', in Ch. Carter (ed.) *Industrial Policy and Innovation*. London: Heinemann.

Bacon, R. and W. Eltis (1976) *Britain's Economic Problem: Too Few Producers*. London: Macmillan.

Beer, S. H. (1966) *British Politics in the Collectivist Age*. New York: Knopf.

Buchanan, J. M. (1975) *The Limits of Liberty*. Chicago/London: University of Chicago Press.

Buchanan, J. M. and G. Tullock (1962) *The Calculus of Consent*. Ann Arbor: University of Michigan Press.

Buchanan, J. M., R. D. Tollison and G. Tullock (eds) (1980) *Towards a Theory of the Rent Seeking Society*. College-Station: Texas A & M University Press.

Cameron, D. R. (1978) 'The Expansion of the Public Economy: A Comparative Analysis', *American Political Science Review*, 72.

Castles, F. G. (1981) 'How Does Politics Matter? Structure or Agency in the Determination of Public Policy Outcomes', *European Journal of Political Research*, 9.

Castles, F. G. (ed.) (1982) *The Impact of Political Parties*. Beverly Hills/London: Sage.

Castles, F. G. and R. D. McKinlay (1979) 'Does Politics Matter: An Analysis of the Public Welfare Commitments in Advanced Democratic States', *European Journal of Political Research*, 7.

Colby, P. W. (1983) 'The Organization of Public Interest Groups', *Policy Studies Journal*, 11.

Crozier, M., S. P. Huntington and J. Watanuki (1975) *The Crisis of Democracy*. New York: New York University Press.

Czada, R. (1983) 'Konsensbedingungen und Auswirkungen neokorporatistischer Politikentwicklung', *Journal für Sozialforschung*, 23.

Dahl, R. A. (1971) *Polyarchy*. New Haven/London: Yale University Press.

Dean, J. W. (1983) 'Polyarchy and Economic Growth', in D. C. Mueller (ed.) *The Political Economy of Growth*. New Haven/London: Yale University Press.

Edmonds, M. (1983) 'Market Ideology and Corporate Power: The United States', in K. Dyson and St. Wilks (eds) *Industrial Crisis*, Oxford: Robertson.

Flora, P. and A. J. Heidenheimer (eds) (1981) *The Development of Welfare States in Europe and America*. New Brunswick: Transaction Books.

Frey, B. S. (1978) *Modern Political Economy*. Oxford: Martin Robertson.

Frey, B. S. (1983) *Democratic Economy Policy*. Oxford: Martin Robertson.

Frey, B. S. and F. Schneider (1978) 'An Econometric Model with an Endogeneous Government Sector', *Public Choice*, 34.

Germann, R. E. (1975) *Politische Innovation und Verfassungsreform*. Bern: Haupt.

Grant, W. (1982) *The Political Economy of Industrial Policy*. London: Butterworths.

Hankel, W. and R. Isaak (1981) *Die moderne Inflation*. Köln: Bund-Verlag.

Hankel, W. and F. Lehner (1976) 'Die gescheiterte Stabilitätspolitik und ihre politischen Bedingungen', *Hamburger Jahrbuch für Wirtschafts- und Gesellschaftspolitik*, 21.

Hayward, J. E. S. (1976) 'Institutional Inertia and Political Impetus in France and Britain', *European Journal of Political Research*, 4.

Heisler, M. O. (1979) 'Corporate Pluralism Revisited: Where is the Theory?', *Scandinavian Political Studies*, 2.

Herbert, R. and R. W. Hoar (1982) *Government and Innovation: Experimenting with Change*. Washington, DC: National Bureau of Standards.

Hewitt, C. (1977) 'The Effect of Political Democracy on Equality in Industrial Societies: A Cross-National Comparison', *American Sociological Review*, 42.

Hibbs, D. (1977) 'Political Parties and Macroeconomic Policy', *American Political Science Review*, 71.

Hibbs, D. and H. Fassbender (eds) (1981) *Contemporary Political Economy. Studies on the Interdependence of Politics and Economics*. Amsterdam: North-Holland.

Ionescou, G. (1975) *Centripetal Politics: Government and the New Centers of Power*. London: Hart-Davis; McGibbon.

Katzenstein, P. J. (1984). *Corporatism and Change*. Ithaca, NY: Cornell University Press.

Katzenstein, P. J. (1985) *Small States in World Markets*. Ithaca/London: Cornell University Press.

Keman, H. (1984) 'Politics, Policies and Consequences: A Cross-National Analysis of Public Policy-formation in Advanced Capitalist Democracies 1967–1981', *European Journal of Political Research*, 12.

Keman, H. and D. Braun (1984) 'The Limits of Political Control: A Cross-National

Comparison of Economic Policy Responses in Eighteen Capitalist Democracies', *European Journal of Political Research*, 12.

Keman, H. and F. Lehner (1984) 'Economic Crisis and Political Management', *European Journal of Political Research*, 12.

Keno, H. (1980) 'The Conception and Evaluation of Japanese Industrial Policy', in K. Sato (ed.) *Industry and Business in Japan*. London: M. E. Sharpe/Croom Helm.

Kriesi, H. P. (1982) 'The Structure of the Swiss Political System', in G. Lehmbruch and Ph. C. Schmitter (eds) *Patterns of Corporatist Policy-Making*. Beverly Hills/London: Sage.

Krueger, A. O. (1974) 'The Political Economy of the Rent-Seeking Society', *American Economic Review*, 64.

Lecher, W. and J. Welsch (1983) *Japan — Mythos und Wirklichkeit. Eine kritische Analyse von Ökonomie und Arbeit*. Köln.

Lehmbruch, G. (1977) 'Liberal Corporatism and Party Government', *Comparative Political Studies*, 10.

Lehmbruch, G. (1983) 'Interest Intermediation in Capitalist and Socialist Systems: Some Structural and Functional Perspectives in Comparative Research', *International Political Science Review*, 4.

Lehmbruch, G. (1984) 'Concertation and the Structure of Corporatist Networks', in J. Goldthorpe (ed.) *Order and Conflict in Contemporary Capitalism: Studies in the Political Economy of West European Nations*. Oxford: University of Oxford Press.

Lehmbruch, G. and P. C. Schmitter (eds) (1982) *Patterns of Corporatist Policy-Making*. Beverly Hills/London: Sage.

Lehner, F. (1979) *Grenzen des Regierens*. Königstein: Athenäum.

Lehner, F. (1983a) 'The Vanishing of Spontaneity: Socio-Economic Conditions of the Welfare-State', *European Journal of Political Research*, 11.

Lehner, F. (1983b) 'Pressure Politics and Economic Growth: Olson's Theory and the Swiss Experience', in D. C. Mueller (ed.) *The Political Economy of Growth*. New Haven/London: Yale University Press.

Lehner, F. (1984) 'Consociational Democracy in Switzerland: A Political-Economic Explanation and Some Empirical Evidence', *European Journal of Political Research*, 12.

Lehner, F. (1985) 'Modes of Interest Intermediation and the Structure of Political Power: An Investigation into Political Efficacy', Paper for the XIIIth IPSA World Congress, Paris.

Lehner, F. (1986) 'The Political Economy of Distributive Conflict', in F. C. Castles et al. (eds) *Managing Mixed Economies: The Impact of Political Institutions*. Berlin: de Gruyter (forthcoming).

Lehner, F. and B. Homann (1987) 'Consociational Decision-Making and Party Government in Switzerland', in R. S. Katz (ed.) *Party Governments: European and American Experiences*. Berlin: de Gruyter.

Lehner, F. and H. Keman (1984) 'Political Economic Interdependence and the Management of Economic Crisis', *European Journal of Political Research*, 12.

Lehner, F. and U. Widmaier (1983) 'Market Failure and Growth of Government: A Sociological Explanation', in C. L. Taylor (ed.) *Why Governments Grow*. Beverly Hills/London: Sage.

Lehner, F., K. Schubert and B. Geile (1983) 'Die strukturelle Rationalität regulativer Wirtschaftspolitik', *Politische Vierteljahresschrift*, 24.

March, J. G. and J. P. Olsen (1984) 'The New Institutionalism: Organizational Factors in Political Life', *The American Political Science Review*, 78.

Mueller, D. C. (1983) 'The Political Economy of Growth and Redistribution', in D. C. Mueller (ed.) *The Political Economy of Growth*. New Haven/London: Yale University Press.

OECD (1982) *The Search for Consensus. The Role of Institutional Dialogue Between Government, Labour and Employers*. Paris: OECD.

OECD (1985) *Science and Technology Indicators Basic Statistical Series — Volume B Gross National Expenditure on R & D*. Paris: OECD.

OECD (1986) *OECD Science and Technology Indicators No. 2 R & D, Invention and Competitiveness*. Paris: OECD.

Offe, C. (1972) 'Politische Herrschaft und Klassenstrukturen', in G. Kress and D. Senghaas (eds) *Politikwissenschaft*. Frankfurt a. M.: Fischer.

Okita, S. (1980) *The Developing Economies and Japan*. New York: Columbia University Press.

Olson, M. (1965) *The Logic of Collective Action*. Cambridge: Harvard University Press.

Olson, M. (1982) *The Rise and Decline of Nations*. New Haven: Yale University Press.

Olson, M. (1983) 'The Political Economy of Comparative Growth Rates', in D. C. Mueller (ed.) *The Political Economy of Growth*. New Haven: Yale University Press.

Paloheimo, H. (1984a) 'Distributive Struggle and Economic Development in the 1970s in Developed Capitalist Countries', *European Journal of Political Research*, 12.

Paloheimo, H. (1984b) 'Distributive Struggle, Corporatist Power Structure and Economic Policy of the 1970s in Developed Countries', in H. Paloheimo (ed.) *Politics in the Era of Corporatism and Planning*. Tampere/Ilmajoki: The Finnish Political Science Association.

Paloheimo, H. (1984c) 'Pluralism, Corporatism and the Distributive Conflict in Developed Capitalist Countries', *Scandinavian Political Studies*, 7. (New Series).

Panitch, L. (1977) 'The Development of Corporatism in Liberal Democracies', *Comparative Political Studies*, 10.

Pempel, T. J. and K. Tsunekawa (1979) 'Corporatism Without Labour? The Japanese Anomaly', in P. C. Schmitter and G. Lehmbruch (eds) *Trends Toward Corporatist Intermediation*. Beverly Hills/London: Sage.

Popper, K. R. (1960) *The Poverty of Historicism*. London: Routledge & Kegan Paul (2nd edn).

Richardson, J. (ed.) (1982) *Policy Styles in Western Europe*. London: Allen & Unwin.

Richardson, J. and R. Henning (eds) (1984) *Unemployment. Policy Responses of Western Democracies*. Beverly Hills/London: Sage.

Rokkan, S. (1966) 'Norway: Numerical Democracy and Corporate Pluralism', in R. A. Dahl (ed.) *Political Opposition in Western Democracies*. New Haven: Yale University Press.

Rose, R. (1979) 'Ungovernability: Is there Fire Behind the Smoke?', *Political Studies*, 27.

Rothwell, R. and W. Zegveld (1981) *Industrial Innovation and Public Policy: Preparing for the 1980s and the 1990s*. London: Frances Pinter.

Sato, K. (ed.) (1980) *Industry and Business in Japan*. New York: Sharpe.

Scharpf, F. W. (1977) 'Public Organization and the Waning of the Welfare State: A Research Perspective', *European Journal of Political Research*, 5.

Scharpf, F. W. (1981) 'The Political Economy of Inflation and Unemployment in Western Europe: An Outline', *Discussion Paper IIM/LMP* 81–21. Berlin: Wissenschaftszentrum Berlin.

Scharpf, F. W. (1983) 'Economic and Institutional Constraints of Full-Employment Strategies: Sweden, Austria and West Germany 1973–1982', *Discussion Paper IIM/LMP* 83–20. Berlin: Wissenschaftszentrum Berlin.

Schmidt, M. G. (1982) *Wohlfahrtstaatliche Politik unter bürlichen und sozialdemokratischen Regierungen*. Frankfurt a. M.: Campus.

Schmidt, M. G. (1982a) 'Does Corporatism Matter? Economic Crisis, Politics and Rates of Unemployment in Capitalist Democracies in the 1970s', in G. Lehmbruch and P. C.

Schmitter (eds) *Patterns of Corporatist Policy Making*. Beverly Hills/London: Sage.

Schmidt, M. G. (1983) 'The Welfare State and the Economy in Periods of Economic Crisis: A Comparative Study of Twenty-three OECD Nations', *European Journal of Political Research*, 11.

Schmidt, M. G. (1984) 'Politics and Unemployment. Rates of Unemployment and Labour Market Policy in OECD Nations', *West European Politics*, 7(1).

Schmidt, M. G. (1985) *Der schweizerische Weg zur Vollbeschäftigung*, Frankfurt a.M.: Campus.

Schmitter, P. C. (1977) 'Modes of Interest Intermediation and Models of Societal Change in Western Europe', *Comparative Political Studies*, 10.

Schmitter, P. C. (1981) 'Interest Intermediation and Regime Governability in Western Europe and North America', in S. Berger (ed.) *Organizing Interests in Western Europe*. New York: Cambridge University Press.

Schmitter, P. C. and G. Lehmbruch (eds) (1981) *Trends Toward Corporatist Intermediation*. Beverly Hills/London: Sage.

Schubert, K. (1987) 'Politics and Economic Regulation', in F. Lehner and M. Schmidt (eds) *The Political Management of Mixed Economies. Comparative Studies on OECD Nations*. Beverly Hills/London: Sage.

Streissler, E. (1973) *Die schleichende Inflation als Problem der Politischen ökonomie*. Zürich: Schulthess.

Tokunaga, S. (1983) 'Die Beziehungen zwischen Lohnarbeit und Kapital in japanischen Großunternehmen', *Leviathan*, 11.

Wachter, M. L. and S. M. Wachter (eds) (1983) *Toward a New US Industrial Policy*. Philadelphia: University of Pennsylvania Press.

Widmaier, U. (1978) *Politische Gewaltanwendung als Problem der Organisation von Interessen*. Meisenheim: Hain.

Wildenmann, R. (1967) *Macht und Konsens als Problem der Innen- und Außenpolitik*. Köln/Opladen: Westdeutscher Verlag. 2nd edn.

Wilensky, H. L. (1976) *The New Corporatism. Centralization and the Welfare State*. Beverly Hills/London: Sage.

Wilks, St. (1983) 'Liberal State and Party Competition: Britain', in K. Dyson and St. Wilks (eds) *Industrial Crisis*. Oxford: Robertson.

Zysman, J. (1983) *Governments, Markets and Growth*. Ithaca/London: Cornell University Press.

4

Institutional accommodation to full employment: a comparison of policy regimes

Gøsta Esping-Andersen

1. Institutional problems of full employment

Pre-war reformist writers foresaw that full employment with welfare policies would establish a both more humane and more productive capitalism. Liberals, such as Beveridge, and social democrats, such as Wigforss and Myrdal, were in basic agreement on this point. They placed their faith in the promotion of Keynesian welfare state policies.

It was to these issues that Michael Kalecki addressed his now classic analysis of the 'political aspects of full employment' (Kalecki, 1943). In his view, the principal problem was how capitalism could be accommodated to the new balance of class power. Kalecki identified two distinct responses: one, a regime in which the 'political business cycle' constitutes the favoured stabilization policy. In this model, the pressures of wages and decaying worker discipline are managed by government-induced slumps. Accordingly, full employment is attained only intermittently during business cycle peaks.

Kalecki is, alas, vague with regard to the alternative regime, and makes only the claim that full employment capitalism must develop new social and political institutions which will reflect the increased power of the working class.

In economies with private enterprise and public commitments to full employment and social justice, the issue of institutional accommodation condenses into the problem of how labour's redistributional power will not jeopardize the need for balanced economic growth. The central question is how to turn potential zero-sum conflicts into positive-sum trade-offs that are consistent with both sustained price stability and full employment. What kind of institutional framework will permit private enterprise and a chronically powerful working class to coexist?

The question confronted all the advanced industrialized capitalist democracies over the postwar era. In most nations, the leap into peace was taken with strong ideological commitment to sustained full employment. To be sure, its articulation ranged from a de facto constitutional character (as in Norway) to generally good intentions (as in the United States and West Germany).

Promises notwithstanding, nations faced the practical task very differently. In some countries, like Great Britain, the United States and Sweden, the distributional dilemmas of full employment emerged immediately after the war, while in others the issue would not surface for many years.

In reality, a genuinely sustained full employment performance has been both temporally and cross-nationally infrequent. Only very few nations (Norway, Sweden and Switzerland) have been capable of consistently securing unemployment levels below 2–3 percent over the entire postwar era. For the majority of cases, full employment has been confined to the brief interlude between 1960 and 1974.

Bordogna (1981) makes a useful distinction between the handful of countries in which a binding full employment commitment actually obtains (such as Norway and Sweden) on the one hand, and nations which, on the other hand, have typically resorted to stop-go policy with associated unemployment as a means to regulate wage pressures. The distinction follows Kalecki's original regime scenarios, but, in the light of postwar developments, it inspires new questions. First, what conditions a nation's choice between these two regime alternatives?

Second, which institutional arrangements and, equally salient, which policy instruments are adopted to contain the wage pressures that a fully employed working class is likely to exert? New institutional structures may, as Kalecki anticipated, be necessary requirements. But they are unlikely to be sufficient unless they are capable of producing policy instruments, on the basis of which zero-sum conflict can be overcome.

Third, there are at least two crucial conditions that fundamentally alter the original conception of how to deliver full employment. One is the emergence of global economic integration. It is analytically necessary to distinguish the full employment issues of the phase of international economic expansion (between the late 1950s and 1973) from the post-1973 era. In this perspective, the remarkable post-1973 performance of nations such as Norway and Sweden demands special attention. Have these nations, via institution-building and policy solutions, managed to cut the Gordian knot of the Phillips-curve dilemma? The other is the radically altered meaning that full employment has been given. Originally, the full employment definition was, by and large, confined to the population of able-bodied men; it has been successively stretched to encompass yet another half of a nation's population, principally women and the disabled. Statistically, this might entail a revolutionary augmentation of the full employment clientele.[1]

In addressing the leading question raised in this paper, my conclusions will be of a pessimistic nature. I shall argue that, despite fundamental differences in institutional accommodation and policy choice (especially since the late 1970s), advanced capitalist democracies appear to converge in the incapability of ensuring both full employment and balanced economic growth. This holds for 'political business cycle' regimes as well as for the illustrious Swedish and Norwegian examples. The principal reason has to do with the limited means available (within any kind of institutional framework that has, so far, been tried in capitalism) to channel zero-sum conflicts into workable bargains. Within the range of limited means, the welfare state came to play a dominant (and problematic) role.

In the final analysis, the kind of bargain or accord required in the pursuit of full employment or any other policy objectives presumes the preservation of private entrepreneurial discretionary powers. Thus the tools available to obtain wage restraint or other sacrifices will be largely limited to the public domain. Not surprisingly, social policy became the chief arena within which distributional solutions were sought. However, this has come to place the welfare state in a double-bind: it is given responsibility for both full employment performance *and* distributional harmony. The two functions, as I shall discuss, are inherently incompatible.

2. Institutional models and policy regimes in the postwar era

For most nations, the period between the 1930s and the 1950s was a historical watershed for socio-political realignment. Novel institutional arrangements were built to manage distributional conflict. Several distinct models are discernible. One, exemplified by the celebrated Swedish case, was premised on powerful, all-encompassing and centralized trade unions that, usually in liaison with a governing (or governable) labour party, were willing to engage in central nation– or industry–wide negotiations with employers. This institutional matrix was based on labour's recognition of the rights and prerogatives of private industrial ownership, implying that neither unions nor labour governments would interfere with decision-making of private firms. The terrain of both collective bargaining and politics was therefore limited to distributional questions of the social product. In brief, it was recognized that labour's power resources would not, and could not be mobilized to alter the boundary between public and private. In this model, the power of Labour compelled strongly phrased commitments to both full employment and social rights: the presence of both powerful, cohesive and class-encompassing interest organizations secured an institutional arrangement of stable 'social accords' with only modest free-rider and prisoner-dilemma problems. Distributional conflicts could, in large measure, be managed through sophisticated and long-term modes of political exchange.

The other basic model of postwar institutional alignment, perhaps best exemplified by the United States, is characterized by incomplete or fragmented class organizational formation in both markets and politics. Lacking institutional means for comprehensive negotiations of distributional issues, both free-rider and prisoner-dilemma problems are likely to be pervasive, and distributional struggles will tend to be particularistic and temporally short-sighted. Under such conditions, labour is likely to favour maximization strategies in bargaining, thus augmenting the need for occasional strong anti-inflationary measures. Further, lacking undisputed institutional recognition from employers, labour movement strength becomes, in itself, an object of conflict. In this kind of system, organizational power will indeed be viewed as a major obstacle to balanced economic growth.

These two polar cases resemble closely the distributional coalitions identified in Olson (1982) and two of the full employment models in Schmidt (1987). They obscure, of course, a rich variety of postwar institutional expressions. The majority of nations exhibit complex mixes of both, and follow their own unique evolution through the postwar decades. The task here, however, is not to elaborate an exhaustive catalogue of institutional models, but to trace how distinctly contrasting systems pursued solutions to the full employment problem. The following examination will predominantly focus on three regimes: the United States, Scandinavia and West Germany; the latter is of particular interest, since it moves in the Nordic direction following the rise of Labour in the late 1950s and early 1960s, but reverts back to anti-inflationary priorities in the 1970s.

3. The crystallization of institutional arrangements in the postwar era

Many countries emerged from the Second World War with fairly solid promises of social-democratization, commitments to social citizenship and the abolition of unemployment. In the United States, this was established with the New Deal reforms in social security, agrarian subsidies and active employment promotion. The Democratic party, under Roosevelt, installed itself as an American equivalent to the Scandinavian 'red-green' alliance of farmers and workers, and with a largely similar programmatic platform. Lacking in the United States were nationally strong and cohesive 'red' and 'green' class organizations. The coalition was, instead, brokered by the political system, and it remained fragile due to the South's insistent rejection of welfare and employment policies that would raise labour costs and emancipate the Black population. Roosevelt's decision to revert to balanced-budget orthodoxy in 1936–7 may have been a technical mistake, but it was viewed as politically necessary. This, the first case of a 'political business cycle' designed to calm down wage and price developments, was in the immediate postwar years augmented by conservative attacks on both the social security reforms and on the full employment promise contained in the (strongly) formulated Wagner bill and the (weaker) Taft-Hartley act. The pioneering steps towards a modern advanced Welfare state that the New Deal embodied were effectively stopped in the period between 1945–50 (Skocpol, 1987). Price stability was institutionalized as the first order priority of any government; the chief policy-mix for its attainment became restrictive budgetary policy coupled with anti-inflationary 'political business cycles', especially in response to the inflationary threats of the Korean War. Until the mid-1960s, there were no welfare state advances, and unemployment levels remained quite high. The relative political independence of the Federal Reserve Bank provided an important institutional means with which to ensure the long-term priority of price stability.

Other nations confronted, with the United States, similar dilemmas immediately after the war. The postwar Labour government in Britain presided over a powerful mandate for welfare state institutionalization along the lines of the Beveridge Plan, and an equally strong consensus for full employment. The successful implementation of both helped fuel strong inflationary pressures. Labour's response was the imposition of an incomes policy with wage and price controls that soon estranged the trade unions. The lack of internal cohesion in the trade unions meant, first of all, that a viable political exchange, or bargain, between wages and future gains was impossible to forge. Secondly, it meant that the trade union movement was institutionally incapable of sponsoring strategic alternatives to either unacceptable incomes policies or to an endless parade of stop-go policies. As Higgins and Apple (1981) argue in their fascinating comparison of Britain and Sweden, the 'positive-sum' solution launched by the Swedish LO in the same years and under similar circumstances could not emerge in Britain; not due to lack of policy creativity, but due to institutional barriers.

Nordic social democracy is often portrayed as the model of balanced full employment welfare state growth.[2] The Nordic countries confronted, like Britain and the United States, the dilemma between the promises of redistribution and full employment, and the hard realities of inflationary spirals. In these small, open economies, too much demand fuels direct and immediate balance-of-payments crises. The problem, therefore, is that competitiveness is jeopardized by too much wage push. Positioned similarly, Nordic social democracy came to diverge.

In Denmark, the Labour movement was politically side-lined during the critical years of postwar institution building. The labour-farmer alliance that carried Denmark through the Depression with a full employment welfare state programme was curtailed, as the powerful (liberalistic) farmers insisted on budgetary austerity and price stabilization policy in order to maintain agrarian exports. Hence, welfare state reforms and full employment in Denmark were not part of the political formula until after the late 1950s. Intermittent wage and price pressures (such as during the Korean War) were, like in the United States and Britain, managed through the 'political business cycle' of stop-go policies.

Within Scandinavia, as well as among all the capitalist democracies, it was therefore only Norway and Sweden that were capable of translating the full employment commitment into reality. These two nations shared, with Denmark, a social democratic breakthrough that inaugurated active welfare- and employment-policies in the 1930s. The foundations were similar: strong universalist trade unions and a labour party capable of dominating the political coalition of farmers and workers that, in the first place, permitted social democratic ascendance.

The decisive institutional contrast to Denmark, however, was that the Norwegian and Swedish trade union movements were far more unified and capable of central co-ordination of bargaining; the farmers were both politically and economically more marginal. Unlike in Denmark, the Norwegian and Swedish Labour parties were capable of dominating the political terrain because there was no possibility of a unified bourgeois coalition alternative. Therefore, these labour movements presided over a powerful mandate for both full employment and welfare state reforms. As in Britain, the mandate was implemented over the immediate postwar years, compelling the labour movements to find more permanent and stable solutions to the problem of wage/price pressures.

In Sweden, the issue arose in the late 1940s as the balance-of-payments situation began to deteriorate. As in Britain, the Social Democratic government saw no alternative but to ask the unions to acquiesce to a wage freeze through incomes policy. The wage controls were naturally most effective among the weaker, and least effective among the strongest workers. This imposed upon the trade unions two problems: one, a future scenario of repeated incomes policies would likely break the unity and solidarity of the union movement; two, incomes policies meant that wage restraint would unequally subsidize profits. The active labour market policy, designed by Gösta Rehn and Rudolf Meidner and promoted by the trade union movement as an alternative to incomes policy became, in Sweden, the instrument through which an accommodation to full employment was pursued. The instrument was brilliant in its simplicity: across-the-board solidarity wage pressure coupled with generous and active labour market programmes to absorb, retrain and move the workers made redundant in the decaying industries. The policy was, concomitantly, designed to favour dynamic industries with generous profits and an ample supply of highly qualified manpower. Finally, it was assumed that the inevitable wage pressures would be contained through (countercyclical) budgetary restraint.

The application of this instrument presumed the presence of two crucial institutional conditions. One, centralized and solidaristic trade union organization in political synchrony with government policy; two, employer confidence and willingness to sustain high investment levels.[3] These institutional preconditions obtained, by and large, until the 1970s, permitting a 'positive-sum' resolution to the problem of full employment wage pressures.

The Norwegian response was parallel to the Swedish, but with its own institutional peculiarities. First and foremost, postwar Norwegian Labour governments enjoyed absolute parliamentary majorities, and could count on an unusually pervasive political consensus. The bourgeois parties were, in fact, co-signatories of the postwar documents that gave binding commitments to the establishment of the welfare state and full employment. The institutional arrangement was, from the beginning, designed for 'neocorporatist' interest intermediation. Government boards would, in collaboration with the unions, set wage guidelines in conjunction with economic growth targets. The most important instrument used to assure compliance with wage guidelines was government's overpowering control over industrial credits and investments. Thus, the trade unions were in a position to trust that wage restraint would be accompanied by investments. In this sense, credit policy became the Norwegian equivalent to Sweden's active labour market policy. Both are designed to channel labour's full employment bargaining power into positive–sum directions; both are only applicable in institutional settings where labour and capital command internal organizational consensus, are capable of relatively far-sighted political exchange, and can, in concert with government translate narrow interests into national interests.

West Germany represents a third variant of postwar development. Rapid economic growth with price stability was, in the celebrated 'social market' model, allowed to flow from a combination of laissez-faire market conditions and restrictive fiscal and monetary policy; the public budget was explicitly prohibited from growing faster than GDP. These, however, would likely fail in their application unless supported by favourable institutional conditions. Aside from the unique circumstances of postwar West Germany (foreign occupation, massive devastation, territorial division), the crucial conditions condense into two major factors. The extraordinarily strong autonomy of the German Central Bank, the 'Bundesbank', has been one of the basic institutional means for containing wage and public expenditure growth through restrictive monetary policies. Two, the de facto marginalization of both the Social Democratic party and the trade unions; three, a constant and massive supply of (well-qualified) manpower (from the Eastern territories) which for long prevented the labour movement from exercising much wage-push. In this respect, the German formula is equivalent to the Italian (with its capacity to draw on Southern labour) and, to an extent, also the American (Hispanic labour).

As long as labour supply outpaced industrial job expansion, the German 'economic miracle' could proceed without inflationary wage pressures and without effective political claims for major social reform. But the need for institutional realignment presented itself when the labour supply dried up in the early 1960s.

The institutional adaptation to labour's emergent redistributional power began with the formation of the 'Grand Coalition' between the CDU and the SPD in 1966; Ludwig Erhard's neo-liberalist economic orthodoxy was shelved in favour of Schiller's Keynesianism with 'Globalsteuerung'. Considerable faith was placed in the capacity of 'Konzertierte Aktion' to regulate the unavoidable wage pressures that full employment would entail. 'Concerted Action' was intended to provide unions, employers and government with an institutional framework within which distributional targets could be co-ordinated. The realignment of German politics took a second crucial step with the formation of the SPD-FDP coalition in 1969. This alliance promoted the major policy instruments designed to accommodate the novel matrix of power. Of critical importance were the Swedish-style active manpower programme and substantial improvements in social benefit programmes.

4. The international convergence of full employment

An international convergence of full employment emerged in the 1960s. In its wake evolved a surprising similarity in the choice of regulatory instruments, even within fundamentally divergent institutional systems. Principally, the welfare state emerged as the favoured outlet for distributional stand-offs and threatening wage pressures. With full employment, labour demanded a renegotiation of the initial postwar 'social contract'. Unemployment levels declined sharply from the 1950s to the 1960s. For 1950–60, the average in the United States was 4.5 percent, in Germany 4.6 percent, in Denmark 4.3 percent, and in Norway and Sweden 2.0 and 1.8 percent respectively. Except for the United States, the other nations converged during the 1960s at approximately 1.5–2.0 percent unemployment.[4]

A robust time-series on wage pressures back to the Second World War is difficult to construct. A fairly comparable measure would be to compute the elasticities of annual change in hourly compensation with respect to annual change in output per hour within manufacturing industries. However, high elasticities in just one year may not necessarily denote wage pressure, only the first effect of negotiated wage increases that then are absorbed the following year. Hence, a solution is to identify the presence of significantly high elasticities over two years or more. Table 1 presents an overview of such wage pressure periods for selected nations.

The only cases of significant wage pressure in the 1950s occur in Sweden (where full employment obtained) and the United States in 1951–2 (when unemployment levels were a record low: 3.2 and 2.9 percent). Otherwise, significant wage pressures in these, as in most other nations, emerged in the 1960s and culminated between 1969 and 1973 (Flanagan et al., 1983; Ulman and Flanagan, 1971; Crouch and Pizzorno, 1978; Sachs, 1979).

The growing wage pressures of the 1960s coincided with declining profitability, inflation and balance-of-payments difficulties. The new situation gave rise to four major responses. One was deflationary policy in response to acute overheating. This was attempted in Italy, France and Denmark

TABLE 1
The incidence of significant wage pressures in selected
OECD nations, 1950–83[1]

I : Years with significant wage pressure	II: Years with significant wage moderation
Ia: The United States	
1951–2	1962
1965–7	1968
1969–70	1971
1972–4	1976–7
1978–9	1981–3
Ib: West Germany	
1962–3	1953–4
1970–1	1959
	1967–8
	1976
Ic: Sweden	
1951–2	1955–7
1957–8	1959
1971–2	1963–5
1975–7	1967–8
	1973–4
	1978–80
	1982–3

[1] Wage pressure is defined as annual rate of change in manufacturing hourly compensation divided by annual rate of change in output per manhour in manufacturing. The underlying data are based on national and OECD National Accounts Statistics. Note, that prior to 1962, hourly compensation does *not* include employer social contributions, but only earnings. The identification of 'significant' wage pressures/moderation has been done by taking substantial deviations from the trend-line. Since each nation has its unique trend-line, the decision-method has been fitted to each.

(1963), in West Germany (1965), in the UK and Sweden (1966) and, if we here include devaluations, also in the UK, Denmark and Norway in 1967. The deflationary measures were primarily in response to sudden balance-of-payment difficulties and, except perhaps for the German, they were relatively mild. They can, at any rate, not be interpreted as a return to the 'political business cycle' logic in Kalecki's use of the term. They were one-shot crisis measures.

The second response was incomes policy, ranging from explicit and comprehensive deals to vaguer and more indirect efforts to persuade unions to restrain themselves. An early and illustrious forerunner of the former type was the Danish 'package solution' (Helhedsløsningen) of 1963, in which government — in consultation with all important interest organizations — pieced together an array of public benefits for all in return for private sector restraint on incomes and consumption. This is a pioneering example of how full employment pressures came to catalyse welfare state expansion.

The capacity for workable incomes bargains varied according to class organizational cohesion and capacity for political exchange. France's attempt in 1964 included only public sector workers, but it was hoped that their wage restraint would trickle down (which it did not). The policy was applied for several years and helped trigger the cataclysmic strike and wage explosions of 1968 (Ulman and Flanagan, 1971; Crouch and Pizzorno, 1978). In Britain, statutory incomes policy was applied in 1966 (with a six-month wage freeze) but, like in France, culminated in strikes and deteriorating relations between the TUC and the labour party (Crouch, 1977 and 1978). In Germany, the new Grand Coalition's Konzertierte Aktion formula, inaugurated in 1966, sought to include the trade unions in setting wage guidelines. These were followed the next two years but, due to the lack of 'social symmetry' (i.e. wage restraint was coupled with a profits boom), the result was a proliferation of wildcat strikes and a consequent wage explosion in 1969 (Müller-Jentsch and Sperling, 1978).

The third response to the new full employment order was institutional rearrangements to accommodate labour's novel power: the emergence of 'neocorporatist' structures of interest-intermediation and concertation. The literature on the 'neocorporatist' phenomenon is very large.[5]

This, as we know, failed in Britain, France and Italy, and was, at best, a fragile experiment in Germany. In countries where the preconditions were appreciably more fertile, such as in Scandinavia and Austria, the structures of interest concertation were strengthened, especially with regard to the battery of instruments available for distributional bargains. Thus, in Sweden, opportunities for bargains were substantially improved by the development of the (ATP) pension funds, the active labour market policy apparatus and the investment reserve system (Martin, 1981; Esping-Andersen, 1985), all of which incorporated the trade unions as key decisionmakers. In Norway, likewise, the institutional network of public credit- and investment-agencies was extended, permitting new deals such as redistribution in favour of poorer and less developed regions. New institutions, with the primary objective of involving labour movements in negotiating distributional priorities, sprang up in nations where they could succeed as well as in nations where such modes of political exchange remained structurally abortive.

Equally importantly, such attempts at institutional realignment were coupled with frantic searches for distributional outlets. One avenue lay in investment-promotion policies, designed to assure that wage discipline would result in new jobs. The other, increasingly dominant, lay in welfare state promotion of the 'deferred wage', that is, promises to improve future social benefits in return for present wage restraint. Both lead to a tremendous expansion of the public budget.

Finally, the fourth response was to mobilize new manpower reserves. One approach was to invite foreign guestworkers to fill the surplus of vacancies; the other was to encourage greater female labour force participation. The former response came to dominate in Germany, Switzerland, Austria; the latter dominated in Scandinavia.[6]

5. The incompatibilities of sustained full employment

As the 1960s drew to a close, most nations had experienced prolonged full employment and, despite major institutional realignments and a variety of policy responses, a new stable equilibrium had not been found. The changed balance of class and organizational power was reflected in growing inflationary pressures (Hirsch and Goldthorpe, 1978), strains within the trade unions as well as between unions and the Labour parties (Crouch and Pizzorno, 1978), proliferating strike activity, and diminishing business profitability.[7] Also, as was illustrated in Table 1, wage pressures escalated in the period 1969–73.

As we have discussed, governments and interest organizations tried to find escape routes from the full-employment pressures of the 1960s. However, the various solutions permitted, at best, only temporary breathing room and were, by and large, incapable of longer-term accommodation. First, neither government-induced slumps, nor the inclusion of new manpower reserves, managed to effectively alter the durable full-employment scenario. Second, the trade-offs for wage restraint that were negotiated in the incomes policy settlements of the 1960s were generally not sufficient to pacify workers' demands, in particular when wage restraint produced profit booms, or when real incomes were affected by inflation. Thirdly, the mix of incomes policies, redistributive wage bargaining and inflation provoked intense equity conflicts in the labour market. On the one hand, wage differentials were upset; on the other hand, privileged groups were often capable of compensating with wage drift.

The result was a burst of new distributional bargains. The basic problem that confronted most countries was how to dampen prices and labour costs, strengthen the balance-of-payments situation, and how to assure sustained investment in the light of declining profitability. In distributional terms, the question was how to formulate alternatives to wage improvements. The political and economic conditions that prevailed during the late 1960s and early 1970s ruled out deflationary policy solutions.

The growing tensions and decaying solidarity within the trade unions meant, in addition, that new quid-pro-quos would have to be more attractive to the rank-and-file, and that they would have to help restore solidarity. The welfare state became the cornerstone instrument of wage restraint. But, compared to the 1960s, the 'deferred wage' embodied in benefit improvements and new social programmes was substantially more costly.

The deferred social wage strategy is quantitatively evident in most nations. Weisskopf (1985) has, for example, shown that the (trended) ratio of social wages to private wages leaped from one business cycle to another. The sharpest increases occurred between the business cycle of the late 1960s (roughly 1963–8/9) and its successors in the early 1970s (1968–71 and 1971–4/5). Table 2 illustrates the rise of the social wage from 1965–82 in seven countries.

TABLE 2

The relative growth of the 'deferred' social wage: the elasticity of average annual growth of social transfer payments over average annual growth of earned wages and salaries, 1962–82

	1962–5	1965–9	1969–73	1973–8	1978–82
Denmark	1.02	1.07	1.04	1.04	1.07*
Norway	1.04	1.06	1.07	1.01	1.05
Sweden	1.07	1.07	1.04	1.16	1.05
Germany	1.00	1.02	0.98	1.08	1.02
Netherlands	1.13	1.13	0.91	1.08	1.06
UK	1.03	1.06	1.00	1.11	1.10
US	0.99	1.05	1.10	1.06	1.06

* 1978–81

Sources: OECD, *National Accounts*. Detailed Tables. Current Volumes. Paris: OECD.

The deferred social wage strategy found variable expression depending on each nation's institutional matrix. In the United States, it took two principal forms. One, negotiated employee benefit improvements (such as health care and occupational pensions) within the corporate sector.[8] Two, social benefit improvements, typically in conjunction with elections. Lacking a firm class- or electoral-base, the political exchange model typical of a European social democracy finds its American equivalent in the institutional framework of election maximization.

Hence, only one incumbent president (Jimmy Carter, in 1979/80) went to elections on the backdrop of deflationary policies. In the United States, virtually all major improvements in social benefits coincided with either congressional or presidential election years. Tufte (1978) shows that nine out of thirteen legislated social security improvements occurred in an election year. However, what is not evident from Tufte's analysis is the role that election maximization policies also play in counteracting wage-push. The social wage ratio remained fairly constant in the United States during the entire 1950s and up until the mid-1960s. This was a period in which wages generally lagged behind productivity, and in which unemployment levels remained high. The situation was sharply reversed after 1965.

From the period 1962–5 to 1965–9, the annual average elasticity of hourly compensation over productivity tripled (Sachs, 1979). It was also in these years that the second American welfare state expansion occurred (Myles, 1984).

If we omit the War on Poverty (which was principally designed to align the poor and black electorates to the crumbling Democratic party coalition), the Johnson administration inaugurated Keynesian stimulus policies (the 1964 tax cut), legislated medicaid/medicare, relaxed eligibility require- ments, and passed two major raises in social security benefits (1965 and 1967).

It was, paradoxically, the Nixon administration that gave the social wage strategy full prominence. During the years 1969–72, the federal govern- ment legislated huge increases in social security benefits, introduced indexation, extended coverage substantially, and passed the guaranteed pension (SSI). Pensions, as a percentage of wages, rose sharply. These improvements coincided with the application of an incomes policy (the wage/price controls) in late 1971. But they were beyond doubt also tailored to winning the 1972 presidential elections. Within the American institu- tional logic, however, the latter motive certainly does not preclude the former.

Major social wage bargains were the order of the day in the late 1960s and early 1970s. Explicit bargains took place in Sweden in 1973, when unions agreed to moderate wage claims in return for a legislated abolition of employee pension contributions. In Denmark, the social wage consti- tuted, since the early 1960s, the only real outlet for wage pressures. Thus, in virtually every case of formal incomes policy, negotiated wage restraint, or devaluation, workers' income restraint was offset with benefit improve- ments and social reforms. As in most other countries, this pattern climaxed in the early 1970s when pensions were upgraded, and major improvements were legislated in unemployment and sickness cash-benefit programmes. The result was, in fact, the development of the world's most generous cash- benefit programmes. And, in Germany, the SPD government's capacity to persuade the trade unions to abide by the wage guidelines within the Konzertierte Aktion was intimately connected to its programme for upgrading the German welfare state. Following the employment promotion act, government passed the law on wage continuation during illness in 1969 — one of the DGB's top-priority demands over the preceding decade. But the trade unions' wage restraint during the initial years of social democracy was followed by a new wave of militancy and wage push (wages as a share of national income jumped from 6.13 percent in 1968 to 66.3 percent in 1974/5). A second phase of major welfare state improvements came in 1972 and included substantial pension hikes, a guaranteed mini- mum pension and liberalized access to early retirement. Like its 1971 American counterpart, this was a blend of social wage bargains and election maximization, since the CDU attempted to overbid the SPD's planned pension reform for electoral reasons.

The deferred social wage presupposes a willingness among workers to delay the consumption increase that their bargaining power would otherwise permit them to enjoy immediately. It is, however, a complex bargaining item. Broad acquiescence assumes a solidarity not only among the wage earners themselves, but also between the wage earners and those most likely to be the immediate beneficiaries, meaning primarily the old. The deferred social wage strategy is caught between two simultaneous motives: it is meant to moderate wage claims, but also inflation. Yet, substantial growth in welfare state expenditures must invoke higher taxes; and, it is possible that rapid public spending growth under conditions of full employment will add to existing inflationary pressures. Hence the search for alternative, and less costly, instruments for induced moderation.

The major alternative that presented itself in the late 1960s and early 1970s involved various schemes to democratize working life and enhance workers' influence over enterprise decision-making. These were attractive from the point of view of welfare state finances and spoke also to the trade unions' internal legitimacy problems. The extension of workers' rights became a major trade union priority. This was evident in the passage of 'industrial democracy' legislation in Norway, Sweden and, to a lesser extent, Denmark in the early 1970s; a parallel case is the West German conflict over the extension of 'Mitbestimmung' in the mid-1970s. In Sweden, the trade-off was both explicit and of substantial proportions. With a series of laws, workers were given representation on company boards, job-tenure rights, a large degree of control over safety and health conditions, and even over technology decisions.

If social wage expansion strained governments' budgets, industrial democratization led to severe strains and, in reality, to naked conflict as it jeopardized accustomed employer sovereignty. Its passage meant a de facto departure from the 'class consensus' upon which the postwar welfare state and full employment model has been premised. And, in Sweden at least, it hardly succeeded in dampening workers' lust for wages.

The incompatibilities of either approach soon became evident. Extended worker control legislation could never provide a positive-sum solution acceptable to employers and has, since its passage, been systematically and powerfully attacked by employer organizations and by conservative parties. It has, undoubtedly, added to the strained circumstances in which collective negotiations have found themselves during the past ten years. And it has also — due to its explicit break with the original 'social contract' — undermined the general conditions for class consensus that, by and large, prevailed over the postwar era in the Scandinavian countries.

The incompatibilities of the social wage bargains are considerably more complex. Their weakness does not seem to be that they catalyse rank-and-file rebellions against their labour leaders, as Leninist analyses were ready to predict. Rather, the incompatibilities lie in their fiscal consequences. Under conditions of employment and output growth, the revenue requirements that an expanded social wage implies can be met without significant increases in the tax rate. The early and mid-1970s, however, were a period in which growth declined and inflation spiralled. The result was inevitably that taxes on average worker households rose dramatically.[9] Table 3 clearly illustrates the problem. Workers ended up footing much of the bill for the deferred wage.

TABLE 3
The tax burden on average worker households, 1965–80,
in Denmark, Sweden, West Germany and the United States.
Average personal tax (incl. social contributions) and marginal tax rate.
Percent of worker earnings. Family with one earner and two children

	Denmark		Sweden		Germany		United States	
	A	M	A	M	A	M	A	M
1965	18	26	22	26	17	20	13	15
1970	26	49	30	45	21	28	15	20
1975	33	53	33	59	26	33	16	31
1980	37	59	33	59	26	34	19	24

Notes: A = Average income tax and social security contribution
M = Marginal tax rate
For Denmark, Sweden and Germany, the marginal tax rates for 1980 are actually 1982.
For Sweden, the average tax for 1970 is estimated.
Sources: OECD, *The Tax/Benefit Position of a Typical Worker*. Paris: OECD, 1981; and (unpublished) data from an ongoing project on distributional conflicts in eighteen OECD nations, conducted by Walter Korpi and Gøsta Esping-Andersen.

The combination of inflation and tax growth forced the trade unions into wage bargaining strategies that often were detrimental to economic stability and continued full employment. In some situations, nominal wage increases would have to be in the magnitude of 20–30 percent just to deliver a 2–3 percent real wage growth. For the trade unions, therefore, tax reductions became a first-order priority and a major item for bargaining against wage restraint. In Sweden, the legislated re-financing of social contributions in 1973 provided a brief respite, but the real issue was marginal taxes. Failure to bring down either taxes or inflation effectively led to the wage explosion in 1975. It was not until 1981 that a major reform helped reduce the marginal tax rate and so, even in the context of an international economic crisis and growing strains of the full employment commitment, the unions were compelled to continue their wage maximization bargaining. Wages grew faster than productivity in the years 1975–77, and again in 1981.

In Denmark, the situation was even more dramatic, in part due to the welfare state's almost exclusive reliance on the direct income tax; and, in part, due to stronger inflation and more rapidly rising marginal tax rates. Thus, by the early 1970s, many households found themselves in the situation that additional labour supply would have directly negative effects on disposable income. The result was the famous tax revolt in 1973, led by Mogens Glistrup's new Progress party. From then on, none of the frequently shifting and parliamentarily weak cabinets could impose additional income taxes to offset rapidly rising public expenditures.

In Britain, as Klein (1985) observes, the logic was similar. Following a period in which the Labour government increased public expenditures in return for wage restraint, it was forced (in 1978) to appease the TUC's demand for considerable tax cuts.

In the United States, as one would predict, the pressure for compensatory tax reductions did not emanate from well-entrenched interest organizations, but instead from (initially) local and (later) national tax revolts. These gave, in 1981, a virtually unchallengeable mandate to the Reagan administration's tax cut, despite a broad expert-consensus regarding its detrimental effects for the economy.

6. The re-emergence of employment as the quid pro quo for wage restraint

The typical, advanced OECD country, be it Denmark, the United States or West Germany, encountered the 1973 OPEC price shock, the collapse of the Bretton Woods monetary order, falling industrial profits, and international trade-stagnation in a contradictory way. From one side, the deferred wage strategy and the general consolidation of social citizenship rights compelled very large public expenditures; from the other side, governments' capacity for additional tax revenue extraction was effectively constrained. The common denominator was an impending fiscal crisis that, over the next decade, could not find resolution in the traditional economic growth dividend, nor in expenditure cuts.

The conditions that came to prevail after 1973 also made the full employment commitment more difficult to honour. The welfare state found itself saddled with the additional responsibility of upholding full employment or, at least, of averting large-scale unemployment. If the deferred social wage strategy, with its ensuing tax constraints, was a convergent national response to the full employment wage problem before 1973, the post-1973 era gave rise to new fundamental divergences.

The political emphasis on price stabilization versus sustained full employment differed between systems, but a significant differentiation also emerged with respect to the means adopted to sustain employment. A cross-national comparison of the situation after 1973 and especially of that after 1979 suggests that none of the prevailing institutional models have been capable of furnishing full employment *and* sustained balanced growth.[10] Counter-inflationary policies based on restrictive monetary and fiscal policies produce unemployment; employment-promotion policies based on a menu of choices ranging from countercyclical fiscal or monetary policies to active employment creation and large-scale production subsidies have proved incapable of delivering balanced growth. The one obvious alternative, namely employment promotion in return for effective and substantial wage restraint, has, so far, been institutionally blocked.

Trade union organization constitutes one important obstacle to full employment maintenance during prolonged economic stagnation. Whether employment expansion is to be pursued via massive new investments in the private sector or via public sector (service) job growth, it has to be financed with a reduction of disposable wages. Since, however, the representational domain of trade unions is generally confined to employed workers, the solidarity that was mobilizable for a social wage- or tax-based bargain is likely to be much more difficult to marshall for employment promotion programmes directed at the non-employed; especially since it stipulates actual real income decline, not merely a declining rate of real income growth. Due to job security laws, moreover, the average unionized worker is unlikely to identify his personal future with a scenario of unemployment.

The second major obstacle has to do with fiscal imbalance of the welfare state. Decaying revenue extraction capacity is matched by rapidly growing social wage commitments, augmented by rising unemployment. Under such conditions, government budget deficits provide one of the few means by which the welfare state is capable of serving the double-barrelled demands for social welfare and full employment.

And the third important obstacle lies in the logic of economic rejuvenation that advanced industrialization and heightened international competition impose; namely, that the marginal employment dividend of new industrial investments is low, and that a restoration of international competitiveness requires either lower labour costs or significant redundancies through rationalization. But, reduced labour costs and redundancies have become directly connected with welfare state performance. A cut in the former entails a reduction of employer social contributions; redundancies assume the presence of welfare state programmes, like early retirement, to absorb laid-off workers. In summary, no matter how the obstacles are perceived, the welfare state emerges as the principal focus of conflict.

The three models that came to characterize the postwar responses to full employment, exemplified in the differences between the United States, Scandinavia and West Germany, retain their distinctiveness with regard to the patterns of political accommodation to the post-1973 conditions. In one model (the United States), the dominant characteristic is a mix of political business cycle management and market regulation; in the second model (Scandinavia), the welfare state becomes the leading force in sustaining full employment — partly as direct employer, and partly through subsidies; and in the third model (Germany), we find a blend of conservative austerity policies and welfare state promoted dis-employment of older workers. In the two former models, employment continues to grow; in the latter, it contracts. In all, the welfare state is forced to absorb costs for which it is not financially equipped. In neither is a return to stable, full employment-based growth imminent.

As will be recalled, the United States entered the post-1973 era with a substantial rise in social expenditures that, of course, were not matched with tax- and social contribution hikes. The institutionally self-financed social security system faced bankruptcy, especially as unemployment reduced revenues and, in concert with demographic change, raised outlays. A major source of increased government tax-revenue was the effect that inflation had on escalating incomes into higher tax-brackets. And it was this which provoked broad support for tax reductions.[11]

The Carter Administration's ability to counter both inflation and unemployment was severely constrained by its limited financial means and policy options. One approach, the expansion of public sector jobs, was fiscally (and politically) barred. The liberalized access to early retirement at age sixty-three helped firms shed some less productive manpower, but further strained social security finances. The hope of introducing an active manpower policy was aborted by concerted business resistance. The CETA (Comprehensive Education and Training Act) programme helped absorb large numbers, but was hardly more than a parking lot for labour reserves.

The clear policy priority was anti-inflationary business cycle regulation that permitted high unemployment. The increase in employment and growth during 1978 and 1979 was accompanied by a resurgent wage-push (the elasticity of wage-growth over productivity growth, 1978–9, was approximately 1.30). Carter's (electorally fatal) response was deflationary measures in 1979.

The very deep recession that ensued produced the highest unemployment rates since the Depression (with annual averages of 9.5 percent in 1982 and 1983). And, in contrast to previous slumps, the core unionized labour force was severely affected. This spurred the trade unions, especially the larger industrial federations, to sponsor deals both at the level of collective bargaining and in the political arena. The idea was to sacrifice wages against employment security and job-promotion policies. Employment-based trade-offs did occur sporadically through private bargains (in autos, for example), but did not resonate well with the new Reagan Administration, whose priorities centred on a swift dismantling of CETA, tax reductions, welfare cutbacks, de-regulation, and anti-inflationary policies.

Although antithetical to the notion of government employment promotion, the Reagan Administration(s) has nevertheless sought recourse to stimulation programmes. For one, the soaring public budget deficits coupled with large defence purchases stimulate demand. Government net lending as a percent of GDP grew from 1.4 percent in 1980 to about 5 percent in 1983.[12] Secondly, the 1981 tax cuts were a de facto government subsidization of businesses. Corporate income taxes as a percent of corporate receipts declined from 20 percent (1980) to 11.4 percent (1983).[13]

Despite an actual decline in the share of government employment, and despite very high unemployment rates (until 1984), the United States rate of employment growth has been very strong.

This performance, spectacular as it is, cannot be explained by reference to Reagan's de facto reflationary policies, since the trend has been strong throughout the 1970s. It is, however, the case that the employment performance during the early 1980s coincides with a policy regime that creates severe economic imbalances, including extraordinarily large deficits on the public budget and on the external trade accounts. Debt service payments as a percent of current federal government outlays were more than 11 percent in 1983.

Norway and Sweden are among the very few nations that have been capable of upholding full employment since 1973. Both nations managed, until the recession of the 1980s, to hold open unemployment under 3 percent. Their record unemployment rate was reached in 1983 with about 3.5 percent. This performance testifies to the strength of the binding full employment commitment that reigns, and it suggests the possibility that these two countries have produced an institutional system in which the basic economic dilemmas of capitalism are resolvable. A closer scrutiny, however, suggests that this is not the case.

The conditions that pattern Norway's policy alternatives are naturally unique due to the impact of the oil economy. The oil revenues have afforded Norway a means of financing both incomes and employment simultaneously that few other countries enjoy. Oil incomes were the basis of Norway's extraordinary Keynesian reflation policy after 1973. Borrowing on future revenues, the government-designed income agreement of 1974 increased government spending by 1 billion Kroner, and gave major tax reductions to employees. This expansionary incomes policy was repeated in subsequent years, culminating in 1977 with a 2 billion Kroner increase in outlays (Esping-Andersen, 1985: 244). These income binges, in the context of full employment, pushed labour costs 25 percent above the OECD average, thus impairing economic competitiveness.

This would have been a ready-made case for heavy unemployment had it not been for government's recourse to production- and wage subsidies. It has been estimated that, in the late 1970s, every fifth Norwegian worker's job owed its existence to public subsidies (Haarr, 1982). However, the sheer volume of production subsidies is staggering. As a percent of GDP, they grew from 5.3 in 1972 to 7.7 in 1978. By 1983, they had declined to 6.1 percent. This is about fifteen times the American rate, three times the West German, and about twice the (high) Danish rate.

The result was, of course, enormous budget deficits (that were eliminated via oil revenues) and, more seriously, a long-term impairment of industrial competitiveness. With declining oil revenues in the future, the costs of upholding full employment are bound to become unbearably high. A third, uniquely Scandinavian, response to rising unemployment has also been adopted in Norway, although to a lesser extent than in Denmark and Sweden. This includes expansion of welfare state jobs (an annual growth rate of about 3.5 percent in the 1970s) and active manpower programmes, including retraining and sheltered employment.

The Swedish full employment performance is the more impressive in that there was no manna from the sea. Moreover, badly orchestrated fiscal policy during the early 1970s placed the Swedish economy in a very unfavourable position. First, in reaction to severe wage push and overheating, the Social Democratic government manufactured a relatively deep recession in 1971–3. The deflationary measures helped arrest income- and consumption growth, but Sweden lost out on the booming international markets that prevailed then and was forced to absorb considerable unemployment within the active labour market apparatus. Secondly, the prolonged income restraint fuelled a wage explosion in 1975–7 which, as in Norway, undermined Sweden's economic competitiveness abroad. In 1976, when the Social Democrats were defeated, it was evident that their longstanding 'middle-way' formula had exhausted its capacity to accommodate full employment to balanced growth. Aside from wage push and sagging competitiveness, investment rates were exceedingly sluggish, inflation high, and real GDP growth low. The social democratic full employment hegemony was maintained during the unstable bourgeois cabinets that reigned from 1976 to 1982. Swedish politics, however, remained imprisoned in an institutional system that no longer functioned: wages were difficult to contain; taxes, impossible to raise; public expenditures impossible to cut; and deflationary policies were out of the question.

The remaining option was to accumulate large government deficits to finance employment. Crisis-industries were granted colossal subsidies; swelling inventories were subsidized across the board (amounting to 2 percent of GDP in 1977); the labour reserves absorbed in active labour market programmes mushroomed. The only other outlet available was to escalate welfare state employment. During the 1970s, average annual growth in public employment was 5 percent. As in the United States, but under welfare state auspices, Sweden actually expanded total employment in a stagnant economy.

The effort to sustain full employment was costly. By 1980, the government deficit was 10.4 percent of GDP; growing to almost 12 percent in

1983. The size of this deficit must be understood in connection with government taxation which, by the 1980s, amounted to 50 percent of GDP.

Sweden's tax-extractive capacity is both unique and intimately related to the solidarity that supports the welfare state and full employment. Additional increases, however, appear blocked. The Social Democratic government that was re-installed in 1982 was not only saddled with huge deficits, but also with the need to finance major new investments. Its capacity to rely on the unions to sacrifice wages for the sake of the common good would not appear high in light of the growing unrest within the labour movement. In 1982, the powerful metal worker union broke ranks with the employers. Growing tensions emerged between private and public sector federations. In the 1970s, Swedish distributional conflicts turned into a zero-sum game that was only precariously patched up by deficit-financed welfare state intervention. That it was precarious is reflected in the evaporation of the longstanding consensus between capital and labour. In its place developed a remarkable polarization.

Social democracy's way out of the dilemma is premised on the wage earner funds ('economic democracy'), introduced in combination with the devaluation and the economic crisis programme in 1982–3. The principle is to make effective wage discipline acceptable because, in return, workers as a collective receive part of the ensuing profits in the form of added revenues to the ailing pension funds, and in the form of collective investment capital for future jobs and wages. In a Kaleckian sense, the wage earner funds constitute a novel attempt at institutional accommodation to full employment; they serve to channel labour's power into positive-sum trade-offs. Yet, their capacity to do so assumes that business is prepared to participate. But, in contrast to social democracy's previous institutional innovations, the wage earner funds' mark, from the point of view of business, an additional incursion into the rights of property ownership which is totally unacceptable. Thus, if it can be argued that any form of institutional accommodation to full employment must rest on an underlying social contract, one would have to predict that the wage earner funds' strategy is likely to shipwreck.[14]

The spectre of a bold new era of social democracy in West Germany was put to rest only a few years after the SPD came to power. West Germany did not confront the 1973 oil crisis in a particularly opportune way. Both private and social wages had grown sharply over the preceding years, profits had declined, inflationary pressures were strong, and Germany's export competitiveness was weakened. With a rise in unemployment after 1973, the SPD naturally opted for expansionary measures. Yet, its countercyclical budget clashed with the Bundesbank's insistence on restrictive monetary policy to stabilize the currency and prices. The Bundesbank's mandate was the strongest, and the government was forced instead to restrict welfare expenditures and tolerate rising unemployment. Austerity policies designed to bring down inflation persisted until the brief 1978–9 reflation.

The Keynesian breakthrough, coupled to active labour market policy, was therefore aborted. The trade unions saw, in this context, little reason to maintain an obligation to the kind of neocorporatist settlements that Konzertierte Aktion implied. Yet, they were barred from exerting wage pressures due to the tight money policies and rising unemployment levels. Wage restraint in the 1970s was therefore a function of the political business cycle; not of negotiated bargains. Indeed, the unions found that there was precious little about which there could be bargaining.

In direct contrast to Scandinavia, the welfare state was not permitted to furnish the double task of social equality and employment promotion. To cover the rising costs of unemployment and pensions, the government was forced in 1977, 1981 and again in 1982 to impose real cuts in social and manpower programme expenditures and, simultaneously, raise tax contributions. Most importantly, social democracy's ability to absorb unemployment in active manpower programmes was effectively vetoed, as was its freedom to expand welfare state employment. In spite of general fiscal austerity, government began to run budget deficits. Modest as they were in comparison to either Scandinavia or the United States (5.7 percent of GDP in 1975; 0.3 percent in 1980, and about 1 percent in 1983), they were not politically acceptable.

Two major policies to combat unemployment remained possible in West Germany. One, to extradite foreign workers; the other, to encourage early retirement among older workers in the hope that this would promote both productivity and jobs for younger workers. This approach, typical of most continental European countries, caused a substantial decline in overall employment. In Germany, the participation rate of males, aged 60–65, declined from 75 percent in 1970 to 44 percent in 1981.[15] Yet, despite the labour force contraction, unemployment levels continued to rise (to more than 8 percent in 1983). Tight money supply policies inhibit both consumption and investments.

The dis-employment strategy characteristic of West Germany may have produced productivity gains for industry, but it saddles the welfare state with the same kinds of fiscal imbalances found in Scandinavia. The major cause here is that dis-employment escalates transfer payments and diminishes social contributions. Hence, to rebalance the public budget, considerable benefit cuts or tax hikes are necessary.

The narrow scope for alternative policies in West Germany, and especially the blocked prospects of bargaining for additional employment, helps explain the trade unions' recourse to a policy of redistributing scarce jobs. Thus, work-time reduction emerged as a major demand, first in 1976 with a demand for a one-hour across-the-board reduction — a proposal which was rejected by the separate union federations. Instead, the IG Metall demanded a 35-hour week combined with a 5 percent wage compensation. Backed by strikes in 1978, the strategy was defeated. So was its successor in 1984.

The German approach to stabilization policies have imposed three extraordinary costs: one, fiscal pressures on the welfare state; two, suboptimal utilization of manpower;[16] three, sluggish investment behaviour.

7. Conclusions

This chapter has tried to construct a new interpretation of old data. The issues dealt with here have been extensively examined before. There is a huge literature on postwar macroeconomic policies, incomes policies, the full-employment experience, the welfare state, on trade unions and neo-corporatist concertation, on declining governability and the economic crisis that beset advanced capitalist nations since the early 1970s.

Despite this accumulation of knowledge and wisdom, a new interpretative exercise seems warranted. First, with a few (very important) exceptions, there has been little effort devoted to study the interconnections between many of the powerful structural changes that took place over the past forty or so years.[17] This seems to me to be particularly the case with the relationship between full employment, economic stabilization policies, and the welfare state. Our intellectual forebears saw these as intricately linked in their scenarios of a new and more democratic capitalism. Contemporary scholarship has gone its own, specialized ways. The deferred wage concept, as Myles (1984) points out, affords us an analytic means by which the welfare state re-enters as an endogenous variable in the study of postwar political economy.

Secondly, the early 1970s not only created a break in the logic of postwar social, political and economic evolution, but also gave birth to a new analytical problem for social science: the study of capitalism in crisis. It strikes me that the new, post-1973 'crises-analyses' are largely disconnected from the scholarship and the phenomena that preceded them. The interpretation offered here is one effort to explore the direct links between the politics of the full employment-growth era, and the politics of the new 'crisis' era.

One of the most central questions of the postwar decades has been how to deliver upon the promise of both equality, full employment and efficiency. The answer that Kalecki provided, namely via new political and social institutions, will, in itself, hardly stir controversy. On the other hand, if Kalecki has in mind an institutional reordering whereby the rights of private entrepreneurship would be seriously weakened, the issue is quite another one.

The success of postwar capitalism lies in its capacity to harmonize democracy with private property. The synthesis of these two institutions was made possible by the 'social contracts' of the 1930s and 1940s, where

labour committed itself to respect the sanctity of entrepreneurial prerogatives in return for the freedom to conduct distributional struggles
unhindered.

The stability of the postwar decades had a lot to do with the capacity
of class and interest organizations to find institutional arrangements within
which this fundamental quid-pro-quo would be operationable. But, if the
social contract was a constant, the institutional arrangements came to
diverge sharply across nations. This played a vital role in shaping not only
the strength and durability of the full employment experience, but also
the capacity for arriving at stable and workable mediations between policy
goals and distributional priorities.

Whatever institutional structure came to prevail, a common feature of
postwar nations is their rising incapability of managing the altered balance
of power which full employment brought about. The basic difficulty lay
in finding acceptable outlets for impending zero-sum conflicts. As we have
noted, the sanctity of property rights meant that the state came to constitute the realm of the possible. The concept of political exchange connotes
therefore two things: the capacity for deferring the fruits of power, and
the dependence on the political arena for managing distributional power.

Our cursory overview has, however, shown that the scope for trade-
offs in the state can be quite extensive. Political exchanges have involved
government credit, investments, nationalizations and subsidies, taxation,
employment and welfare policy. The welfare state emerged as the major
outlet for full employment pressures, principally in the shape of the
deferred social wage.

But, in whichever form it takes, the viability of a deferred wage strategy
depends ultimately on one's ability to collect upon it in the future. This
has proven itself the Achilles' heel of the deferred wage. For reasons of
bargaining, labour would have to insist against tax increases; for reasons
of competitiveness, corporations would similarly refuse. As a consequence,
the welfare state found itself in a situation in which it was either compelled
to renounce on its original obligations, or to finance the deferred wage
by deficits — thereby only delaying the zero-sum confrontation.

The nation's ability to balance distributional demands in a full employment situation worsened considerably as world-wide trade and growth
stagnated. But it clearly also worsened because existing distributional
outlets approached exhaustion. Yet, empirical evidence suggests that the
limits of a deferred wage strategy are not necessarily strictly financial.
That is, governments' capacity to increase taxes to accommodate rising
expenditures appears to be positively related to the strength of working-
class power mobilization and societal corporatism (Schmitter, 1981). Thus,
a nation's capacity for 'solidarity' is closely associated with economic
policy options. This is also a key-factor in a country's ability to move
beyond the conventional policy instruments. The case par excellence is

Sweden, where the deferred wage strategy was increasingly exhausted by a combination of forces: one, internal trade union problems with cohesion and legitimacy; two, the incapacity to bargain nominal wages to compensate for both taxes and inflation; three, the growing disbelief that wage restraint was reciprocated by sustained entrepreneurial investment. These factors led the trade unions to question their traditional adherence to the sanctity of property rights. The trade unions rediscovered a slogan from the 1930s: 'Democracy cannot stop at the factory gates', demanded a renegotiation of the original contract, and launched, first, worker control legislation and, subsequently, economic democracy with collective wage earner funds. These became in the 1970s and early 1980s the core trade-off policies. Their introduction, unlike the trade-off policies of the 1950s and 1960s, were, from the point of view of business, non-negotiable and unacceptable. They were thus the legislative victories of power, not of societal corporatism and interest intermediation.

In this way the democratization of property rights became both a novel type of stabilization politics (the Social Democratic government managed to persuade effective wage restraint against wage earner funds) and at the same time a source of de-stabilization. Although they may one day become acceptable to business, the politics of workers' control are certainly not so at present. Thus, in Sweden the only possible social democratic formula for a combined action of equality, full employment and efficiency is precariously upheld by slim parliamentary majorities. It still takes two to tango and, in a world with free capital movements, your partner may choose not to dance.

Notes

This is a revised version of a paper presented at the ECPR workshops in Barcelona, March 1985. Many of the principal ideas contained herein derive from Goldthorpe (1984) and from longstanding discussions with John Myles. I am also grateful for comments and criticisms received from Hans Keman, John Eivind Kolberg and Manfred Schmidt. The analyses presented here would have been superior had I been able to incorporate all their suggestions.

1. Between 1950 and 1980, female labour force supply doubled in Sweden and the United States (from 23 to 47, and from 22 to 40 percent, respectively). In Germany, female activity rates grew only from 31 to 34 percent (ILO, *Yearbook of Labor Statistics*, 1960 and 1983).

2. The following discussion is heavily based on Esping-Andersen (1985). A model of postwar political-economic development that is closely parallel to the Scandinavian is the Netherlands. In part, the Netherlands followed quite similar welfare state policies and strong full employment commitments; in part, balanced non-inflationary growth was pursued via an impressively consistent consensus around incomes policies (Ulman and Flanagan, 1971; Braun and Keman, 1986).

3. In fact, the model also assumes that employers are highly organized and capable of cohesion, and that the 'weaker' and decaying capitalists' political sway is marginal. It takes two to make centralized, solidarity-wage bargaining work.

4. The total OECD average for 1960–7 was 3.1 and for 1968–73, 3.4 percent. In the

United States, unemployment rates began first to decline sharply after 1964 (OECD, *Historical Statistics, 1960–83*, Paris: OECD, 1985; and Maddison, 1982).

5. For some important and representative treatments, see P. Schmitter (1981); P. Schmitter and G. Lehmbruch (1979); Lange (1984); Lehmbruch '(1984); Panitch (1980); Cameron (1984); and Regini (1984).

6. The numbers were large. At its peak, foreign workers accounted for more than 9 percent of the labour force (1973) in Germany; in Austria, more than 7 percent (1973); and for Sweden, the corresponding percentage is approximately 5 percent (including Finns), and about 3 percent (excluding Finns).

7. The profit share (net profit as a percent of net value added in manufacturing) declined precipitously between 1960–7 and 1968–73 for most countries, including the United States, Germany, the UK, Sweden and Denmark (OECD, *Historical Statistics 1960–83*, Paris: OECD, 1985; Flanagan et al., 1983; Glyn and Sutcliffe, 1972; Edgren et al., 1973; Martin, 1985; Nordhaus, 1974).

8. Employer contributions to private pension plans, as a percent of the total wage bill, grew from 5 percent in 1970 to 7.3 percent in 1975 (OECD, *National Accounts, 1962–79*, Vol. 2. Paris: OECD, 1981).

9. On the employer side the result was parallel. Non-wage labour costs (primarily social contributions) skyrocketed. As a percentage of total, they rose (1965–75) from 17 to 23 percent in the US, 19 to 32 percent in Sweden, and from 30 to 34 percent in Germany (SAF, 1976 and 1984).

10. By sustained balanced growth we here mean economic growth over the medium term which is not bought at the expense of seriously accumulating balance-of-payments deficits or public sector deficits, disinvestment, or inflation.

11. Note, however, that the first wave of tax revolts focused on the property tax that spiralled in the wake of inflation.

12. Omitting social security funds and including both current and capital accounts, the 1983 deficit was equal to 8.3 percent of GDP.

13. Note, however, that the 1981 tax cuts for business followed a long period in which government tax expenditures implicitly furnished a massive subsidy towards corporations. Break (1980) shows that, in the period 1970–80, tax expenditures in favour of corporations grew almost three times faster than Federal government income tax revenue.

14. The rather rosy picture of economic revitalization that is presented in a recent survey (OECD, 1985) is not necessarily incompatible with the gloomier scenario presented here. Our point is, that a *sustained* revitalization is unlikely to occur as long as its institutional framework is under serious dispute.

15. In Germany, total employment declined by an average −0.7 percent from 1973–83; the figure for Belgium (1979–83) is −1.1; for Austria (1979–83), −0.5; but, for the OECD as a whole, employment *grew* by an average of 1.1 percent (1973–9) and 0.2 percent (1979–83).

16. The national differences are clearly brought out in the following figures of total labour force participation as a percent of population, 15–64 years old:

	Germany	United States	Sweden
1971	69.3	66.8	74.9
1983	64.8	72.8	81.3

Source: OECD, *Historical Statistics* (Paris: OECD, 1985: Table 2.5)

17. One of the most comprehensive synthetic overviews is found in J. Goldthorpe (1984).

References

Bordogna, L. (1981) 'The Political Business Cycle and the Crisis of Keynesian Politics'. Paper presented at the American Sociological Association Meetings, August, in Toronto.

Braun, D. and H. Keman (1986) 'Politikstrategien und Konfliktregulierung in den Niederlanden', *Politische Vierteljahresschrift*, 27(1).

Break, G. F. (1980) 'The Role of Government: Taxes, Transfers and Spending', in M. Feldstein (ed.) *The American Economy in Transition*. Chicago: University of Chicago Press.

Cameron, D. (1984) 'Social Democracy, Corporatism, Labour Quiescence, and the Representation of Economic Interest in Advanced Capitalist Society', in J. Goldthorpe (ed.) *Order and Conflict in Contemporary Capitalism*. Oxford: Oxford University Press.

Crouch, C. (1977) *Class Conflict and the Industrial Relations Crisis*. London: Heinemann.

Crouch, C. (1978) 'The Intensification of Industrial Conflict in the United Kingdom', in C. Crouch and A. Pizzorno (eds) *The Resurgence of Class Conflict in Western Europe since 1968*, Vol. 1. New York: Holmes & Meier.

Crouch, C. and A. Pizzorno (1978) *The Resurgence of Class Conflict in Western Europe since 1968*, Vols 1 & 2. New York: Holmes & Meier.

Edgren, G., K. O. Faxén and C.-E. Odhnev (1973) *Wage Formation and the Economy*. London: Allen & Unwin.

Esping-Andersen, G. (1985) *Politics against Markets: The Social Democratic Road to Power*. Princeton: Princeton University Press.

Flanagan, R., D. Soskice and L. Ulman (1983) *Unionism, Economic Stabilization, and Incomes Policies*. Washington DC: The Brookings Institution.

Glyn, A. and R. Sutcliffe (1972) *British Capitalism. Workers and the Profits Squeeze*. London: Penguin.

Goldthorpe, J. (1984) 'The End of Convergence: Corporatist and Dualist Tendencies in Modern Western Societies', in J. Goldthorpe (ed.) *Order and Conflict in Contemporary Capitalism*. Oxford: Oxford University Press.

Haarr, A. (1982) *I Oljens Tegn*. Oslo: Tanum.

Higgins, W. and N. Apple (1981) *Class Mobilization and Economic Policy: Struggles over Full Employment in Britain and Sweden, 1930–80*. Stockholm: Arbetslivcentrum.

Hirsch, F. and J. Goldthorpe (eds) (1978) *The Political Economy of Inflation*. London: Martin Robertson.

Kalecki, M. (1943) 'Political Aspects of Full Employment', *Political Quarterly*, 14.

Klein, R. (1985) 'Public Expenditure in an Inflationary World', in L. Lindberg and C. Maier (eds) *The Politics of Inflation and Economic Stagnation*. Washington DC: The Brookings Institution.

Lange, P. (1984) 'Unions, Workers, and Wage Regulation: The Rational Bases of Consent', in J. Goldthorpe (ed.) *Order and Conflict in Contemporary Capitalism*. Oxford: Oxford University Press.

Lehmbruch, G. (1984) 'Concertation and the Structure of Corporatist Networks', in J. Goldthorpe (ed.) *Order and Conflict in Contemporary Capitalism*. Oxford: Oxford University Press.

Lindberg, L. and C. Maier (eds) (1985) *The Politics of Inflation and Economic Stagnation*. Washington DC: The Brookings Institution.

Maddison, A. (1982) *Phases of Capitalist Development*. Oxford: Oxford University Press.

Martin, A. (1981) 'Economic Stagnation and Social Stalemate in Sweden', in US Congress, Joint Economic Committee, *Monetary Policy, Selective Credit Policy, and Industrial Policy in France, Britain, West Germany, and Sweden*. Washington DC: Government Printing Office.

110   Coping with the economic crisis

Martin, A. (1985) 'Wages, Profits, and Investment in Sweden', in L. Lindberg and C. Maier (eds) *The Politics of Inflation and Economic Stagnation*. Washington DC: The Brookings Institution.

Müller-Jentsch, W. and H. J. Sperling (1978) 'Economic Development, Labour Conflicts and the Industrial Relations System in West Germany', in C. Crouch and A. Pizzorno (eds) *The Resurgence of Class Conflict in Western Europe since 1968*, Vols. 1 & 2. New York: Holmes & Meier.

Myles, J. (1984) 'Does Class Matter? Explaining America's Modern Welfare State'. Paper presented at the Center for the Study of Industrial Societies, University of Chicago, (November).

Nordhaus, W. (1974) 'The Falling Share of Profits', in *Brookings Papers on Economic Activity*, 1. Washington: The Brookings Institution.

OECD (1985) *Sweden — Economic Survey*. Paris: OECD.

Olson, M. (1982) *The Rise and Decline of Nations*. New Haven: Yale University Press.

Panitch, L. (1980) 'Recent Theorizations of Corporatism: Reflections on a Growth Industry', *British Journal of Sociology*, 31.

Regini, M. (1984) 'The Conditions for Political Exchange: How Concertation Emerged and Collapsed in Italy and Great Britain', in J. Goldthorpe (ed.) *Order and Conflict in Contemporary Capitalism*. Oxford: Oxford University Press.

Sachs, J. (1979) 'Wages, Profits and Macroeconomic Adjustment: A Comparative Study', in *Brookings Papers on Economic Activity*, 2. Washington: The Brookings Institution.

SAF (1976), *Wages and Total Labour Costs for Workers, 1965–75*. Stockholm: SAF.

SAF (1984) *Wages and Total Labour Costs for Workers, 1972–82*. Stockholm: SAF.

Schmidt, M. G. (1987) 'The Politics of Labour Market Policy, in F. G. Castles, F. Lehner and M. Schmidt (eds) *The Political Management of Mixed Economies*. Berlin: de Gruyter.

Schmitter, P. and G. Lehmbruch (eds) (1979) *Trends toward Corporatist Intermediation*. Beverly Hills/London: Sage.

Schmitter, P. (1981) 'Interest Intermediation and Regime Governability in Contemporary Western Europe and North America', in S. Berger (ed.) *Organizing Interests in Western Europe*. Cambridge: Cambridge University Press.

Skocpol, T. (1987), 'The Limits of the American New Deal', in G. Esping-Andersen, L. Rainwater and M. Rein (eds) *Stagnation and Renewal: The Rise and Fall of Social Policy Regimes*. New York. M. E. Sharpe (forthcoming).

Tufte, E. R. (1978) *Political Control of the Economy*. New Haven: Yale University Press.

Ulman, L. and R. Flanagan (1971) *Wage Restraint: A Study of Incomes Policies in Western Europe*. Berkeley: University of California Press.

Weisskopf, T. (1985) 'Worker Security and Productivity Growth: An International Comparative Analysis', unpublished paper. Department of Economics, University of Michigan (July).

5

The compatibility of economic, social, and political goals in incomes policies

A comparative analysis of incomes policy developments in ten West European countries in the 1970s

Klaus Armingeon

Introduction

In the 1970s the Western European economies experienced the third post-war boom in incomes policies (cf. Braun, 1975). Compared to the previous periods of frequent use of incomes policies, the wage and price regulations of the 1970s were to a large extent voluntary understandings between governments, unions and (often) employers. These informal understandings and 'social contracts' (cf. Flanagan et al., 1983) meet the criterion of neocorporatist policies; that is they were intended as voluntary concertations of public policies and policies by powerful interest groups in order to reach common macroeconomic goals such as full employment and price stability (cf. Lehmbruch, 1982, 1983).

How can it be explained that governments opted so often for neo-corporatist incomes policies? One explanation could point to the assumed increased economic efficacy of voluntary wage restraint. In general, economists agree on the limited efficacy of incomes policies (OECD, 1980; Meyer-Thoms, 1978). Some of the deficiencies of the instrument are attributed to its statutory mode. Low compliance of unions is one of the major flaws of such a dictated wage policy. In case of voluntary agreement the probability that unions are willing to adhere to the wage norm is higher than in the case of statutory regulation. This could be the reason why policy makers opt for the neocorporatist solution.

A competing argument, however, stresses that neocorporatist policies avoid certain possible unwanted social, economic, and political side effects of statutory regulation, such as major societal conflicts, decline of willingness of unions to co-operate with government bodies in other policy fields, or open conflicts between government and unions (cf. Streeck and Schmitter, 1985: 127–9). Due to the goal of avoidance of negative side-effects, and not, or not primarily, due to reasons of economic efficacy, governments aspire to neocorporatist strategies. Statutory policy would be the second best solution, if a voluntary agreement could not be concluded. Only in the case when governments do not have such additional goals, or the policy is thought to tackle a problem other than rising prices, and/or low international competitiveness, is it to be expected that statutory incomes policy is preferred to a voluntary one. The sole example in the 1970s of Northern and Central European governments who are willing to accept major conflicts with unions are Mrs Thatcher's executives since 1979. An example of incomes policies which are not intended to bring down the rate of inflation and increase the international competitiveness are statutory settlements of union-employer conflicts which otherwise would escalate into mass strikes.[1]

The explanatory power of both sets of arguments was tested by analysing incomes policy developments in ten West European countries (Austria, Belgium, Denmark, Finland, Federal Republic of Germany, Ireland, the Netherlands, Norway, Sweden, and the UK) in the 1970s.

The following section considers the economic record of neocorporatist incomes policies. It turns out that in this respect their efficacy is low, and in most cases lower than that of statutory regulations. Some reasons for this are discussed subsequently. A direct test of the 'political' hypotheses is not possible. This would require a survey among members of government, asking them why they used a certain type of policy. However, indirectly these assumptions are confirmed, if it can be shown, that — under specified conditions — governments aspire to voluntary solutions; and that only if these are not feasible do governments decide to use the statutory regulation. Empirical evidence for such a sequence of policy decisions and for the underlying conditions are presented in the last part of this chapter.

Incomes policies in the 1970s: the economic record
Incomes policies denote direct interventions by governments or public administration into the development of prices of factors of production (Cassel and Thieme, 1977; OECD, 1980). Usually the focus of these interventions is the modification of the expenditure on wages.[2] We will differentiate between two modes of incomes policies: the neocorporatist and the statutory. Among the neocorporatist techniques a distinction will be made between 'social contract' and informal policies. 'Social contract' policies are formal, usually written, understandings between government, trade unions, (often) employers and (sometimes) other interest groups. The core of such a 'social contract' is the concertation of private wage policy with public policy. The parties to the agreement sign it voluntarily, and they take responsibility for the implementation of their respective agreed policies. The key difference between this and an informal neocorporatist policy is the level of formality: informal policies are not announced as binding vis-a-vis the public and they have the character of gentlemen's agreements.

Examples of the 'social contract' policies are the package deals in

Norway and Finland (cf. Schwerin, 1980; Anckar and Helander, 1983; Uusitalo, 1983), the 'National Understandings for Social and Economic Development' in Ireland 1979–81 (cf. Addison, 1979; 1981; O'Brien, 1981) or the 'Social Contract' in the UK (cf. Barnes and Reid, 1980; Crouch, 1979).

Examples of informal neocorporatist policies are the processes of wage-price regulation in Sweden until 1976 (cf. Fulcher, 1976; Martin, 1979; Kuhn, 1981) or in Austria (Marin, 1982; Lang, 1978).

Table 1 contains data on the periods of various incomes policies and on 'policy-off' periods (non-interventions) in ten West European countries in the 1970s.

As already mentioned, four of the above listed incomes policies were not primarily a response to the economic problem of wage/price pressure but to the social problem of aggravating conflicts between unions and employers. All other incomes policies were responses to the threat of high wage increases leading to high rates of inflation, low international competitiveness, or low profits of employers.

In Table 2 data on the development of wages and prices are presented. The indicator for price developments is yearly averages of the first differences of the consumer price index changes for the respective period. Wage developments were measured as gaps between changes in real productivity and changes in real wages in manufacturing in the respective period. If wage increases exceed increases in productivity, the difference will be negative and according to wage-push hypotheses inflationary effects are to be expected. Two variants of these wage gaps were calculated. The first is based on real wages in manufacturing, the other is based on contractual wages. The former indicates the final wage development, i.e. the outcome of the distributional conflict, the latter indicates the result of bargaining on collective agreements, i.e. the output of collective bargaining.

For each country these indicators were calculated for the various policies and for the whole period under consideration. The cells of Table 2 are subdivided into three rows. The first row contains data on the development of prices, the second on the final wage development, and the third on the output of collective wage bargaining. For example, in the case of Belgian statutory incomes policy, the rate of inflation decreased yearly by 3.8 percentage points. On the average, real productivity increases exceeded that of real wages by 4.8 percentage points, and the real wage changes agreed upon in collective bargaining have been 5.0 percentage points lower than the increase of real productivity.

Four conclusions can be drawn from the data in Table 2:

1. Except for the case of the Netherlands, prices rose less or about equally in 'policy-on' periods compared to 'policy-off' periods. But still, in most cases they rose.

TABLE 1

Periods of incomes policies in ten West European countries (1970–80)

Country	Statutory incomes policy	Non-intervention	Informal neocorporatist incomes policy	'Social contract' neo-corporatist incomes policy
Austria			1/70–2/80	
Belgium	1/76–2/76		1/70–2/75; 1/77–2/80	
Denmark	1/75–2/80	1/70–2/70; 1/73–2/74	1/71–2/72	
Finland	1/78–2/78	1/73–2/73; 2/77–2/80		1/70–2/72; 1/74–1/77; 1/79–2/80
Germany, Fed. Rep.		1/70–1/75	1/70–1/77	
Ireland		1/70–1/75	2/75–1/79	2/79–2/80
Netherlands	1/71; 1/74–2/74; 1/76–2/76; 1/80–2/80	1/70–2/70; 2/71–2/72	1/75–2/75; 1/77–2/77	1/73–2/73
Norway	1/78–2/79		1/70–2/75; 1/80–2/80	1/76–2/77
Sweden		1/77–2/80	1/70–2/76	
United Kingdom	1/73–1/74	1/70–2/72; 2/78–2/80	2/74–1/75; 2/77–1/78	2/75–1/77

Sources: Armingeon, 1983; Flanagan et al., 1983

Notes: Data refer to half-years. If various modes of incomes policies were pursued in a half-year or if there was a change between an incomes policy and a period of non-intervention, the respective half-year was classified according to the policy which is pursued the longest time in this half-year. A problem of classification occurred in the case of the statutory policy of 1973/74 in Finland. It was pursued between 1 April 1973 and 31 March 1974.

2. In most countries, in periods of neocorporatist wage regulation, prices rose more compared to periods of statutory policy and less compared to periods of non-interventions.

3. This might be due to the development of wages. In most cases statutory as well as neocorporatist incomes policy was successful in curbing the rate of increase of contractual wages to such a degree that real wage increases did not exceed increases in productivity.

4. Obviously both policies were modified when they were implemented. Judged by the data — which are of limited reliability — this modification was stronger and has had (following a wage-push hypothesis) more disastrous effects in the case of neocorporatist incomes policies. Obviously private and public policy makers sign agreements in accordance with macroeconomic developments but they are not able to implement the policies as they are agreed upon.

Of course the data of Table 2 are not the result of an econometric analysis of the effect of incomes policy on the development of prices and wages. Rather it is a test whether macroeconomic data developed as they should according to the incomes policy programme. Measured by what policy makers have declared, the economic performance of incomes policy was poor; especially in the case of neocorporatist strategies.

Deficiencies of the incomes policy instrument
The low efficacy of incomes policies can be explained generally by its theoretical and structural deficiencies. According to one set of arguments, the policy fails since inflation is not caused by wage push; hence there is no sense in applying the instrument. The second strand of reasoning points to the fact that at least when the policy finishes, the groups who have suffered from wage and price restraint try to regain what they have lost (cf. OECD, 1980).

The data of Table 2 suggest that it is in the process of policy implementation that the neocorporatist instrument has its major weakness. In the literature at least two major hypotheses have been developed, dealing with that problem.[3] The first starts from the assumption that members do not accept the moderate wage policy of union leaders. The second relates the failure of the policy to conflicts among wage earners. These conflicts arise because the wage policy modifies wage differentials.

According to the first hypothesis the main problem is the conflict of interest between leaders and members of union: members always want more, whilst leaders are 'responsible'. When designing their policies, they take into account the general state of the economy. For this problem, there exists an organizational solution: a high level of centralization of collective bargaining and a strongly unified union movement gives union leadership the power to force all groups of wage earners to adhere to one national wage norm (cf. Streeck, 1981; Crouch, 1982; Panitch, 1976;

TABLE 2

The development of prices and wages by type of incomes policy (1970–80)

Country	Statutory incomes policy	Non-intervention	Informal neo-corporatist incomes policy	'Social Contract' incomes policy	1970–80 resp. 1970–9
Austria	(a) −3.6 (b) 4.8 (c) 5.0				(a) 0.3 (b) −1.0 (c) −1.2[1]
Belgium			(a) 0.6 (b) −2.9 (c) −2.5		(a) 0.3 (b) −2.1 (c) −1.8
Denmark	(a) −0.5 (b) −1.4 (c) 2.9	(a) 3.4 (b) −4.0 (c) 3.8[1]	(a) 0.4 (b) −3.1 (c) 2.9		(a) 0.7 (b) −2.5 (c) 3.1[1]
Finland	(a) −4.4 (b) 3.9 (c) 6.7	(a) 3.9 (b) −0.9 (c) 4.5		(a) 0.8 (b) −0.6 (c) 3.4	(a) 0.9 (b) −0.2 (c) 3.9
Germany, Fed. Rep.		(a) 0.6 (b) 0.6 (c) 1.0	(a) 0.4 (b) 2.1 (c) 0.4		(a) 0.3 (b) 1.7 (c) 0.6
Ireland		(a) 1.9 (b) −2.2[2] (c) n.a.	(a) −4.4 (b) 2.4[2] (c) n.a.	(a) 4.9 (b) n.a. (c) n.a.	(a) 1.0 (b) −0.9[2] (c) n.a.
Netherlands	(a) 1.5 (b) 0.8 (c) 2.4	(a) −1.5 (b) −2.3[3] (c) −0.4[3]	(a) −0.9 (b) −2.8 (c) −2.4	(a) 0.2 (b) −1.2 (c) 1.5	(a) −0.1 (b) −1.6[3] (c) −0.1[3]

Norway	(a) −2.2 (b) 2.5 (c) 5.4	(a) 2.1 (b) −2.3[4] (c) 3.6[4]	(a) −1.3 (b) −3.1 (c) 2.9	(a) 0.7 (b) −1.4[4] (c) 3.8[4]
Sweden	(a) 0.9 (b) 0.4 (c) 3.3	(a) 1.1 (b) −1.6[5] (c) 3.1[5]		(a) 1.0 (b) −0.9[5] (c) 3.2[5]
United Kingdom	(a) 2.1 (b) 0.8 (c) n.a.	(a) 2.3 (b) −1.2 (c) n.a.	(a) −7.7[6] (b) 1.3[6] (c) n.a.	(a) 1.1 (b) −0.5 (c) n.a.

Notes: 1) 1971–9; 2) 1971–8; 3) 1970, 1972–9; 4) 1970, 1972–9; 5) 1972–9; 6) In the case of the UK several years have to be excluded from calculation due to the changes from informal to 'Contract' policy and vice versa. If no distinction is made between the two modes of neocorporatist policy, the data for voluntary incomes policies are: Inflation: −0.1 and Wages: 2.2

row (a): averages of the first difference of the rate of inflation (1970–80)

row (b): averages of the gap between changes of real productivity and real wages in manufacturing (1970–9)

row (c): averages of the gap between changes of real productivity and real contractual wages in manufacturing (1970–9)

If there were various modes of policies, respecting a change from or to non-intervention within a year, this year was excluded from calculation of the respective indicator.

Sources: *Rate of inflation:* OECD, 1981; *Austria and Federal Republic of Germany:* wages for Austria from ILO (various years); contractual wages and wages for Germany: Österreichisches Statistisches Zentralamt (ed.): (various years); Sachverständigenrat zur Begutachtung der gesamtwirtschaftlichen Entwicklung (1982). Productivity (real gross domestic product divided by civilian employment) was calculated with data from the same OECD publications as the respective data for the other countries. *All other countries:* Armingeon, 1983: 141–2, 307–8.

1979; Bergmann et al., 1976).[4] If these conditions are met, neocorporatist incomes policy can be successfully put into effect.

Data on the degree of centralization of collective bargaining and on concentration of national union systems are given in Table 3. They suggest that a high degree of centralization and concentration is not a necessary condition for the economic success of neocorporatist incomes policies. In addition neither the emergence nor the duration of neo-corporatist incomes regulation are directly dependent on centralization and concentration.

The key to this missing dependence of neocorporatist strategies on organizational structures might be that little empirical evidence is available for the underlying assumption of the hypothesis. Survey data indicate that members agree with union leaders' moderate stance in collective bargaining, in particular if unemployment is high and prices are rising (cf. Bergmann and Müller-Jentsch, 1977: 88; Bierbaum et al., 1977: 92; Lewin, 1980: 99).

More credit can be given to an explanation which relates major problems of implementation of neocorporatist incomes policies to intra-organizational and intra-class conflicts: due to timing of policy, to the coverage of the wage agreement or of the law, and often due to flat rate elements included in the policy, wage differentials are distorted. Often they are altered in an egalitarian direction. This is opposed by those groups of wage earners and union members, which suffer from the policy.

The timing of the introduction of the policy will create differentials between those unions who have already agreed on wage settlements and those whose potential agreements are pre-empted by the introduction of wage restraint.

The larger the coverage of the policy, the lesser the possibility for certain groups to secure extra gains due to above-average productivity in the respective sector. Thus, traditional wage differences between certain industries can be narrowed.

Most West European unions pursue solidaristic wage policies aiming at a more egalitarian wage structure. Often this means the use of flat rate elements in pay bargaining so that low wage groups improve their position compared to high wage groups (cf. Pfromm, 1978). Actually such egalitarian wage policies were included in most neocorporatist arrangements.

The restoration of established wage differentials in and between industries can take place immediately the national neocorporatist policy is implemented. This distinguishes the voluntary policy from the statutory, and might explain some of the efficacy of the latter, as long as it lasts. In cases where trade union leaders try to prevent this modification of national incomes policy they risk member discontent. Thus neocorporatist incomes policies can only be pursued and supported by trade unions if

TABLE 3

Indicators of centralization and concentration of national trade union systems (1970–9)

Country	Overall union density (Percentage of unionized wage and salary earners in dependent civilian employment) Average 1970–9	Percentage share of major union confederation in total union membership. Average 1970–9	Degree of centralization (Major union [confederation] decides on collective agreements — at national level = high — at regional, industrial level = medium — at local, plant level = low)
Austria	59.2	100.0 (ÖGB)	high
Belgium	74.8	49.8 (CSC)	medium
Denmark	68.8	72.4 (LO)	high
Finland	74.4	66.8 (SAK)	medium
Germany, Fed. Rep.	37.8	85.0 (DGB)	medium
Ireland	57.8[1]	93.0[2] (ICTU)	low
Netherlands	39.5	62.1 (NVV+NKV; FNV)	medium
Norway	60.2[3]	73.8[3] (LO)	high
Sweden	79.5	63.3 (LO)	high
United Kingdom	51.2	90.2 (TUC)	low

Notes: 1) 1971, 1975, 1976, 1979; 2) 1979; 3) 1970, 1972–9.

Sources: Union density: Visser, 1983 except of Belgium, Finland and Ireland. *Membership figures* for Belgium: letter by CSC to the author; Ireland: letter by Department of Labour to the author and Trade Union Information, Summer 1980, Nos. 252–7; Finland: Pehkonen 1981. *Wage and salary earners* (civilian employment): OECD, 1983. For Ireland, these figures were not available for 1975 and 1976. For these years, union density was calculated on the basis of the average of the data for 1974 and 1977. *Degree of centralization:* Armingeon, 1983, chap. 2.

there is a possibility of avoiding or mitigating such intra-class conflicts due to voluntary restraint. There are two main mechanisms relieving unions involved in neocorporatist wage agreement from intra-organizational strain, and thus allowing for long-term union co-operation. Common to both mechanisms is the fact that individual members and member groups can to a certain extent modify the central and solidaristic wage norm.

The first mechanism is the possibility of a second round of wage bargaining at a lower level of the union organization in addition to national bargaining. This informal bargaining contributes to a high wage drift, i.e. a large difference between contractual and actual wage increases. On the other hand, high drift endangers the success of any national wage policy, making any agreement at the national level nothing more than a minimum norm for shop floor bargainers. Obviously this was what happened to much of the neocorporatist incomes policies, considering the differences between wage and contractual wages in Table 2.

The second mechanism is the possibility of non-compliance with the voluntary national agreement. This is a mechanism widely used in Finland and Ireland. Unions are not forced (Finland) or cannot be forced (Ireland) to comply with the national agreement. If they think they would do better without voluntary incomes policy, they can opt out. Through this mechanism, potential troublemakers are excluded from the national incomes policy.

Both mechanisms stabilize the neocorporatist incomes policy in terms of duration, and both contribute to low anti-inflationary efficacy of the policy: unions (and employers' organizations) can pursue strategies only to the degree and as long as members do not oppose the decision of leadership. And in the case of voluntary wage restraint members will not oppose it if there is the possibility of modifying developments of wage structure (and to a lesser extent of wage levels) brought about by the national neocorporatist arrangement.

Policy preferences of governments

In the preceding parts empirical evidence has shown that incomes policy has had limited success in lowering inflation rates. Neocorporatist wage regulations were especially inefficient in combating inflation. This might be due to certain structural deficiencies of voluntary incorporation of interest organizations into public policy-making. In addition to problems of incomes policies common to all types of wage restraint, these deficiencies further contribute to the low economic efficacy of neocorporatist strategies. Hence, the emergence of neocorporatist wage regulation cannot be explained by its increased level of efficacy compared to statutory policy.

On the other hand, governments frequently have pursued neocorporatist incomes policies in the ten countries under consideration. According to the second explanation of the evolution of neocorporatist techniques, it is to be expected that governments prefer neocorporatist to statutory policies since the former avoid the negative 'side-effects' of the former.

Before governments decide on the mode of the policy, however, two general preconditions for pursuit of an incomes policy have to be met: (a) There must be an economic problem (usually rising prices) and government must feel under pressure to intervene in the economy in order to solve this problem. (b) Whether the mode of intervention is a wage policy depends on whether governments are convinced that incomes policy has some value in mitigating the economic problem.

Once both preconditions are met, we hypothesize that governments will prefer neocorporatist regulation. Whether such a solution can be realized depends on: (a) whether the government is willing to attune its policies with the unions, and (b) whether the government is able to realize these policies agreed upon with unions (and employers). This includes government being willing and able to grant certain compensations for union wage restraint to the extent wished by the unions. (c) As far as unions (and employers' organizations) are concerned, the policy can be pursued as long as it does not endanger organizational stability. This is the case as long as the two conflict-mitigating mechanisms can be used.

Given both preconditions, our hypothesis suggests that statutory incomes policies or abstention from wage legislation will result if a neocorporatist incomes policy cannot be realized. This hypothesis is confirmed by the incomes policy developments in the countries under study.[5]

In the UK 1972 and in Belgium 1976 governments were not willing to grant compensations for wage restraint demanded by the unions. These governments were not politically very close to the unions (UK), respectively to one major confederation (Belgium, FGTB). In both Belgium and the UK neocorporatist solutions were not reached, and the two governments subsequently felt under pressure to introduce statutory regulation. In the Netherlands in 1977/8 after Mr van Agt took office, bargaining on a neocorporatist wage agreement failed. But here the government, being opposed by the Social Democratic union federation, did not introduce wage legislation until 1980.

In Finland 1973, Denmark 1979, and Sweden 1976 after voluntary tuning of public and union policies, governments failed to obtain the majority in parliament for the package, and therefore were not able to grant compensations. After these failures, in Denmark the government introduced wage legislation, whilst the Finnish and Swedish governments abstained from directly influencing union wage behaviour. The end of the British 'Social Contract' was mainly due to its equalizing effects on wages, and its rather low wage norms which were opposed by union members and sub-units of unions. However, its end was also explained by the failure of government to fully realize the social reforms demanded by the unions.

Some attempts at neocorporatist incomes regulation were unsuccessful on grounds of intraorganizational problems of trade unions. After 1977/8 the British TUC lost the ability to pursue centralized wage policies like the ones between 1975 and 1977. These policies have — according to the unions — distorted wage differentials. This has created inter-union conflicts, based on blaming the policy because of its equalizing effects and not because it generally lowered wage increases. In 1978, the Norwegian government and unions agreed on the need for wage restraint without compensations financed by expansionary public budgets. The unions feared the non-organized groups would not be bound by a voluntary agreement on wage stop between the Social Democratic Government and the LO. Thus both sides supported legislation freezing wages. In 1979 parliament passed a law which stipulated that wage increases drawn up in agreements signed voluntarily by LO cannot be exceeded by other non-unionized groups. This law was founded on the stated goals of preserving unions' ability to co-operate. Comparable laws were introduced in the Netherlands (1977) and for a limited period in Ireland (1973).

In the case of all successfully bargained neocorporatist incomes policies, the conditions were met, that (a) for unions (and employers) mechanisms were available for absorbing intra-organizational conflict; and that (b) governments were willing and able to attune their policies to the degree wished by the unions.

Certain political circumstances are conducive to this process of concertation of private and public policies: politically there should be a similarity between economic theories (defining an economic problem and its solution), goals (i.e. goals of a particular set of policies), and values (defining means and ends) of governing parties and those of trade unions. The greater this similarity the easier it is to reach voluntary agreement. This explains the frequent emergence of neocorporatist incomes policy in periods when the government is composed of political parties close to trade union(s). In cases where there are basic divergences between the goals and values of governments and of unions, the concertation of union and public policies becomes difficult (cf. Headey, 1970; Armingeon, 1982; Halle, 1984).

A case in point is the Dutch attempt at a neocorporatist solution for the collective agreements in force in 1973. This voluntary agreement was reached when the government was made up of parties which were not politically close to the major union confederation. Members and sub-units of this socialist confederation stated that there could be no co-operation based on trust with a government which did not include the PvdA (Labour Party). The union leader demanded that the government make binding promises: if the unions moderated their wage claims they would want to know exactly what the government would give in return. There were also conflicts within government. Some ministers refused to create public policy in bargaining situations with trade unions. Under these problematic circumstances it was only with difficulty that a loose social contract emerged out of collective bargaining. In other countries where the political composition of the trade union movement is mirrored by party composition of government, the problem of arriving at an agreement is much smaller. Rather than conduct collective bargaining over sharply conflicting claims, it is sufficient to tune policies finely. Underlying these policies are common goals and values of trade unions and their allied political parties. So far there is reason to assume that in some cases this concertation is symbolic politics (for the UK cf. Dürr, 1981). Issues are settled in public long after they have been settled in programmes of the organized labour movement. This may explain why public policy outcomes do not change significantly due to neocorporatist policies (Armingeon, 1983: 152–78).

Conclusion

In this paper empirical evidence was provided for a more general hypothesis that public economic policy is determined not only by purely economic but also by political and social goals of government. This implies that in its economic policy, government chooses the mode of policy with the fewest negative side effects — even if this reduces the economic success of the intervention, which could have been reached if another mode of regulation would have been selected.

Of course our analysis is based on policy developments in ten West European countries in the 1970s. Changing general economic, social and political conditions in the 1980s could lead to changing conclusions. In addition, our empirical evidence for the policy preferences is only indirect by inferring from sequences of policy formation on preferences of governments. A direct test of this hypothesis is hard to realize: survey data are not available that might demonstrate for which reasons members of governments select particular policy instruments. Further restrictions have to be made concerning the results of the analysis of the economic effects of incomes policies: it measured whether macroeconomic data developed as they were expected to when the policy was in force. This method of calculation does not allow estimates of the relative share of the policy variable in the explanation of the macroeconomic developments, but this was not our research question. We only wanted to see whether the economic ends were achieved when the policy was pursued.

Notes

This paper analyses data which have been collected in the course of a research project on neocorporatism directed by Professor G. Lehmbruch and located at the University of Konstanz. The project was supported by the Stiftung Volkswagen Werk. For helpful comments I thank the editors, Oda van Cranenburgh and Margaret Herden. For any shortcomings I alone am responsible.

1. These are the statutory regulations in Denmark 1975, 1977 and — less unequivocal — in the Netherlands 1974 and 1975. Their primary function was not to decrease wage costs but rather to solve the social problem of avoiding a major strike caused by deadlock in collective bargaining between employers and unions. In all four cases, government avoided eruption of social conflict by making law the mediation proposal (accepted by the unions) or the unions' last offer. These governments have been politically close to the major trade union confederation. In this respect, these policies are the results of a coalition of organized labour against capital in order to preserve social peace (cf. Windmuller and de Galan, 1979: 171ff.; van Waarden, 1981; Flanagan et al., 1983: 475, 477).

2. The following analysis will not consider incomes policies confined only to a limited number of plants or industries. For extensive descriptions of incomes policy developments see Armingeon (1983) and Flanagan et al. (1983). The empirical analysis in this paper is based on Armingeon, 1983.

3. Since in practice incomes policy is mainly wage restraint, the discussion will be confined to trade unions and wage earners/salaried employees.

4. For a more detailed discussion of this institutional hypothesis see Armingeon, 1986.

5. One case of statutory wage legislation will not be considered: the failure in continuation of neocorporatist incomes policy in Finland 1978 was due to technical reasons in an economic emergency situation. Both sides of industry have agreed to wage legislation under these specific conditions.

References

Addison, J. T. (1979) *Wage Policies and Collective Bargaining Developments in Finland, Ireland, and Norway*. Paris: OECD.

Addison, J. T. (1981) 'Incomes Policy: The Recent European Experience', pp. 187–245 in R. F. Elliot and J. L. Fallick (eds) *Incomes Policy, Inflation and Relative Pay*. London: Allen & Unwin.

Anckar, D. and V. Helander (1983) *Consultation and Political Culture*. Helsinki: The Finnish Society of Sciences and Letters.

Armingeon, K. (1982) 'Determining the Level of Wages: the Role of Parties and Trade Unions', pp. 225–82 in F. G. Castles (ed.) *The Impact of Parties*. Beverly Hills/London: Sage.

Armingeon, K. (1983) *Neo-korporatistische Einkommenspolitik*. Frankfurt: Haag & Herchen.

Armingeon, K. (1986) 'Formation and Stability of Neo-Corporatist Incomes Policies', *European Sociological Review*, 2 (2): 138–47.

Barnes, D. and E. Reid (1980) *Governments and Trade Unions. The British Experience, 1964–1979*. London: Heinemann.

Bergmann, J. and W. Müller-Jentsch (1977) *Gewerkschaften in der Bundesrepublik. Band 2*. Frankfurt: Aspekte.

Bergmann, J., O. Jacobi and W. Müller-Jentsch (1976) *Gewerkschaften in der Bundesrepublik. Band 1*. Frankfurt: Aspekte (2nd ed).

Bierbaum, C., J. Bischoff, D. Eppenstein, S. Herkommer, K. Maldaner and A. Martin (1977) *Ende der Illusionen? Bewußtseinsveränderungen in der Wirtschaftskrise*. Frankfurt/Köln: EVA.

Braun, A. R. (1975) 'The Role of Incomes Policy in Industrial Countries since World War II', *IMF Staff Papers*, XXI: 1–36.

Cassel, D. and H. J. Thieme (1977) *Einkommenspolitik*. Köln: Kiepenheuer & Witsch.

Crouch C. (1979) *The Politics of Industrial Relations*. Glasgow: Fontana.

Crouch, C. (1982) *Trade Unions: The Logic of Collective Action.* Glasgow: Fontana.

Dürr, K. (1981) *Konflikt und Kooperation. Die Situation der Arbeitsbevölkerung, das System der Arbeitsbeziehungen und die Strategien der Gewerkschaftsbewegung in Großbritannien in den 70er Jahren.* Frankfurt: R. G. Fischer.

Edelman, M. and R. W. Fleming (1965) *The Politics of Wage-Price Decisions. A Four-Country Analysis.* Urbana: University of Illinois Press.

Flanagan, R. J., B. W. Soskice, and L. Ulman (1983) *Unionism, Economic Stabilization, and Incomes Policy: European Experience.* Washington, DC: Brookings Institution.

Fulcher, J. (1976) 'Class Conflict: Joint Regulation and Its Decline', pp. 51–97 in R. Scase (ed.) *Readings in the Swedish Class Structure.* Oxford: Pergamon.

Halle, A. (1984) 'Funktionsverlust des Parlaments durch Neokorporatismus?', *Zeitschrift für Parlamentsfragen,* 15: 380–91.

Headey, B. W. (1970) 'Trade Unions and National Wages Policies', *The Journal of Politics,* 32: 407–39.

ILO (ed.) (various years) *Yearbook of Labour Statistics.* Geneva: ILO.

Kuhn, K. (1981) 'Neo-Korporatismus in Skandinavien', pp. 209–29 in U. von Alemann (ed.) *Neokorporatismus.* Frankfurt/New York: Campus.

Lang, W. (1978) *Kooperative Gewerkschaften und Einkommenspolitik. Das Beispiel Österreich.* Frankfurt: Lang.

Lehmbruch, G. (1982) 'Introduction: Neo-Corporatism in Comparative Perspective', pp. 1–28 in G. Lehmbruch and Ph. C. Schmitter (eds) *Patterns of Corporatist Policy-Making.* Beverly Hills/London: Sage.

Lehmbruch, G. (1983) 'Neokorporatismus in Westeuropa: Hauptprobleme im internationalen Vergleich', *Journal für Sozialforschung,* 23: 407–20.

Lewin, L. (1980) *Governing Swedish Trade Unions.* Cambridge, Mass./London: Harvard University Press.

Marin, B. (1982) *Die Paritätische Kommission. Aufgeklärter Technokorporatismus in Österreich.* Wien: Internationale Publikationen.

Martin, A. (1979) 'The Dynamics of Change in a Keynesian Political Economy: The Swedish Case and Its Implications', pp. 88–121 in C. Crouch (ed.) *State and Economy in Contemporary Capitalism.* London: Croom Helm.

Meyer-Thoms, G. (1978) *Lohn- und Preiskontrollen als Instrument der Stabilitätspolitik.* Bochum: Brockmeyer.

O'Brien, J. (1981) *A Study of National Wage Agreements in Ireland.* Dublin: The Economic and Social Research Institute.

OECD (1980) 'Incomes Policy in Theory and Practice', pp. 33–50 in OECD *Economic Outlook, Occasional Studies,* July.

OECD (1981) *Economic Outlook 29,* July, 29. Paris: OECD.

OECD (1983) *Labour Force Statistics.* Paris: OECD.

Österreichisches Statistisches Zentralamt (various years) *Statistisches Handbuch für die Republik Österreich. Neue Folge.* Wien: Österreichisches Statistisches Zentralamt.

Panitch, L. (1976) *Social Democracy and Industrial Militancy. The Labour Party, the TUC, and Incomes Policy, 1945–1974.* Cambridge: Cambridge University Press.

Panitch, L. (1979) 'The Development of Corporatism in Liberal Democracies', pp. 119–46 in Ph. C. Schmitter and G. Lehmbruch (eds) *Trends Toward Corporatist Intermediation.* Beverly Hills/London: Sage.

Pehkonen, J. (1981) *Parties and Trade Union Organizations: Some Preliminary Analyses and Comparisons of Their Functional Preconditions. The Case of Finland.* Tampere: University of Tampere, Department of Political Science, Occasional Papers 28.

Pfromm, H. A. (1978) *Solidarische Lohnpolitik.* Köln/Frankfurt: Bund-Verlag.

Sachverständigenrat für die Begutachtung der gesamtwirtschaftlichen Entwicklung (1982) *Investieren für mehr Beschäftigung. Jahresgutachten 1981/1982*. Stuttgart/Mainz: Kohlhammer.

Schwerin, D. S. (1980) 'The Limits of Organization as a Response to Wage-Price Problems', pp. 71–106 in R. Rose (ed.) *Challenge to Governance*. Beverley Hills/London: Sage.

Streeck, W. (1981) *Gewerkschaftliche Organisationsprobleme in der sozialstaatlichen Demokratie*. Königsstein/Ts.: Athenäum.

Streeck, W. and Ph. C. Schmitter (1985) 'Community, Market, State — and Associations? The Prospective Contribution of Interest Governance to Social Order', *European Sociological Review*, 1: 119–38.

Uusitalo, H. (1983) 'Incomes Policy in Finland: Economic and Social Effects in a Comparative Perspective', *Scandinavian Political Studies*, 6 (1): 1–25.

van Waarden, F. (1981) 'Politisering van het loonfront en economisch politiek', pp. 25–39 in A. Teulings (ed.) *De nieuwe vakbondstrategie*. Alphen/Brussels: Samson.

Visser, J. (1983) *Trade Unions 1950–1980: A Quantitative Assessment of the Development of Union Membership and Union Density in Ten West-European Countries*. Florence: European University Institute.

Windmuller, J. T. and C. de Galan (1979) *Arbeidsverhoudingen in Nederland*. Utrecht/Antwerpen: Spectrum (3rd edn).

III

POLICY STRATEGIES, IMPLEMENTATION AND OUTCOMES

6

Political strategies to overcome the crisis: policy formation and economic performance in seventeen capitalist democracies

Hans Keman and Tibert van Dijk

1. Introduction

An increasing number of people hold the view that the ways in which governments cope with the economic crisis are ineffective and unconvincing to the public (Coughlin, 1980; Hibbs and Madsen, 1980). The resulting resignation about the decreased potential of economic policy-formation is in marked contrast to the optimism that prevailed among economists, political scientists as well as politicians until the mid-seventies. After the Second World War the Keynesian approach suggested that business fluctuations and economic growth could be managed in line with objectives. This view posited that both unemployment and inflation could be checked if fiscal and monetary policies were properly applied. This approach differs from the 'neo-classical' one, in that neo-classicists claim that fine tuning or detailed public control of the economy is not possible. On the contrary, they implicitly argue that with a certain degree of state *non*-intervention the recession can be overcome.

In the 1970s the limits of economic policy became increasingly clear: rates of inflation and unemployment rose dramatically and simultaneously, and on the macroeconomic level it became apparent that state intervention may very well lead to an ineffective or even a counter-productive performance (cf. Frey, 1983). The leader of the British Labour Party, James Callaghan, described the end of the 'Keynesian Era' as follows:

> We used to think that you could spend your way out of a recession and increase employment by cutting taxes and boosting government spending. I tell you in all candour that that option no longer exists and that insofar as it ever did exist, it only worked by injecting a bigger dose of inflation into the economy, followed by a higher level of unemployment, at the next step. (quoted in Armstrong et al., 1984: 427)

Many leaders of governments (and of the opposition of course) have voiced similar opinions since the mid-1970s. The message is clear: the 'Golden Age' of managed capitalism is definitively over (cf. Maddison, 1982). It is not surprising then, that both economists and political scientists started to investigate alternative approaches of economic policy-formation and to look for a different policy-style to overcome the crisis. Most changes, if any, concerned a simple defensive move towards policies of austerity in order to cope with the severest economic crisis since the war. Yet a look at the literature concerning the interdependence of politics and economics shows that the array of alternative approaches and strategic possibilities is much wider. Apart from the much quoted monetarist response, the view of 'Supply-siders' became popular, and recently we see the ascent of 'Rational expectations' model as a bold attempt to combine diagnosis and therapy (Nell, 1984).

However, it appears not only important to formulate the right theoretical answer, but it also becomes apparent that the corresponding style of economic policy-formation affects to a large extent the economic performance of a society (Keman, 1984; Scharpf, 1985). In other words, we need not only to investigate the best theoretical alternative, but we must also increase our knowledge about how to put theory into practice. Important for analysing this matter is therefore the interaction between politics and economics. This relationship is predominantly manifested in the behaviour of political parties and governments on the one hand, and the representatives of social and economic interests on the other.

In this paper we set out to investigate seventeen advanced capitalist democracies between 1964 and 1982. The following three research questions will be our point of departure:

1. the extent to which there was a change in economic policy-making before and after 1973 and 1979;[1]
2. the extent to which a strategy of state intervention has led to a better economic performance in each period;
3. the nature of the factors that account for the cross-national and inter-temporal variation in both policy formation and economic performance.

In Section 2 we will present the theoretical arguments related to these questions. In Section 3 we shall discuss our research design, and in Section 4 the empirical variation in economic strategies. In Section 5 we look at the relationship between the economic strategies and economic performance. Finally, in the concluding section, we shall discuss the economic outcomes in terms of whether there exists an 'optimal' strategy for 'coping with crisis' in advanced capitalist democracies.

2. Strategies of economic policy formation in advanced capitalist democracies

During the period up to 1973 a broad consensus was established between the major parties of Left, Right and Centre, that the present economic system and the way it operates constitutes a 'mixed economy'. That is to say, a capitalist economy of which a large part is (re)distributed, consumed and thus steered by the state. In addition, the political parties accepted certain responsibilities such as to provide various welfare services and infra-structural needs for capital, as well as to maintain more or less full employment. This active mode of state intervention has prompted some writers to suggest that the private sector in capitalism may be withering away (Offe, 1983; Therborn, 1984; Esping-Andersen, 1985; Stephens, 1979; Keman, 1979).

In this chapter our emphasis will be mainly on the existing *strategies of state intervention* which are thought to be essential and beneficial for the economic well-being of a country (Katzenstein, 1984, 1985; Scharpf, 1983, 1985; Braun and Keman, 1986), rather than using broad but vague conceptions of the state in late capitalist society. Our notion of strategy combines two levels of analysis which are often confounded: structures and agencies. The structure is represented in the institutional setting which shapes the interaction between politics and economics (e.g. the degree of market regulation by the state) and the international economic environment which constrains domestic policy-making (as e.g. in small and open economies). The process of interaction is manifested in the way actors operate within these structures (Keman and Lehner, 1984: 122–4). A government is an example of an agency, which is able to change certain relationships, but within a given structure (such as the operating 'rule of law'). In short, political and economic structures influence the actions of certain political and societal actors, but that does not mean that this relationship is causal by definition or pre-determined.

In most developed countries Keynesian economic management dominated the strategy of state intervention during the 1960s and the early 1970s.[2] It was based on the assumption that active and expansionist demand management could successfully regulate the deficiencies and instabilities of capitalist (re)production. The influence of Keynesian prescriptive theory has contributed to an extension of public control of the economy and to increasing levels of welfare expenditures. 'Keynesianism' is a good example of what we mean by our notion of strategy: it was considered as an economically appropriate way to 'control' the business cycle of a national economy. Hence, without disturbing the essential characteristics of the capitalist structure of modern society, both state-agencies and societal actors were expected and allowed to play an active part in the perseverance of highly industrialized democracies. It should be noted, however, that as a strategy its application was only possible because of the extant degree of consensus which produced an integration of societal views, goals and means (Scharpf, 1983: 4–6). From this description of 'Keynesianism' it will be clear that strategy can be dominant for some time, but is never in an absolute sense dominating (Abercrombie and Turner, 1978). Even during the heyday of 'Keynesianism' there were other competing views on the management of capitalist economies (Friedman, 1962; Nell, 1984; Ashford, 1984). Since 1973 it is obvious that 'Keynesianism' is no longer a dominant current in political and economic thinking. From then on other strategies of state intervention such as monetarism gained influence.

This description of a strategy of state intervention is in our opinion not yet complete as an analytical concept. It is necessary to extend it with a more dynamic dimension, since the above description is more or less based on general conditions rather than on specific processes. We introduce therefore here Poulantzas' ideas on 'conjunctures' (concurrent political and economic developments), which stress the continuing interdependence between structures and actors. The degree to which the conditions for a successful strategy are available are, in this view, dependent on the positive relationship between political consensus and socio-economic co-operation on the one hand, and the systemic characteristics of the polity on the other (Poulantzas, 1978). This relationship is primarily embodied in the specific process of interaction between state-agencies and (organized) interests and its societal manifestations (i.e. more or less consensus and co-operation). We consider this relationship between politics and economics and the related process of interaction between structure and actors as being 'variable'. We will call this complexity *intermediary conjuncture* (cf. Braun and Keman, 1986). We posit that the extent to which the intermediary conjuncture is characterized by a positive relationship between state and society will contribute to the feasibility of a strategy of state intervention in terms of an optimal political and economic performance.

Our notions concerning 'strategy' and 'intermediary conjuncture' will be investigated by paying attention to both structural features of capitalist democracies and the way political and socio-economic actors limit the scope of policy formation in periods of economic crisis. In the following section we shall develop a typology of four different but related strategies that can be discerned taking both social and economic dimensions of 'Welfare State Capitalism' (Jones, 1985) as a point of reference.

2.1 *Four strategies of state intervention*

Our definition of welfare state is based on a distinction we wish to make between two related concepts of the welfare state: namely 'social', indicating the activities of the state concerning the regulation and provision of social security, health, and education; and 'economic', indicating the capacity of the state to direct a growing part of the national income in order to control the private economy (Therborn, 1984: 26). In our opinion these concepts can only be separated analytically, and are in reality always related (Keman, 1985; Esping-Andersen, 1985; Gough, 1979; Mishra, 1984). The Keynesian approach, for instance, combined these two dimensions and was the guideline for most leftish or progressive governments during the sixties and the early seventies.

Since the so-called stagflation crisis in the 1970s, however, the utility and accuracy of Keynesian management of the private and the public economy has been doubted by many (OECD, 1981; Woolley, 1982). Instead of Keynesianism, Monetarism and Fiscal Conservatism (cf. Cameron, 1982) became increasingly fashionable as an alternative strategy of state intervention in the late seventies. The main argument of the Monetarists is (and has always been since the late 1950s) that the 'market' has a strong self-regulating capacity and that governments only need to maintain favourable conditions for the functioning of markets. It is argued that state intervention does not stabilize economic cyclical movements but instead reinforces instability. In the short run increased state intervention may have a positive effect on, for example, the unemployment rates, but in the long run it will only cause inflation and consequently more unemployment. Thus governments, trying to reduce unemployment, will cause inflation (cf. Nell, 1984: p. 13; Gould et al., 1981). Hence in the end Keynesian management of the economy will only reduce the self-regulative capacity of market forces. Thus the main task of the state should be to regulate the money supply to accommodate the rate of real economic growth, since failure to control money-supply will lead to more unemployment and inflation in the long run (Gould et al., 1981; Ashford, 1984; Cameron, 1985). Friedman, the leading advocate of the monetarist approach, also stresses the fact that the functional activities of the modern state, and especially the welfare state and its tax burdens, should be reduced to the minimum possible. This approach is not only an alternative doctrine, but it is also a point of departure for a strategy of state (non)-intervention. It derives from the monetarist claim that interventionist governments, no matter how well-intended, have almost invariably done more harm than good (Friedman, 1962, 1983).

Another group of theorists could be labelled as 'fiscal conservatives'. Their political-economic beliefs or theories originate from the Austrian School (Von Mises; Hayek). Their ideas are strongly based on methodological individualism, a laissez-faire approach to economics which regards state intervention as bound to fail, because planning and regulating the behaviour of individuals is impossible. Their views, on state intervention in general and on economic policy formation in particular, are related to those of the monetarists. The main difference lies in the pace of action: they argue that the more rapidly the rate of inflation is reduced and the welfare state dismantled, the quicker and longer-lasting the economic recovery will be. Whereas monetarists still see a positive role for some state regulation with the help of 'fine-tuning' the supply of money (OECD, 1982). This is not the case with the fiscal conservatives: they wish a bare minimum of state intervention both in a regulative and in a fiscal fashion (Ashford, 1984; Cameron, 1982).

This view has recently been enhanced by a 'new' approach in the debate on 'free market conservatism' (cf. Nell, 1984). This is the so-called 'rational expectations' theory, which simply assumes that all (economic) agents involved understand that state intervention cannot have a positive impact on employment and output, and can only affect prices; therefore, these actors anticipate and negate governmental adjustments, moving the economy directly to a 'natural rate of unemployment' without suffering higher inflation. The essential ingredient of this view is the psychological premise that economic decisions are based more or less exclusively on expectations of future inflation and development (see for this: Nell, 1984: 119 ff; Lindberg, 1985: 43).

Finally, another alternative approach that has received attention, particularly in the USA, is 'supply-side economics'. This is an off-shoot of the neo-classical synthesis as presented by Samuelson (Frey, 1983). 'Supply-siders' clearly represent the idea that markets have a stabilizing function, resulting in optimal outcomes. Therefore this school believes in deregulation (to clear markets from state intervention), tax-cuts (to stimulate demand) but are not afraid of budget deficits (Gould et al., 1981). Although supply-siders in principle abhor state intervention, they do not regard budget deficits as a great problem as long as governments deregulate and cut tax rates to a point that economic growth will be stimulated sufficiently to remove these deficits (Wanninski, 1978). They believe that the money supply adapts to market pressures like any other supply. In contrast to monetarists they do not support the view that 'fine-tuning' is feasible.

These competing views on the relationship between politics and economics have different consequences for the formulation of strategies of state intervention. This formulation always refers to two dimensions. On the one hand, there is the role and size of the public economy and the threat of 'crowding out' private investments and deficit spending; on the other hand, there is the range of social welfare activities of the welfare state. Both dimensions differ cross-nationally according to the strategy chosen, which in turn reflects both societal views and related political goals. We posit that it is precisely this interaction between societal views and political goals that influences not only the choice of strategy but also the feasibility of adapting to the chosen strategy. In some countries there is a gradual, but distinct, dismantling of the social welfare state after 1973, in others a more discrete change of the economic welfare state. These developments are a manifestation of change in the strategy of state intervention and an expression of the apparent changing interaction between political and socio-economic actors. In order to be able to analyse this development and change in strategy, we have developed a typology using our dual concept of the welfare state.

FIGURE 1

Typology of the dual concept of the welfare state

| | | Social Welfare State | |
		Strong	Weak
Economic Welfare State	Strong	1) Keynesian Welfare State	3) General Monetarist Strategy
	Weak	2) Super-market State	4) Restrictive Fiscal State

Note:

Strong = High levels of public expenditure and state activity.

Weak = Medium and low levels of public expenditure and state activity.

1. *Keynesian Welfare State*. This strategy has been dominant during the 1960s and early 1970s; it is a combination of (re)distributive policy-making which provides goods and services to improve the well-being of the citizens, and a more equal distribution of rights and income. As a strategy it was considered to be politically feasible in some countries (Sweden being the prime example) and economically appropriate until the mid-1970s (Scharpf, 1981; Therborn, 1984). One of the reasons why it lost support was its tendency towards incrementalism and inertia (Tarschys, 1983, 1985). Decremental budgeting as a means for dealing with inflation seemed almost impossible or did not produce economic recovery in the long run. The enduring economic slump brought about by budget cuts caused political instability and threatened the existing intermediary conjuncture. This was to some extent the outcome of a 'welfare-tax backlash' (cf. Wilensky, 1976; Hibbs, 1985) and because of a declining rate of profitability (cf. Rowthorn, 1980). The final result often has been a further development of stagflation, which produced a fiscal crisis which jeopardized the development of concertation and undermined existing

incomes policies (Braun and Keman, 1986). It may be expected therefore, that only in countries with dominant social democratic party-governments (Schmidt, 1982) or with neocorporatist arrangements (Katzenstein, 1985; Keman et al., 1985) will this strategy of the Keynesian Welfare State be continued.

2. *Supermarket State*. In contrast to the Keynesian Welfare State, the Supermarket State is much closer to pluralist politics and is more sympathetic to regulation through the market, hence the intermediary conjuncture does not permit a high degree of 'welfare statism'. We have called this type of strategy 'Supermarket State' (see also Olsen, 1985) to indicate the rather incoherent policy-making that is often apparent in countries where there is no dominant Social Democratic party or a strong tendency towards neocorporatist arrangements (Katzenstein, 1985). In these countries there is no straightforward choice between economic recovery and maintaining social welfare. The interdependence of politics and economics will be more variable than that. It is like a supermarket: everyone may find something to his or her liking. The Supermarket State is a macroeconomic strategy that differs from monetarism on the one hand, by avoiding rigid budgeting and strict monetary controls, and from Keynesianism on the other, by proclaiming tax-cuts and direct stimuli for the supply-side of the economy (Cameron, 1982; Maier and Lindberg, 1985). The primary target is not social equity, but economic effectiveness. The state should only produce those services, which do not hamper economic recovery. Unlike monetarism, the Supermarket State Strategy is not afraid of deficit-spending. In our view this strategy will be important in those countries and periods in which there is no clear-cut political consensus about the response to the economic crisis or where socio-economic conflict prevails over co-operation.

3. *General Monetarist Strategy*. Monetarism is often defined as being equivalent to 'fiscal conservatism'. This is more the result of the political ideas and rhetoric of Friedman (1962, 1983) and his adepts, and less a logical consequence of the prescriptive monetarist theory as such (Ashford, 1984). Though we do not see it as progressive, as a strategy it is at least sensitive to the political and economic environment (Nell, 1984; Gould et al., 1981). The General Monetarist Strategy aims at a control of the (private) economy by checking the rate of growth of the money supply to be in line with the rate of growth of the real economy (Cameron, 1985: 270). Theoretically the best policy would be the so-called method of 'fine-tuning' (OECD, 1979). However, 'fine-tuning' is dependent on adequate domestic controls and on international economic developments. Thus in practice most monetarist strategies will be confined to simple, general, guidelines for monetary expansion. This strategy does not lend

itself to upholding social welfare related policies, since economic recovery is the dominant goal. This is to a large extent the basic difference between monetarism and the strategy of the Supermarket State, which is more flexible and open to political compromise between social and economic welfare related interests. Thus it appears to depend on the actual behaviour of the political and societal actors whether this strategy can be implemented.

4. *Restrictive Fiscal State*. The final strategy is the exact opposite of the first, and aims at a rapid reduction of too much state intervention, especially in the (private) economy. In this view public expenditure should be at the barest minimum possible and any form of deficit spending or public borrowing must be avoided (OECD, 1982). Its underlying rationale is obvious: the self-regulation of market forces and — if necessary — an economic purge of state intervention is the only way to economic recovery and growth (Nell, 1984). Unlike the preceding strategies, this one is clearly conservative. It is to a large extent based on the ideas of Hayek et al. on the one hand, and on the 'rational expectations' school on the other. State intervention is not only considered to be economically counter-productive, but also politically dangerous. It will be apparent from this description that this strategy is the purest type of all four. We expect that there could be a development towards a more restrictive fiscal stance in a number of countries. Again, of course, this will depend on the inter-mediary conjuncture which is in turn related to more specific, national, conditions and developments.

2.2 *The appropriateness of 'national' strategies*
We expect the choice of a strategy and its timing to be to a large extent contingent on its political feasibility and economic appropriateness. Most of the change can be observed by comparing the period before and after 1973 and 1979. The extent to which this change is more or less distinct will depend on how the political and social forces within a nation interact with each other. Together with certain structural characteristics of a country such as the relationship with the world market and the prevalence of neocorporatist structures (see for this Keohane, 1984; Katzenstein, 1985; Lindberg, 1985) these actor related features will shape the intermediary conjuncture. The better the subsequent political and economic perfor-mance, the more appropriate is the 'national' strategy.

As will be clear from Section 2.1, the contents of each strategy typify party-political distinctions in the left-right mould. It may be expected therefore that a left-wing dominated parliament and government will tend to favour the social *and* economic welfare state as a strategy (i.e. type 1), whereas in countries with a more mixed or conservative complexion of parliament and government, the choice of strategy also depends on the degree to which the socio-economic agents will co-operate. The lesser the co-operation, the more austere and restrictive the choice of strategy. We posit that a failure to co-operate will lead to either a General Monetarist Strategy (3) or a Restrictive Fiscal State (4). The more consensus and co-operation between class organizations and political parties and the less dominating one of the parties or class organizations is, the more likely it will be that a change of strategy is in the direction of the less extreme types (2 & 3). To increase the feasibility of a strategy under an economic recession, there will be a tendency to seek a change from either a more 'statist' or restrictive stance towards a more economically active attitude (Czada, 1983). We expect therefore, if a change takes place, that this change will always be to an adjacent category and that there is a tendency towards the middle (e.g. from 1 to 2 or from 4 to 3) when the intermediary conjuncture is more or less shaped by an integrative socio-political structure and consensus prone actors.

Although a 'national' strategy must be understood primarily in the domestic political and socio-economical context, it is obvious that international economic developments influence national politics. In particular those countries that rely strongly on exports must find ways to implement macroeconomic measures without endangering socio-economic stability and industrial relations. As Cameron (1978, 1984) has shown, capitalist democracies which are strongly integrated into the world market are not only prone to seek domestic consensus and co-operation (Keman, 1984), but also appear to be more flexible in adjusting to economic changes (Katzenstein, 1985). We expect therefore that in countries that are highly related to the international economy, the choice of a strategy will tend to be in favour of a social welfare state. In addition it may also be expected that in capitalist democracies with an open economy and flexible system of political and societal interactions, the change of strategy will be greater than in other countries (Scharpf, 1983).

Apart from choosing a strategy another important matter is of course the degree to which it can actually be implemented. One of the most important aspects in this context is the binding force of a government and thus the degree to which different actors can be compelled to comply. We posit that in countries with a tradition of tripartite socio-economic arrangements, and dominant executive powers a strategy is more prone to 'deliver the goods' than in other countries. The effectiveness of the strategy depends on the degree of routinization, the balance of social forces and the coherence of a strategy (Scharpf, 1981; Dye, 1975). We expect that the more opportunities interest groups and particularly 'distributive coalitions' have to interfere with or to shirk the process of policy-formation, the less effective it will be (Olson, 1982; Lehner and Keman, 1984).

It will be clear that the choice of a strategy is not only dependent on its economic appropriateness and political feasibility, but is also closely connected with certain value-related goals. These goals are the same in almost every country, namely the recovery from stagflation and the promotion of real growth (Keman, 1985; Schmidt, 1986). However, regardless of how unambiguous these goals may appear, the choice of a certain strategy also implies a certain precedence in combating either unemployment or inflation. We expect that both the strategies of 'Keynesian Welfare State' (1) and the 'Supermarket State' (2) will aim for a more active public policy against unemployment, whereas the other two strategies, 'General Monetarism' (3) and the 'Restrictive Fiscal State' (4) will stress the need to reduce inflation by letting the private economy seek its (dynamic) equilibrium by the operation of market forces.

Finally, it should be noted that the eventual results of any strategy are of course more or less an amalgam depending on which factors are relevant. Likewise it is obvious that neither the developed typology nor the possible explanations are mutually exclusive and of an unambiguous nature. As we already stated, the way strategies are formulated, chosen and implemented, depends, by and large, on the intermediary conjuncture. It is in this context of concurrent developments in economics and politics that we have to evaluate the appropriateness of national strategies.

3. Research design

In the light of the above developed typology, we opted for a simple systematic cross national comparison of the main indicators of social and economic welfare. This is in order to arrive at a wide distribution of countries pursuing the different strategies in each period under review. In addition we will compare the strategies with the economic performance of each country in order to obtain a deeper understanding of the relationship between the different strategies and the economic performance (or outcomes). This will be the basis for judging which factors not only influence the strategy-choice, but also which may have an impact on the actual policies pursued. Most of the data relevant for our analysis are directly available from various OECD publications.

In our analysis we included one variable which represents the structural relationship between politics and the socio-economic forces: a comparative scale of the degree of central bargaining, indicating the vertical discipline within class-organizations in combination with the degree of neocorporatism, referring to the way class-conflicts are regulated by means of concertation. This variable is described in detail in Keman (1984: 167). In addition there are two political variables: party differences and the political complexion of government and parliament.[3] Party differences are indicated by the average number of votes gained by respectively the Left, Right and Centre. The divisions between them are based on the analysis of Castles and Mair (1984). Secondly, an index indicating the complexion of parliament and government — as developed in Castles (1982) — has been used. These variables are expected to show the degree to which political actors can effectively influence a 'strategy-choice' (Budge, 1984), whereas the other mentioned variables show the degree to which a positive relationship with economic performance is likely to develop.

The intervening variables employed to indicate the social welfare state and the economic welfare state are the following: *social welfare state* consists of Total Social expenditure as reported in Social Expenditure 1960–90 (OECD, 1985b).[4] In addition we used Direct Taxation and the Rate of Public employment (in percent of total labour force; OECD, 1985c) in order to investigate the willingness of states to employ a Keynesian mode of welfare policy. *Economic welfare state* contains a number of macroeconomic indicators, pointing to specific instruments of economic policy-formation: Total taxation, Money Supply, and Net Lending/ Borrowing capacity (all in percent of GDP; OECD, 1985c). All three variables appear to be fair proxies for the willingness to steer and stimulate economic activities in society. Together with the social welfare state, it is possible to summarize the degree and direction of economic policy-formation: the more of everything means the more Keynesian welfare statism and the less of everything means a development towards a more restrictive fiscal stance; if there is a choice between cuts in taxation and avoiding extending the borrowing capacity, then we posit that this represents the difference between the Supermarket State and General Monetarist Strategy. Finally, if these developments do not occur, then we hold that the strategy of the Restrictive Fiscal State has been chosen in a country.

The dependent variable of our analysis is the economic performance of the countries involved. In most publications a combination of economic growth and the rate of unemployment and inflation is considered as a fair indication of the relative good or bad economic performance on the macro-level (Hunt and Sherman, 1972; Maddison, 1982; Armstrong et al., 1984; Schmidt, 1983b; Paloheimo, 1984; Lindberg and Maier, 1985). In addition we took into account the balance of payments, as this represents the extent to which a country is in a debtor's or in a creditor's position regarding the rest of the world. These four indicators also seem to have a different significance as policy aims in the four strategies we have developed. We therefore constructed three indexes using these four indicators:

1. *overall economic performance*, i.e. the average rank order of each country on all indicators, representing some kind of a yardstick of the general state of the economy;
2. *political performance of the economy*, i.e. we used only the rates of unemployment and inflation to indicate the differential political weight that is attributed to either inflation and unemployment in the various strategies. For, as we already pointed out, a strategy is not only a translation of economic prescriptive theory, but also the result of contested political views;
3. *targets of economic performance*, i.e. the extent to which the economic

aims, considered as targets (cf. OECD, 1979), have been attained or not. To this end, we attributed the relative weight of the four indicators according to the differing theoretical economic approaches.[5]
The data on economic performance are reported in Table 1. The countries under review are all capitalist democracies, which are members of the OECD.[6] The periodization reflects the external events all countries have in common, namely the first and second 'oil shock' (in 1973 and 1979), leading to the economic recession and eventually crisis in all capitalist democracies (Keman and Braun, 1984). We expect that these variables will show to what extent and in what direction the strategy of state intervention varies from the original type of policy-stance (e.g. Keynesian type of welfare statism) to a policy of austerity (e.g. restrictive fiscal statism) as the recession became more severe. Understood in this way, our typology can be considered as a continuum. The discussion of the empirical results of our investigation is the subject of the following sections.

4. Social and economic welfare policy mixes as a strategy

In Table 2, the results of our empirical investigations of strategies of state intervention are presented for each period. The four ideal-types of strategy which we developed in Section 2 appear to be empirically observable. As we explained in Section 3 we distinguish between the social and economic welfare policies of the countries under review, which would indicate the presence or absence of a Keynesian Welfare State. Not surprisingly it turns out that many of the Nordic countries can be considered as typical examples of the Keynesian Welfare State. The Netherlands and Belgium also follow this pattern after 1973 (Castles, 1978, 1982; Stephens, 1979; Flora and Heidenheimer, 1981; Keman, 1985). Finland and Austria seem surprising cases in this table: the first because it is included as an example of a Keynesian Welfare State and the second because it is not. However, the small scale of borrowing capacity together with an emphasis on redistributive measures in Finland explains the coding. In Austria the reverse situation applies, and so it is coded as an example of the Supermarket State (Paloheimo, 1984; Czada, 1983). Italy and the Federal Republic of Germany are typical examples of the Supermarket State: they tend to strike a balance between social and economic welfare. They do so, however, by stressing the importance of economic recovery without extending social welfare. By contrast in the case of France prior to 1981, public borrowing was small and redistributive measures depended on real economic growth. Clearly in France priorities were dictated by economic considerations and not by social welfare (Berger, 1981). This places France in the General Monetarist category. Japan and Switzerland are different again, where the social welfare state can

TABLE 1

Economic performance in capitalist democracies (N = 17), expressed in overall terms, as political values and economic targets between 1964–73, 1974–9 and 1980–3

Country	Overall economic performance			Political performance of the economy			Targets of economic performance		
	1964–73	1974–9	1980–3	1964–73	1974–9	1980–3	1964–73	1974–9	1980–3
Australia	8.00	11.00	9.50	6.00	12.00	10.00	7.40	11.00	8.70
Austria	6.75	5.25	5.50	5.50	2.50	4.50	6.40	5.20	5.20
Belgium	6.25	9.50	13.00	7.50	10.30	12.60	3.00	11.60	15.40
Canada	4.50	7.50	10.25	4.00	10.60	9.60	5.80	8.70	10.20
Denmark	13.50	13.25	11.50	13.30	12.00	12.30	12.00	15.40	10.40
Finland	11.50	12.50	7.75	11.60	10.60	8.00	9.60	11.20	6.20
France	7.25	8.00	11.10	8.30	10.00	13.80	6.70	8.20	10.60
FR Germany	4.50	4.50	8.00	1.60	4.00	4.50	5.00	6.60	9.60
Ireland	15.75	12.75	14.00	17.00	16.00	16.30	15.30	10.80	13.00
Italy	8.75	11.00	12.75	12.50	15.50	14.00	8.80	10.20	10.80
Japan	5.25	5.25	2.25	8.50	10.00	1.60	4.40	4.60	2.00
Netherlands	6.25	5.25	10.00	8.50	6.00	10.60	6.20	6.40	13.20
Norway	10.75	7.00	5.00	7.60	4.30	5.30	10.20	5.00	3.60
Sweden	10.75	8.50	9.75	8.60	5.60	6.60	11.60	9.60	8.20
Switzerland	7.00	5.00	3.10	6.00	1.00	2.00	8.60	7.40	4.20
UK	13.00	12.75	11.50	12.50	13.50	14.30	13.60	13.40	12.30
USA	9.25	9.00	8.50	8.00	9.00	8.00	10.20	8.70	8.70

Notes: A low value indicates a 'good' performance, whereas a high value indicates a 'bad' performance; the values are derived from ranking orders on the various dimensions mentioned in this section; the basic data are reported in *Economic Outlook* 36, OECD, 1984: Tables R1–R10–R12–R13; see Note 5 for the construction of the variables.

TABLE 2

Cross-national distribution of strategies of state intervention between
1964–83 in seventeen advanced capitalist democracies

Country	1964–73	1974–9	1980–3
Australia	SMS (2)	GMS (3)	GMS (3)
Austria	SMS (2)	SMS (2)	SMS (2)
Belgium	SMS (2)	KWS (1)	KWS (1)
Canada	SMS (2)	GMS (3)	GMS (3)
Denmark	KWS (1)	KWS (1)	KWS (1)
Finland	KWS (1)	KWS (1)	SMS (2)
France	GMS (3)	GMS (3)	GMS (3)
FR Germany	GMS (3)	SMS (2)	SMS (2)
Ireland	GMS (3)	SMS (2)	GMS (3)
Italy	SMS (2)	SMS (2)	SMS (2)
Japan	SMS (2)	RFS (4)	RFS (4)
Netherlands	SMS (2)	KWS (1)	KWS (1)
Norway	KWS (1)	KWS (1)	KWS (1)
Sweden	KWS (1)	KWS (1)	KWS (1)
Switzerland	RFS (4)	RFS (4)	RFS (4)
UK	SMS (2)	SMS (2)	GMS (3)
USA	SMS (2)	GMS (3)	GMS (3)

Notes: The numbers in brackets refer to the typology in Section 2.1, whereas the abbreviations
denote the strategies:
KWS = Keynesian Welfare State (1);
SMS = Supermarket State (2);
GMS = General Monetarist Strategy (3);
RFS = Restrictive Fiscal State (4).

better be described as underdeveloped and economic policy-making has
a more ad hoc character than anywhere else (Schmidt, 1985; Pempel,
1982). All in all, the categorization as well as the resulting cross-national
and inter-temporal variation appear to be tenable in the light of our
conceptual design. The main trend in Table 2 appears to be from a social
welfare state to a more divergent pattern. During the first period thirteen
countries can be characterized as social welfare state oriented. After 1973,
however, this pattern changes gradually resulting in nine countries with
either a Keynesian Welfare State (5) or a Supermarket State (4). The
remainder tends towards a policy of austerity and monetarism (8). Seven
countries did not experience a change of strategy: Austria, Denmark,
France, Italy, Norway, Sweden and Switzerland, each representing
different strategies of state-intervention. Below, in Section 4.1, we shall
try to explain the observed difference between countries in more detail.

The shift towards a more economically oriented welfare state seemed
to occur directly after the events of the early seventies, since the number

of those countries increases from seven before 1973 to ten afterwards. It should also be noted that the distribution between Keynesian Welfare State and the General Monetarist Strategy changes over time: the General Monetarist Strategy occurs only three times before 1974 increasing to four after 1973 and then to six after 1979. It seems that the Supermarket State is withering away. This strategy is obviously too loosely organized to be effective during periods of slump and stagflation. This is not the case with the Keynesian Welfare State, which was the most frequently employed strategy directly after the 'oil shock', and remained important after 1979, even though the General Monetarist Strategy was occurring equally frequently. As we stated before, we regard the typology more or less as a continuum, that runs from Keynesian Welfare State through respectively to the Supermarket State and General Monetarist Strategy to the Restrictive Fiscal State. This point is supported by the results in Table 2, since only one country — Japan — does not change to an adjacent category, but to a completely different one: from Supermarket State to Restrictive Fiscal State. As we shall see later on, Japan is an 'outlier' par excellence and will be discussed as such in Section 5.

The main difference between strategies can be attributed to the so-called 'Extraction-Distribution cycle' (Goldscheid and Schumpeter, 1976; Easton, 1979). This cycle is dependent on the relationship between the level of taxation and the degree of governmental distributive outlays. As taxation has a dual purpose of financing expenditures on the one hand, and to redistribution on the other it is relevant for both the social and the economic welfare state. Therefore the rate of total taxation and direct taxation is an important indicator of the different strategies (see also Hibbs and Madsen, 1980; Peacock and Forte, 1981; O'Connor, 1973).

Between 1974 and 1979 total taxation grew considerably by 7.4 percent on average, and since 1980 by 2.5 percent. This slowdown results mainly from economic stagnation. Thus, insofar as there represented a change of strategy it was a movement away from redistribution towards financing the social welfare state through enlarging the borrowing capacity. Therefore, after 1974 government interest payments rose dramatically in many countries. It is interesting to note that, with the exceptions of the Netherlands and Switzerland, in most countries expenditure on government interest payments has risen faster than social welfare expenditures. Both the changes in total taxation and direct taxation can be understood partially as constraints on the choice of strategies. Until 1973 this process was hardly visible and may explain the high number of Supermarket State-cases at that time in which variations in the forms of extraction and distribution were large. Since 1974, however, governments had to reassess the existing extraction-distribution cycle. In some countries this evaluation has led to more governmental borrowing and less increase in taxation (e.g. Canada, Italy and the US), whereas in countries like Denmark and Belgium the state maintained relatively high levels of taxation and had to increase the net borrowing capacity to meet existing and new expenditures.

Social expenditures have remained surprisingly stable over time: only France and Norway show some movement in these over time. After 1973 France moved towards a more austere policy-stance, which was reversed after 1981. Expenditures in Norway also slumped a bit after 1973 but regained their original rank-order position after 1980. Both cases can be explained by specific factors (a Social Democratic president and government in France, and the realization of the North Sea oil riches in Norway). In general, however, social expenditures cannot be considered an important indicator of changing strategies. In our context, social expenditures are apparently better indicators of incrementalism and the routinization (Scharpf, 1983; OECD, 1981) of existing policy-strategies.

Public employment shows more variation than social expenditures. Cross-nationally most Anglo-American countries are above average in public employment together with most of the Keynesian Welfare State countries (Finland and the Netherlands being the exceptions). Changes over time, however, are more interesting, since, unlike social expenditure there seems to be less tendency to incrementalism. Between the mix-sixties and mid-seventies all countries show a modest growth in public employment. However, after 1974 the picture is different: only four countries show a rise in public employment, none of them being an Anglo-American country, but all of them being a Keynesian Welfare State (i.e. Belgium, Denmark, Sweden and Norway). This development shows that public employment is a useful indicator for the difference of strategy-choice. It also demonstrates that policies can be changed at will. For not only did the public employment grow in a number of countries, but it also decreased in Canada and the USA.

In sum: there is cross-national variation in strategy-choice but over time the pattern becomes more uniform. Moreover, one can surmise a trend from social welfare statism to economic welfare statism. Of course, this is hardly surprising, since the 'oil shock' of 1973 and the growing uncertainty of international monetary relations, have led to the most severe economic crisis since the Second World War. What is interesting, however, is the fact that the existing social welfare state is *not* in disarray, only the way it is financed, as we demonstrated in the discussion of the extraction-distribution cycle. It seems therefore plausible to suggest that the change of strategy has to do with the impact of this economic crisis on the size and range of the public economy. We would argue this was primarily concerned with domestic politics on the one hand (Wilensky, 1976 and 1981; Hibbs and Madsen, 1980; Hibbs, 1985), and the relationship of a country to the international economy on the other. Not only the trade posture (cf. Cameron, 1978) of a country matters here, but also the way this affects rates of inflation and unemployment (Lindberg, 1982;

Schmidt, 1987; Braun and Keman, 1987). In order to assess this more fully, we will now examine each type of strategy of state-intervention in more detail.

4.1 *Patterns within strategy-types*

There are some differences to note within the sub-example of *Keynesian Welfare State*. First of all, it is obvious that the extraction-distribution cycle is well developed in most of these countries, except for the Netherlands and Finland (Cameron, 1985). Finland has developed from a more distributive stance towards a more restrictive policy-stance, which after 1979 resulted in a shift to the Supermarket State. The Netherlands slowly developed a high level of direct taxation and has in addition financed its social welfare state by means of its revenues from 'natural gas' export and by its domestic borrowing capacity. Primarily, this type of fund-raising has benefited social expenditures. This is unlike most other Keynesian welfare state countries, which show high public employment rates (Denmark, Finland, Norway and Sweden) or a steadily increasing rate of public employment (Belgium). The other side the extraction-distribution cycle is also important with regard to the 'visibility' of taxes. The Scandinavian countries clearly opt for a course that is predominantly oriented towards direct taxation, whereas the Benelux countries are more reluctant to do this and tend to borrow more. Such an approach also appears to apply to Denmark and Finland.

To a certain extent all the Keynesian Welfare State countries have developed in the direction of financing the welfare state by *both* increasing the net borrowing capacity and the level of taxation. Especially after 1979, this seems to be the case for both Norway and the Netherlands. The main emphasis in the Dutch Keynesian Welfare State is on indirect measures like transfer payments on the one hand, and on some monetarist 'fine tuning' on the other (Braun and Keman, 1986). This latter aspect appears to be variable over time and across most of the Keynesian Welfare States. Apart from Finland, all Keynesian Welfare States appear to be moderately successful in controlling the money supply. This observation accords with the views of Lindberg (1982, 1985) and Cameron (1982, 1985), that one need not follow all the measures suggested by monetarist theory to achieve monetarist targets.

The reason that the Scandinavian countries (apart from Denmark) differ from the Benelux countries is that they can afford more visible ways of administering taxation. This can probably be explained by the dominant party: social democracy in Scandinavia versus christian democracy in the Benelux (see also Kohl, 1984; Cameron, 1984; Becker and van Kersbergen, 1986). In addition, the high degree of similarity of policy-stance can be attributed to the fact that most of these countries showed features of neocorporatist bargaining (Armingeon,

1983; Czada, 1983; Keman, 1984; Paloheimo, 1984; Keman et al., 1985; Crouch, 1985).

Unlike the Keynesian Welfare State, the *Supermarket State* shows a change in quantitative terms, and is less straightforward in its complexion over time. It is clear that in this strategy various, sometimes conflicting, policy instruments have been employed. The combination of policy instrument reflects often an uneasy political compromise, rather than a coherent strategy. Only two countries can be characterized as Supermarket States throughout the whole period: Austria and Italy; and only two other countries have experienced this strategy for a longer period: the FRG since 1974 and the UK up to 1979. In all other cases, the Supermarket State appears to be a temporary strategy. It is our contention that countries often change from this to another strategy, typifying the political instability and the economically loose nature of the Supermarket State as a strategy. In four instances the Supermarket State leads to a more monetarist course (i.e. Australia, Canada, the US after 1974 and the UK after 1979). It is noteworthy that these countries are all characterized by a Westminster type of government (Lijphart, 1984; von Beyme, 1982). In addition, a common feature of these countries is their opposition to active state interference and a dis-inclination to create neocorporatist practices (Keman, 1984; Katzenstein, 1985). Other countries that employed this policy-style shifted towards more welfare statism (Belgium and the Netherlands after 1973) or from an austere policy-stance to less restrictive policies (the FRG and Ireland). This development seems to strengthen our view that inter-mediating socio-economic institutions and actors are important in creating a feasible strategy of state-intervention. This feasibility, however, should not be overestimated, since the strategy's 'success' is found to be temporary and its prime importance appears to be that it can function as a stepping stone to other strategies. Such a function, though, does not necessarily lead to a negative evaluation of the Supermarket State as a strategy of state-intervention. Politically it can fill the gap between affluence and austerity, economically it can create conditions for a more strict manage-ment of the economy. If this is true, its presence indicates an intermediary conjuncture, which is in transition. Therefore its success will be only temporary.

The *General Monetarist Stategy* shows a trend different from the Super-market State: its importance increases steadily. Only France, the FRG and Ireland between 1964 and 1973 showed monetarist features in their policy-stance. After this time, the other countries joined this type of strategy, including the UK after 1979 (and Ireland again). None of the countries under review here persisted with this strategy throughout the whole period. This may point to the fact that this strategy really is intended to *overcome* the crisis, rather than to find a new optimum or a feasible political solution. The most striking feature of the General Monetarist

Strategy countries is that most of them are medium on both total taxation and net borrowing capacity. It appears reasonable to suggest that these countries use their policy-instruments in a moderate fashion, but can only do so by following the path of austerity and a modest level of extraction (which is our basic line of demarcation between Supermarket State and General Monetarist Strategy). The fact that the extraction-distribution cycle is managed more easily in some countries could be a result of their relationship with the world market (Cameron, 1978), as well as their domestic political configuration (Castles, 1981). Ireland and the UK show definitely more 'openness' than the other countries in this group, but they are also less flexible in policy-responses because of domestic political strife (Katzenstein, 1985). General Monetarist Strategy then appears to be a more stern, restrictive version of the Supermarket State. In a sense it is more contingent upon economic theory and less resistant to change, but this is by and large a consequence of its relatively low degree of welfare orientation and a relatively high degree of economic openness.

The latter aspect is obviously different for the two countries that can be characterized as a *Restrictive Fiscal State*: Switzerland and Japan. Both countries are very sensitive to international economic fluctuations (cf. Keohane, 1984), but at the same time appear to be able to cope with it. In the Swiss case, according to Katzenstein (1984) and Schmidt (1985) this is the result of an encompassing consensus and co-operation within the political system and highly decentralized system of industrial relations. The transaction-costs are met by means of its tax-policies: which involve high individual taxation as well as social security and luxury taxation, but comparatively low levels of taxation on corporations, goods and services. In addition, Swiss fiscal policy is flexible and based on balancing the budget or even creating a surplus by net savings (OECD, 1986). The public interest is less 'general welfare' and more the traditional liberal view that each societal actor is responsible for himself. In this view, the state acts more as a safeguard rather than a key actor promoting economic recovery.

In Japan the intermediary conjuncture appears to be quite different from most other capitalist democracies. As long as certain social and economic deficiencies are off-set by sufficient growth, there will be little political protest and socio-economic conflict. Therefore the role of the state of Japan is different: special organized ties between ministries and corporations exist (e.g. MITI; Junne, 1984); policy-making is by and large not implemented by fiscal means but via semi-public/private funding. This type of 'concertation' extends to social welfare activities, which are organized on a decentralized cost/benefit basis (Pempel, 1982; OECD, 1986). Both countries really belong on the opposite extreme of our continuum of state-intervention, because they refrain from direct intervention as much as possible, and if they have to intervene, they only do it on a temporary basis.

All the cases within one type of strategy share close similarities; however, elements of one strategy appear in other strategies, the differences are a matter of degree. The ordering of the countries in our typology therefore shows the latter must be seen as a continuum. In particular the management of the so-called extraction-distribution cycle is more important than the other instruments that make up the cross-national and inter-temporal variation between the different types of strategy. In fact, one could argue that the manner and the extent to which this cycle is managed is the most characteristic and delineating feature of an economic strategy. Indeed, it is important to assess the role and position of the state in determining how and to what extent options and constraints emanating from the relationship between extraction-distribution cycle and economic crisis make a strategy more or less feasible. A number of influences can be taken into account on this question: structural features like the degree of 'openness' of an economy or the level of socio-economic institutionalization on the one hand, and more 'cyclical' phenomena such as the domestic political configuration and party-behaviour in government on the other. Both sets of influences, which reflect the intermediary conjuncture, may explain not only the choice of strategy, but also the extent to which a certain strategy helps to overcome the crisis. In the next section we will examine the correspondence between strategy and performance as well as investigating the factors that explain the observed degree of correspondence.

5. Do strategies of state intervention matter? The 'fit' between a chosen strategy and economic performance

We shall now examine to what extent some strategies are better than others in producing a favourable economic performance. In addition we will investigate to what extent there is a difference between strategies in terms of the pre-eminent aims to be achieved. In the remainder of the section we shall present our findings regarding: a) the relationship between overall economic performance and different strategies; b) the extent to which the strategies have produced outcomes in terms of rates of unemployment and inflation which are considered as political aims; c) the correspondence between the chosen strategy and corresponding economic targets. These different measures of economic performance (which have been operationalized in Section 3) reflect the underlying rationale for our concept of the different types of strategy. In Table 3 we present the cross-national differences on average of these three types of performance.

It is obvious that the path of non-intervention, followed by Switzerland and Japan, appears to have the highest pay-off in terms of overall performance. Yet, one should immediately take into account that both countries are generally considered to be more or less permanent outliers (see e.g. Katzenstein, 1984; Schmidt, 1985; Pempel, 1982). Secondly, one should also bear in mind that only a few countries can afford such

TABLE 3

Average cross-national differences in overall performance, in political
performance and in economic targeting in capitalist democracies (N = 17)

Strategy	1964–73	1974–9	1980–3
Overall performance			
(1) Keynesian Welfare State	11.63	9.33	9.85
(2) Supermarket State	7.61	9.25	8.40
(3) General Monetarist Strategy	9.15	8.88	10.20
(4) Restrictive Fiscal State	7.00	5.13	2.67
Average per period	8.85	8.15	7.80
Political performance			
(1) Keynesian Welfare State	10.30	8.13	9.50
(2) Supermarket State	8.10	10.30	7.75
(3) General Monetarist Strategy	9.00	10.40	12.00
(4) Restrictive Fiscal State	6.00	5.50	1.80
Average per period	8.25	8.60	7.80
Economic targeting			
(1) Keynesian Welfare State	10.90	9.85	10.15
(2) Supermarket State	7.85	9.25	7.95
(3) General Monetarist Strategy	9.00	9.15	10.60
(4) Restrictive Fiscal State	8.60	6.00	3.10
Average per period	9.10	8.55	7.95

Note: Based on the aggregated values of Table 1 and following the division of countries
in Table 2.

a strategy of state intervention which is aiming at a 'minimax' effort
because of the existing intermediary conjuncture. It is difficult to think
of another country under review here which can follow such a trajectory
without a negative feedback effect on the economy or the political system.
Leaving aside the Restrictive Fiscal State as a feasible example to be
followed by other countries, what is the 'second best' solution?

It appears that both the Supermarket State and Keynesian Welfare State
do not do badly if one looks at which countries are above the average
ranking order: in terms of overall results the Supermarket State clearly
performs well before 1974 and after 1979, whereas there does not seem
to be a real alternative or 'next best' strategy between 1974 and 1979.
All strategies, except for Restrictive Fiscal State, score on average in
overall terms. Both Keynesian Welfare State and General Monetarist
Strategy must be considered to be the least successful ones. These results
are quite striking, especially regarding the General Monetarist Strategy:
the most widely advocated alternative to Keynesianism appears to be the

least successful. In whatever period, regardless of how long it has been employed and in whatever way the performance is measured, the strategy is inferior. In another chapter of this book Paul Whiteley has already made clear what is theoretically wrong with this strategy and underpinned his criticism empirically. There is little need to dwell much longer on the subject: the General Monetarist Strategy can be dismissed as insufficient and ineffective.[7] Yet, the countervailing strategy is equally badly equipped to overcome the crisis. It seems, therefore, that the 'Left' alternative of the Keynesian Welfare State may be ideologically important, but in terms of overall performance and economic targeting it is not successful. At the same time, it should be noted that there is little evidence that this strategy is more harmful than the General Monetarist Strategy. The basic point of difference has always been that 'Keynesianism' was detrimental to economic recovery, whereas 'monetarism', which did not even claim to be humane, was supposed to be more effective in the long run. The Keynesian Welfare State performs a little better though if measured politically and in terms of targeting.[8] Viewed in this way, the Keynesian Welfare State is a kind of minimax strategy. However, in the long run, the burden of the social welfare state, which the Keynesian strategy induces, creates a fiscal crisis which can limit the policy room for manoeuvre. This tendency reveals itself particularly after the 'second oilshock' (1979) when the Keynesian Welfare State turns out to be the second-worst of all strategies in terms of performance (see Table 3). Resistance to change, or 'routinization' (cf. Scharpf, 1983) apparently renders the Keyesian Welfare State as more or less ineffective in coping with crisis.

The Supermarket State remains the most intriguing strategy, since it appears to be rather efficient in its functioning. Its political appropriateness is really quite surprising. Between 1974 and 1979 the Supermarket State performed almost as well as the Keynesian Welfare State in terms of political performance. This outcome supports our contention that this strategy of state intervention can indeed be considered as a strategy of transition. Taken in this sense, it apparently reflected between 1974 and 1979 a change of the intermediary conjuncture in a number of countries. Its loose nature may in the end paradoxically contribute to its very success: since it did not raise too high expectations as compared with the Keynesian Welfare State, it is in this way a more flexible strategy. On the other hand, it is more capable of creating acquiescence, since social welfare demands do not tend to overload the political system. Thus it appears that 'muddling through' (cf. Schmidt, 1983a) along the lines of Supermarket State has the highest pay-off if we look at the three measures of performance in all periods. Of course, this does not imply that Supermarket State leads unequivocally to a similar economic performance. On the contrary, the cross-national differences within this type reveal that the level of correspondence between policy-output and outcomes is on average good, but that the variation across the countries is rather high. In general, if we take above average performance in Table 3 as an indicator of success, then it appears that:

— in the period 1964–73 a more or less successful overall performance can be found among all strategies, except for the Keynesian Welfare State; the political performance of the General Monetarist Strategy, was unsuccessful, as were the economic targets of the Keynesian Welfare State;

— in the period 1974–9 the pattern shows a more even distribution: all strategies contain countries that perform well; one could posit that different strategies hardly matter in terms of performance during this period;

— in the period 1980–3 this is no longer the case: Keynesian Welfare State (lx) and General Monetarist Strategy (more) show hardly any success in overall terms; the Supermarket State and Restrictive Fiscal State clearly perform better as strategies, although this is partly a consequence of the fact that some of the poor performance countries have changed to a General Monetarist Strategy.

In sum, there is some degree of correspondence, which became stronger in the Supermarket State and Restrictive Fiscal State, but which does not exist in the Keynesian Welfare State before 1974 and the General Monetarist Strategy after 1980. Again, surprisingly enough, either 'muddling through' or minimal state intervention appear to be the more successful routes to economic recovery. This pattern needs to be explained more fully by examining the specific independent variables.

5.1 *The politics of inflation and unemployment*

In Table 3 we have reported the average political performance, which is indicated by the rates of unemployment and inflation. Many writers have posited that both are politically sensitive issues of prime importance to politics (Tufte, 1978; Hibbs, 1985; Goldthorpe and Hirsch, 1978; Whiteley, 1980; Schmidt, 1982; Keman, 1984; Gerlach et al., 1984). Often political decision-makers have declared either the attainment of less unemployment or less inflation as the pre-eminent target. In many cases this choice has been related to certain strategies: the fight against unemployment with an active economic strategy and against inflation with a more restrictive approach. However, from Table 1 it can be inferred that political performance does not systematically vary according to the strategies pursued, or in relation to an emphasis on either inflation or unemployment (as described in Note 5). Actually, there is a division between 'good' and 'bad' performers within each type of strategy, except in the case of the General Monetarist Strategy (only the US and Canada show some success after 1980; see Note 4). Thus the various strategies are differently related to the rates of inflation and unemployment. This poses the question of the extent that the intermediation between societal actors and the state as well as the political configuration influence state agencies, and produce these cross-national differences in political performance. A closer inspection reveals that the behaviour and strength of political and social actors is important for understanding why countries differ in performance. It appears that after 1973 and 1979 only seven countries experienced a 'good' performance. All these countries (see Table 5), except for Switzerland and Japan, can be characterized either as left-wing oriented or balanced in parliament and government. After 1980 this pattern changes somewhat, since only three out of seven countries can be characterized as 'leftish' in this period. At the same time, these countries show a comparatively strong tendency to neocorporatist arrangements. However, this is not a sufficient explanation from a cross-national point of view. The politics of unemployment and inflation can be explained more fully if we take into account the intermediary conjuncture, which we discussed in Section 2. We argued that the various ways in which this relationship between the structural characteristics of a country and the role actors play within this configuration has a positive influence on a country's performance, can be inferred from three factors: first, the extent to which there is an actual 'consensus' amongst the major political actors (parties and government); second, whether there is a reasonable degree of 'concertation' among the principal socio-economic actors (capital and labour); three, the fact whether or not there is 'co-operation' between the executive and legislature. These factors will have a considerable bearing on the successful implementation of a strategy and hence the economic and political performance. It seems that in particular the concurrent development of a Centre–Left inclination in party behaviour with a relatively high degree of neocorporatism, as well as the availability of efficient executive agencies, often are favourable conditions for a successful political performance.

The data in Table 4 suggest for the conclusion that the coincidence of political consensus, socio-economic concertation and co-operation between state agencies often leads to a more favourable political performance in countries with a strong left or a political balance. Ongoing class conflict and weak state agencies (Weir and Skocpol, 1983; Braun and Keman, 1986) can explain why other countries in the Keynesian Welfare State and Supermarket State mould, like Belgium, Finland, Italy and the UK, suffer from a lower political performance. The lack of such favourable intermediary conjuncture produces this outcome. Of course, this is not a complete answer, but it gives an indication of what conditions must be fulfilled in order to make a certain strategy-choice politically more feasible. However contingent the strategy may be on specific factors and however appropriate the targets can be in economic terms, without a favourable intermediary conjuncture any strategic choice will remain unsuccessful. The influence of the executive state-agencies on the process of implementation must be stressed. It is generally an acknowledged view that a strong

TABLE 4
Political factors in successful countries in terms of political performance

Country	Left votes 1964–83 %	Political complexion 73–9	Political complexion 80–3	Neo-Corporatism	Relation executive/legislative
Austria	48.7	5	5	5	3
FR Germany	43.7	4	3	3	3
Japan	33.8	1	1	3	2
Netherlands	35.5	3	3	4	2
Norway	48.4	5	4	5	3
Sweden	51.4	3	3	5	3
Switzerland	27.3	2	2	4	3

Left votes: see for explanation and operationalization Section 3; *Political complexion* (complexion of government and parliament; Castles, 1982). The values indicate the following: 5 = social democratic dominance; 4 = social democratic preponderance; 3 = balance between Left and Right; 2 = right-wing preponderance; 1 = right-wing dominance.
Neocorporatism: the values indicate the following (Keman, 1984): 5 = strong neocorporatism; 4 = developed neocorporatism; 3 = medium neocorporatism; 2 = weak neocorporatism; 1 = no neocorporatism.
Executive/Legislative: is operationalized following Smith (1976: 260–1): 3 = high degree of co-operation; 2 = medium degree of co-operation; 1 = no co-operation.

executive tends to immobilize innovative policy formation (Wildavsky, 1976; Dye, 1975; Scharpf, 1981). If this holds, then it is likely that a strong executive will harm the implementation of a chosen strategy and hence the resulting political performance.

If we take size of the public economy and the existence of a strong social welfare state as indicators of routinization or immobilism then the hypothesis that policy immobilism inhibits performance does not appear to be very plausible. Strong welfare states such as the Netherlands, Norway and Sweden are capable of performing economically very well, and only Denmark and Belgium are cases in which there appears to be a negative relationship between an extended social welfare state and resistance to change. Actually, one could argue that the arresting influence of the welfare state is more related to the size of the public economy than to the range of social welfare activities. This idea is corroborated by Cameron's analysis of the public economy in relation to economic performance (Cameron, 1982). In this study he shows that it is not the social welfare state that hinders economic performance but in some cases the size of the budget. All in all, there seems to be little evidence that routinization or the existence of a large public economy prevents a positive relationship between strategy choice and performance.

The politics of unemployment and inflation is by and large influenced by the intermediary conjuncture which is expressed in terms of left-right hostility and socio-economic conflict. Little hostility and conflict in combination with a strong executive produce favourable conditions for an optimal response to the crisis. It will be clear, however, that there are other factors which may influence economic performance. The feasibility of economic targets, in particular, does not only appear to be influenced by domestic political factors, but also by the influence of international interdependence.

5.3 *Domestic economic targeting and international interdependence*
Both economic growth and a stable balance of payments are considered as necessary requirements of economic recovery in any prescriptive economic theory. As policy-aims in general they are undisputed, but there are disputes over the means of achieving them. Therefore we have developed an 'economic targeting' variable (see Note 5) which distinguishes the economic performances of the four types of strategy. Economic growth and a stable balance of payments are very much dependent on international economic influences and the degree of interdependence of countries. By assessing the importance of these factors, we intend to explain the cross-national variation in performance in terms of economic targeting. The balance of payments will indicate the extent to which a country is vulnerable to external pressures and is thus able to respond to domestic demands.

For instance, it is argued that open economies are more prone to disturbances in production, employment and consumption, and that this sensitivity could only be cushioned by employing strategies of welfare statism, rather than by reducing state intervention in the economy. However, given the inverse relationship between the degree of openness and the overall size of the economy, an additional explanation may lie in the fact that larger economies are less sensitive to fluctuations of the world economy (OECD, 1985a). Small economies are thus characterized by both a higher degree of openness to the world market and by a higher degree of sensitivity to the world economy in comparison to large economies (Keohane, 1984; Katzenstein, 1985; Braun and Keman, 1987; Cameron, 1984).

It follows from this discussion that the scale of the economy (see for an operationalization Katzenstein, 1985: 106) in combination with the openness of the economy will lead to various intermediary conjunctures and thus to a different choice of strategy. In fact, we expect that the small scale economies, which are more sensitive to the world market, need to adopt the Keynesian Welfare State or Supermarket State strategies since domestic political and socio-economic acquiescence can only be achieved through some degree of social welfare (Cameron, 1978, 1984). The reverse option is expected in the case of large scale and closed economies: they will opt for the strategy of General Monetarism or the Restrictive Fiscal State, since it is expected that their domestic markets are able to foster economic growth. Countries that fall outside either categorization will follow the path of Supermarket State, as this strategy is clearly the most flexible one and thus more feasible in different situations. In Table 5 we have ordered the countries under review according to scale and openness of the economy.

TABLE 5
Scale of economy and degree of openness in seventeen capitalist democracies

Country	Scale of economy	Openness of economy
Australia	small	closed
Austria	small	open
Belgium	small	open
Canada	large	closed
Denmark	small	open
Finland	small	closed
France	large	closed
FR Germany	large	closed
Ireland	small	open
Italy	large	closed
Japan	large	closed
Netherlands	small	open
Norway	small	open
Sweden	small	open*
Switzerland	small	open
UK	large	open*
USA	large	closed

* Borderline cases.
Sources: Scale of Economy: Katzenstein, 1985: 106.
Openness of Economy: OECD, 1985: 116; *National Accounts*, Vols I and II (1983).

Actually, there are only three exceptions to the observed inverse relationship between scale and trade posture: Australia, Finland and the UK. All other countries fit into the expected pattern. The same observation can be made for the extent to which this leads to certain strategies. If we look back at Table 2, only Italy and Switzerland are obvious outliers and Australia and the FRG (after 1973), as well as Finland and the UK (after 1979). We contend therefore that scale and openness of the economy are associated with certain strategies of welfare statism. Yet, it is more interesting to see whether or not these particular strategies work out in terms of the economic objectives.

If we look at Table 3 it is clear that after 1973 all strategies, except for the Restrictive Fiscal State, do not perform well according to the economic targets. Generally speaking, it appears that there is not a strong relationship between the scale and openness of the economy and good and bad performance. After 1979, however, one can observe that small and open economies tend to deteriorate economically more rapidly than the large and closed economies. Apparently the degree of vulnerability (Keohane and Nye, 1977; Krasner, 1981; Keohane, 1984) increases as the economic recession continues.

The exceptions to the pattern are Austria and Switzerland: both perform very well, although they have small and open economies. They have employed different strategies and have a different complexion of government and parliament. What they do have in common though is a very high degree of consensus, concertation and co-operation. It appears therefore plausible to follow Cameron (1984), Keman (1984) and Katzenstein (1984) and to suggest that those features are highly relevant for developing a feasible strategy of state intervention. A feasible strategy is able to intermediate domestic pressures and to adjust to international fluctuations. Such a favourable intermediary conjuncture appears to be less necessary in most of the larger and closed economies than in the smaller open ones. Only Italy and the USA (up to 1979) do not perform according to the economic targets implied by the choice of strategy. The UK is an exceptional case, in so far as it developed from a large and relatively open economy to a slow growing and highly open economy. Obviously this development has resulted in a higher degree of sensitivity with which it cannot cope adequately (Nell, 1984; Armstrong et al., 1984; Gould et al., 1981). Again, it seems that Supermarket State offers the optimal solution. As we stated already, the Restrictive Fiscal State also appears to be adequate, but this strategy of minimal state intervention and maximal performance is only feasible under certain political, socio-cultural and economic circumstances. This concordant intermediary conjuncture can only be found in Japan and Switzerland.

In sum, international interdependence appears to be an important factor in assessing the choice of a strategy and influences the feasibility of economic targets. The vulnerability of a country seems to increase over time when it is a small and open economy and when there is no favourable intermediary conjuncture in terms of political consensus, socio-economic concertation and statist co-operation.

6. Conclusions

The four strategies of state intervention we analysed in this chapter appeared to have had quite dissimilar effects in terms of policy performance. The differences that we observed are ambiguous: on the one hand, countries tend to choose strategies such as the Keynesian Welfare State and the General Monetarist one as time goes by, whereas the other two strategies, the Supermarket State or the Restrictive Fiscal State, are less frequently selected. On the other hand, the latter two strategies paradoxically appear to perform better than the former, particularly after 1979, when the recession turns out to be an economic crisis. This outcome is somewhat surprising since we would have expected that strategies which are considered to be economically appropriate would yield better results. Yet, this outcome supports our view that the relationship between the state-structure and societal agencies is more important for the choice of strategy than economic appropriateness. It also means, whatever strategy is chosen, that there is a high level of uncertainty for both political and decision-makers and societal actors, which in turn may constrain future economic policy-formation.

We have discussed three different types of factors which appear to explain the cross-national and inter-temporal variation in strategy-choice and economic performance and indicate the various forms of intermediary conjuncture that accompany the strategies:

1. Domestic politics of (re)distribution which indicate the degree of political *consensus* in a country;
2. Interaction between socio-economic actors and the state-agencies with respect to welfare statism, indicating the degree of societal *co-operation*;
3. Scale and openness of advanced industrialized economies, being a structural constraint, indicating the *feasibility* of political and societal options.

All three factors have an influence, as we have observed, on both strategy-choice and performance.

During the period before 1973, the choice of strategy was mainly influenced by domestic political struggles for redistribution. During this period of relative affluence, the development of strategies depended more on ideological conflict and historical patterns of welfare statism. This explains to a large extent the presence of the Supermarket State in this period (1964–73) which dominated together with the Keynesian Welfare State. Thus the historical development of the *social* welfare state by and large determined the choice of strategy (Castles, 1981; Flora and Heidenheimer, 1981; Alber, 1982). The outcomes support our view that 'leftish' domestic politics, together with intermediation between state agencies and societal actors, are important factors leading to a particular strategy-choice of the Keynesian Welfare State or the Supermarket State.

The scale and openness of the economy also influences the size and the range of the welfare state as a whole. This process, highlighted by our investigation of the so-called 'extraction-distribution cycle', laid the foundation for the choices made after 1973. It appeared from our analysis that a change of strategy almost always involved going to an adjacent category of our typology. In general, there appeared to be a movement away from the social welfare state towards the economic welfare state. In short, one can surmise a development in strategy-choice from one based on various political options with few economic constraints to the reverse situation in which the economic constraints greatly limited the available political options. Oddly enough, the results of the different strategies cross-cut the two clusters we observed with respect to strategy-choice. Both the Supermarket State and the Restrictive Fiscal State appear to be on average the most successful strategies. The Keynesian Welfare State and the General Monetarist Strategy show a higher degree of variation concerning their performance. These results indicate that it is not only a matter of choosing the best or optimal strategy in terms of economic appropriateness and political priorities, but also the extent to which the intermediary conjuncture favours effective implementation and avoids negative feedback processes.

Strategies of state intervention to cope with an economic crisis are therefore not only difficult to choose, but it is even more difficult to tell which will bring the best outcome. It is clear, however, that if the political-economic circumstances are not mediated by political consensus and social-economic co-operation then hardly any strategy appears to be feasible to cope with the economic crisis, let alone to overcome it.

Notes

We would like to acknowledge the hospitality of the European University Institute, where we both stayed when we developed this chapter. In addition, we would like to thank the University of Amsterdam for the support we received in preparing this chapter, Oda van Cranenburgh (European University Institute/University of Leiden), Dietmar Braun (University of Amsterdam) and Paul Whiteley (Virginia Polytechnic State University/University of Bristol) for their useful comments, and Clare Gardiner (European University Institute) and Mirjam Koldenhof for their assistance.

1. Generally the 'oil shock' and its related consequences are considered to be the watershed between the period of prosperity and adversity. The second 'oil shock' of 1979 indicates another turning point, signifiying the appreciation of the fact that the economic crisis was not of a cyclical nature, but bore structural characteristics that were not easy to overcome (Armstrong et al., 1984; Maddison, 1982; Keman, 1984; Schmidt, 1983a; OECD, 1982b).

2. Unlike many other people we do not hold the view that Keynesianism was an accepted strategy *before* the 1960s. During the period of postwar economic reconstruction most countries did not indulge in deficit spending, nor inflationary cycles. Only since the early 1960s was an economic policy of economic growth and counter-cyclical measures generally accepted and institutionalized (Armstrong et al., 1984; Schmidt, 1986; Braun and Keman, 1986; Keman, 1986).

3. In contrast to Castles (1982) we stress the relative power positions of the Left and Right, rather than using the single largest political party representing either politicial-ideological milieu (see also: Schmidt, 1983a; Keman, 1984).

4. These data are updated using the *National Accounts* Vol. II 1983 (OECD, 1983). It concerns education, health, pension, unemployment compensation and other social expenditures (expressed in GDP and deflated).

5. Expressed in a formula the three indexes are constructed as follows:
   1. *Overall economic performance* =
      $((EG) + (U) + (I) + (BP))/4$
   2. *Political performance of the economy* =
      Keynesian Welfare State: $((2* U) + I))/3$
      Supermarket State: $(U + I)/2$
      General Monetarist Strategy: $(U + (I* 2))/3$
      Restrictive Fiscal State: $((0.5* U) + (2* I))/2.5$
   3. *Targets of economic performance* =
      Keynesian Welfare State: $((2* EG) + (2* U) + BP)/5$
      Supermarket State: $((2* EG) + (2* U) + I + BP)/6$
      General Monetarist Strategy: $((2* EG) + (2* I) + U + BP)/6$
      Restrictive Fiscal State: $((2* EG) + (2* I) + BP)/5$

To some extent the variation in this variable is not only due to differences as attributed, but also to the exclusion of one of the indicators, which is neglected or considered as unimportant in either approach.

N.B.: EG = economic growth; BP = balance of payments. See also: Gould et al., 1981; Nell, 1984. The basic data can be found in OECD, 1984.

6. Luxembourg and Iceland were left out because of the very small scale of their economies. Greece, Spain and Portugal were left out because they were not democracies during most of the first period of our research. Turkey and Yugoslavia are not considered as advanced capitalist democracies.

7. The USA and Canada apparently seem to contradict our harsh verdict, but it should be noted that the recovery of the USA is actually due to its deficit-spending, vast military-oriented subventions to industry and more recently the upswing of the world-market. Canada is closely related to the US-economy as well as to the world-market, so it is less the strategy and more exogenous variation what produced the American-Canadian recovery. See also: Junne, 1984; OECD, *Economic Outlook*, No. 38; Friedman, 1983.

8. It should be noted, however, that there is a division between 'good' and 'bad' performers among the countries within this group: the Netherlands, Norway and Sweden perform better between 1974–9, but then deteriorate afterwards when the upward swing fails to appear.

References

Abercrombie, N. and B. S. Turner (1978) 'The Dominant Ideology Thesis', *British Journal of Sociology*, 29 (2): 149–70.

Alber, J. (1982) *Vom Armenhaus zum Wohlfahrtstaat. Analysen zur Entwicklung der Sozialversicherung in Westeuropa*. Frankfurt/New York: Campus.

Armingeon, K. (1983) 'Neo-korporatistische Einkommens — politik im internationalen Vergleich', *Journal für Sozialforschung*, 23 (4): 441–8.

Armstrong, P., A. Glyn and J. Harrison (1984) *Capitalism since World War II. The Making and Breakup of the Great Boom*. London: Fontana.

Ashford, N. (1984) 'Intellectual Sources of Economic Policy: Thatcher and Reagan', ECPR Joint Sessions Paper, Salzburg.

Becker, U. and K. van Kersbergen (1986) 'Der Christliche Wohlfahrtstaat der Niederlande. Ein kritischer Beitrag zur Vergleichenden Politikforschung', *Politische Vierteljahresschrift*, 27 (1): 61–77.

Berger, S. (ed.) (1981) *Organizing Interests in Western Europe*. Cambridge: Cambridge University Press.

Braun, D. and H. Keman (1986) 'Politikstrategien und Konfliktregulierung in den Niederlanden', *Politische Vierteljahresschrift*, 27(1): 78–99.

Braun, D. and H. Keman (1987) 'Economic Interdependence, International Regimes and National Strategies of Industrial Adjustment', *European Journal of Political Research*.

Budge, I. (1984) 'Parties and Democratic Government: A Framework for Comparative Exploration', *West European Politics*, 7(1): 95–118.

Cameron, D. R. (1978) 'The Expansion of the Public Economy', *American Political Science Review*, 72: 1243–61.

Cameron, D. R. (1982) 'On the Limits of the Public Economy', *Annals of the American Academy of Political and Social Science*, Vol. 459: 46–62.

Cameron, D. R. (1984) 'Social Democracy, Corporatism, and Labor Quiescence in Advanced Capitalist Societies', pp. 143–78 in J. Goldthorpe (ed.) *Order and Conflict in Contemporary Capitalism*.

Cameron, D. R. (1985) 'Does Government Cause Inflation? Taxes, Spending and Deficits', pp. 224–79 in L. N. Lindberg and C. S. Maier (eds) *The Politics of Inflation and Economic Stagnation*.

Castles, F. G. (1978) *The Social Democratic Image of Society. A Study of the Achievements and Origins of Scandinavian Social Democracy in Comparative Perspective.* London/Henley/Boston: Routledge & Kegan Paul.

Castles, F. G. (1981) 'How Does Politics Matter? Structure or Agency in the Determination of Public Policy Outcomes', *European Journal of Political Research*, 9(2): 119–32.

Castles, F. G. (ed.) (1982) *The Impact of Parties. Politics and Policies in Democratic Capitalist States.* London/Beverly Hills: Sage.

Castles, F. G. and P. J. Mair (1984) 'Left-Right Political Scales: Some "Expert" Judgements', *European Journal of Political Research*, 12(1): 73–88.

Coughlin, R. M. (1980) *Ideology, Public Opinion and Welfare Policy.* Berkeley: University of California Press.

Crouch, C. (1985) 'Conditions for Trade Union Restraint' pp. 105–39 in L. N. Lindberg and C. S. Maier (eds) *The Politics of Inflation and Economic Stagnation*.

Czada, R. (1983) 'Konsensbedingungen und Auswirkungen neokorporatistischer Politikentwicklung', *Journal für Sozialforschung*, 23(4): 421–45.

Dye, T. R. (1975) *Understanding Public Policy*: Englewood Cliffs (NJ): Prentice-Hall.

Easton, D. (1979) *A System Analysis of Political Life.* Chicago/London: The University of Chicago Press.

Esping-Andersen, G. (1985) *Politics against Markets: The Social Democratic Road to Power.* Princeton/New Jersey: Princeton University Press.

Flora, P. and A. J. Heidenheimer (eds) (1981) *The Development of Welfare States in Europe and America.* New Brunswick/London: Transaction Books.

Frey, B. S. (1983) *Democratic Economic Policy.* Oxford: Basil Blackwell.

Friedman, M. (1962) *Capitalism and Freedom.* Chicago/London: The University of Chicago Press.

Friedman, M. (1983) *The Tyranny of the Status Quo.* Harmondsworth: Penguin.

Gerlach, K., W. Peters and W. Sengenberger (eds) (1984) *Public Policies to Combat Unemployment in a Period of Economic Stagnation. An International Comparison.* Frankfurt/New York: Campus Verlag.

Goldscheid, R. and J. Schumpeter (1976) *Die Finanzkrise des Steuerstaats. Beitraege zur Politischen Ökonomie der Staatsfinanzen.* (Hrsg. Hickel, R.), Frankfurt a.M.: Suhrkamp.

Goldthorpe, J. (ed.) (1984) *Order and Conflict in Contemporary Capitalism.* Oxford: Clarendon Press.

Goldthorpe, J. and F. Hirsch (eds) (1978) *The Political Economy of Inflation.* London: Robertson.

Gough, I. (1979) *The Political Economy of the Welfare State*. London/Basingstoke: Macmillan.

Gould, G., J. Mills and S. Stewart (1981) *Monetarism and Prosperity?* London/Basingstoke: Macmillan.

Hibbs, D. A. (1985) 'Inflation, Political Support, and Macroeconomic Policy', pp. 175–94 in L. N. Lindberg and C. S. Maier (eds) *The Politics of Inflation and Economic Stagnation*.

Hibbs, D. A. and H. J. Madsen (1980) 'Public Reactions to the Growth of Inflation and Government Expenditures', *World Politics*, 32: 413–53.

Hunt, E. K. and H. J. Sherman (1972) *Economics. An Introduction to Traditional and Radical Views*. (second edn). New York: Harper International.

Jones, C. (1985) 'Types of Welfare Capitalism', *Government & Opposition*, 20(3): 328–42.

Junne, G. (1984) 'Het Amerikaanse Defensiebeleid: een substituut voor industriepolitiek?' *International Spectator*, 38(7): 419–27.

Katzenstein, P. J. (1984) *Corporatism and Change: Switzerland, Austria and the Politics of Industry*. Ithaca/London: Cornell University Press.

Katzenstein, P. J. (1985) *Small States in World Markets*. Ithaca/London: Cornell University Press.

Keman, H. (1979) 'State Intervention and Public Policy in Late Capitalist Society', ECPR Joint Sessions paper, Brussels.

Keman, H. (1984) 'Politics, Politics and Consequences: A Cross-National Analysis of Public Policy Formation in Advanced Capitalist Democracies (1967–1981)', *European Journal of Political Research*, 12(2): 147–70.

Keman, H. (1985) 'Het verschil tussen Succes en Falen van Beleid', pp. 101–18 in H. A. van der Heide and J. Kastelein, (eds) *Succes- en Faalfactoren bij bestuurlijke reorganisaties*, Groningen: Wolters-Noordhoff.

Keman, H. (1986) 'Strategies of Economic Policy-formation: Dutchmen, Dutch Diseases and Dutch Crossings', ECPR paper, Gothenburg.

Keman, H. and D. Braun (1984) 'The Limits of Political Control: A Cross-National Comparison of Economic Policy Responses in Eighteen Capitalist Democracies', *European Journal of Political Research*, 12(1): 101–8.

Keman, H. and F. Lehner (1984) 'Economic Crisis and Political Management: An Introduction to Political Economic Interdependence', *European Journal of Political Research*, 12(2): 121–30.

Keman, H., J. Woldendorp and D. Braun (1985) *Het-Neo-Korporatisme als Nieuwe Politieke Strategie. Krisisbeheersing met en (door) overleg?* Amsterdam: CT-Press.

Keohane, R. (1984) 'The World Political Economy and the Crisis of Embedded Liberalism', pp. 15–38 in J. Goldthorpe (ed.) *Order and Conflict in Contemporary Capitalism*.

Keohane, R. O. and J. Nye (1977) *Power and Independence. World Politics in Transition*. Boston/Toronto: Little, Brown and Company.

Kohl, J. (1984) 'Zur Entwicklung des Oeffentlichen Sektors in den westlichen Wohlfahrstaaten: Thesen und empirische Befunde vergleichender Analysen', paper for the Friedrich Ebert Stiftung, Bonn (mimeo).

Krasner, S. D. (1981) *Defending the National Interest. Raw Material Investments and US Foreign Policy*. Princeton (NJ): Princeton University Press.

Lehner, F. and H. Keman (1984) 'Political-Economic Interdependence and the Management of Economic Crisis', *European Journal of Political Research*, 12(2): 213–20.

Lehner, F., M. G. Schmidt and F. G. Castles (eds) (1987) *The Political Management of Mixed Economies*. Berlin: De Gruyter.

Lijphart, A. (1984) *Democracies. Patterns of Majoritarian and Consensus Government in 21 Countries*. New Haven/London: Yale University Press.

Lindberg, L. N. (1982) 'Intellectuals and Economics as Policy Profession: Reflections on the Retreat from Keynesianism and from the Interventionist State', IPSA paper, Rio de Janeiro.

Lindberg, L. N. (1985) 'Models of the Inflation-Disinflation Process', pp. 25–50 in L. N. Lindberg and C. S. Maier (eds) *The Politics of Inflation and Economic Stagnation*.

Lindberg, L. N. and C. S. Maier (eds) (1985) *The Politics of Inflation and Economic Stagnation*. Washington DC: The Brookings Institution.

Maddison, A. (1982) *Ontwikkelingsfasen van het kapitalisme*. Utrecht/Antwerpen: Het Spectrum.

Maier, C. S. and L. N. Lindberg (1985) 'Alternatives for Future Crises', pp. 567–88 in L. N. Lindberg and C. S. Maier (eds) *The Politics of Inflation and Economic Stagnation*.

Mishra, R. (1984) *The Welfare State in Crisis. Social Thought and Social Change*. Brighton: Wheatsheaf Books.

Nell, E. J. (ed.) (1984) *Free Market Conservatism*. London: Allen & Unwin.

O'Connor, J. (1973) *The Fiscal Crisis of the State*. New York: St. Martins Press.

OECD (1979) *Monetary Targets and Inflation Controls*. Paris: OECD.

OECD (1981) *Welfare State in Crisis*. Paris: OECD.

OECD (1982a) *Budget Financing and Monetary Control*. Paris: OECD.

OECD (1982b) *Employment in the Public Sector*. Paris: OECD.

OECD (1983) *National Accounts of OECD-countries*, Vol. II. Paris: OECD.

OECD (1984) *Economic Outlook 36*. Paris: OECD.

OECD (1985a) *The Role of the Public Sector, Economic Studies 4*. Paris: OECD.

OECD (1985b) *Social Expenditures 1960–90. Problems of Growth and Control*. Paris: OECD.

OECD (1985c) *Historical Abstracts, 1960–83*. Paris: OECD.

OECD (1986) *The Observer*, No. 138. Paris: OECD.

Offe, C. (1983) 'Competitive Party Democracy and the Keynesian Welfare State: Factors of Stability and Disorganisation', *Policy Sciences*, 15: 225–46.

Olsen, J. P. (1985) 'Administrative Reform and Theories of Organization', paper for the European University Institute Conference on Democratic Theory, Florence (mimeo).

Olson, M. (1982) *The Rise and Decline of Nations*. New Haven/London: Yale University Press.

Paloheimo, H. (ed.) (1984) *Politics in the Era of Corporatism and Planning*. Tampere: Finnish Political Science Association.

Peacock, A. and F. Forte (1981) *The Political Economy of Taxation*. Oxford: Basil Blackwell.

Pempel, T. J. (1982) *Policy and Politics in Japan. Creative Conservatism*. Philadelphia: Philadelphia University Press.

Poulantzas, N. (1978) *State, Power and Socialism*. London: New Left Books.

Rowthorn, B. (1980) *Capitalism, Conflict and Inflation*. London: Lawrence and Wishart.

Scharpf, F. W. (1981) 'The Political Economy of Inflation and Unemployment in Western Europe: An Outline'. Berlin: International Institute of Management and Labour Market Policy (mimeo).

Scharpf, F. W. (1983) 'Economic and Institutional Constraints of Full Employment Strategies: Sweden, Austria and West Germany (1973–1982)'. Berlin: International Institute of Management and Labour Market Policy (mimeo).

Scharpf, F. W. (1985) 'Beschäftigungspolitik in der Krise', *Leviathan*, 1: 1–22.

Schmidt, M. G. (1982) 'The Role of the Parties in Shaping Macroeconomic Policy', pp. 97–176 in F. G. Castles (ed.) *The Impact of Parties. Politics and Policies in Democratic Capitalist States*.

Schmidt, M. G. (1983a) 'The Welfare State and the Economy in Periods of Economic Crisis: A Comparative analysis of Twenty-three OECD Nations', *European Journal of Political Research*, 11(1): 1–26.

Schmidt, M. G. (1983b) *Westliche Industriegesellschaften*, Vol. 2 of Pipers Wörterbuch zur Politik. Munich: Pipers Verlag.

Schmidt, M. G. (1985) *Die Schweizerische Weg zur Vollbeschäftigung*. Frankfurt/New York: Campus Verlag.

Schmidt, M. G. (1987) 'The Politics of Labour Market Policy', in F. Lehner, M. G. Schmidt and F. G. Castles (eds) *The Political Management of Mixed Economies*.

Smith, G. (1976) Politics in Western Europe. London: Heinemann.

Stephens, J. D. (1979) *The Transition from Socialism to Capitalism*. London/Basingstoke: Macmillan.

Tarschys, D. (1983) 'The Scissors Crisis in Public Finance', *Policy Sciences*, 15: 205–24.

Tarschys, D. (1985) 'Good Cuts, Bad Cuts: The Need for Expenditure Analysis in Decremental Budgetting', *Scandinavian Political Studies*, 4(5): 261–85.

Therborn, G. (1984) 'The Prospects of Labour and the Transformation of Advanced Capitalism', *New Left Review*, 145 (May-June): 5–38.

Tufte, E. R. (1978) *The Political Control of the Economy*. Princeton (New Jersey): Princeton University Press.

von Beyme, K. (1982) *Parteien in Westlichen Demokratien*. Munich: Piper.

Wanninski, J. (1978) *The Way the World Works*. New York: Basic Books.

Weir, M. and T. Skocpol (1983) 'State Structures and Social Keynesian Responses to the Great Depression in Sweden and the United States', *International Journal of Comparative Sociology*, 24(1) & 24(2): 4–29.

Wildavsky, A. (1976) *Budgeting. A Comparative Theory of Budgetary Processes*. Boston/Toronto: Little, Brown & Co.

Wilensky, H. L. (1976) *The 'New Corporatism'. Centralization and the Welfare State*. London/Beverly Hills: Sage.

Wilensky, H. L. (1981) 'Leftism, Catholicism and Democratic Corporatism: The Role of Political Parties in Recent Welfare State Development', pp. 345–82 in P..Flora and A. J. Heidenheimer (eds) *The Development of Welfare States in Europe and America*.

Whiteley, P. F. (ed.) (1980) *Models of Political Economy*. Beverly Hills/London: Sage.

Woolley, J. (1982) 'Monetarism and the Politics of Monetary Policy', pp. 148–60 in *Annals of the American Academy of Political and Social Science*.

7

The economic policy strategies of the Nordic countries

Jan Otto Andersson

1. Introduction

For several years a group of social researchers from the different Nordic countries have met two or three times a year in order to make a joint study of the economic policies in Scandinavia. The first project concerned the evolution and mechanics of income policies. The results were published in a special issue of *Nordisk Forum* (No. 28, 1981).

Our next step was more ambitious. We wanted to analyse not only income policies, but the whole range of economic policies, and at the same time to strive for a more coherent theoretical framework suited for comparisons of the different countries. The effort resulted in a special issue of *Nordisk Tidskrift för Politisk Ekonomi* (1984) containing five country studies, and in a manuscript for a book called *Norden dagen derpå* (Scandinavia the Day After). This chapter is based on the results of the work of the group.[1]

The intention of our investigation was to study whether the 'economic-policy models' had changed as a consequence of the problems and pressures which characterized the 1970s. The idea was to compare the 'models' of the 'Golden Age' in the 1950s and especially 1960s with the experiences during the 'Phase of Blurred Objectives' (using two terms introduced by Angus Maddison). After intensive discussions our concept of a national economic-policy model was scaled down to that shown in Figure 1.

Since all the Nordic countries are small open economies their economic structure is above all determined by the way in which they are linked to the world economy. In our study the principal indicator for the economic structure therefore became the main exporting sectors of the different countries. In this chapter I will use the degree of one-sidedness in the export structure of a country for choosing the order in which the countries will be treated.

The main component of the politico-institutional relations in our study was the relative strength of the working class and the kind of 'class compromise' that established a certain political balance in the country. In the historical description of the rise of the different models we tried to show how the development of the economic structure influenced the

FIGURE 1

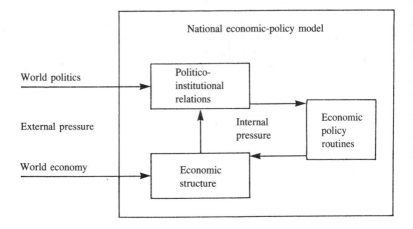

mobilization of the different classes and the kinds of alliances or 'historical projects' that came to dominate.

Although we, of course, were interested in the possible changes in the economic structure and the political relations, our main object was to look at whether and how the economic policy routines were affected by the different pressures. In this chapter the focus will very sharply be on this aspcct, and thereby there is the risk that our deeper and broader intentions are lost. Furthermore, the presentation will mostly be restricted to the external economic pressures, although the different types of internal pressures in the Nordic countries are of great interest, and certainly quite important for the developments of the economic policy routines. I am well aware that the choices I have made can give a too shallow picture of the project. For this I have to apologize to my associates.

The chapter is made up of two parts. In the first, the different national models of the Golden Age are described, and in the second I will try to answer the question if and how the economic policy routines were changed as result of the new challenges. In conclusion I will make some general remarks.

2. The Nordic models in the Golden Age
During the period of spreading of 'fordism' (a term used especially by the French so-called regulation-school) in the advanced capitalist countries, all the Nordic countries underwent a rapid economic and social development. However, this impressive assimilation of new production and consumption norms was carried through in a rather stable framework of economic policy routines. In each of the five countries it is possible to

discern a certain national pattern of economic regulation, which was not challenged during the Golden Age of rapid economic transformation.

The patterns of economic regulation, as well as the economic structures and the political constellations, varied a lot between the different countries. Therefore it is possible to speak of five Nordic models instead of only one. Of course, there were also many similarities, but in relation to the rest of the industrialized capitalist world, these similarities cannot usually be said to have been specific to the Nordic countries. As the presentation will show it is also quite problematic to speak of a 'Scandinavian model', common for Denmark, Norway and Sweden, although such an expression has sometimes been used in the international discussion.

2.1 *Iceland — seeking stability through inflation*

The Icelandic model of the postwar decades was based on the fishing industry as the main exporting sector, a kind of profitability-guarantee for this sector, a profit-sharing system linking the incomes of the fishermen to those of the fishing industry, and a widespread system of indexation linking the incomes of the rest of the economy to the fishing sector and inflation. A particular feature of Iceland was not only the split between fishermen and other wage earners, but a split inside the political labour movement, which tended to give the bourgeois parties a clear political dominance.

The fishing industry has had a dominating role in Iceland's economy. In the 1960s some 90 percent of all export incomes came from this sector alone. It is therefore no surprise that the main aim of economic policy has been to guarantee the incomes and investments of this sector, despite the large fluctuations in the quantities caught and in the export prices. During fat years the fishing industry has been allowed to keep and to spend its earnings. During lean years the state has taken measures in order to guarantee the profitability, and avoid bankruptcies. Such measures have been generous devaluations, interest subventions, credit guarantees, and a costly system to stabilize prices.

The axis of the class compromise in Iceland has been between the fishing capitalists and the fishermen. The latter have been integrated into the model through a profit sharing system, giving them a direct interest in the profitability of the main exporting sector. Increasing export incomes have, therefore, rapidly led to wage increases and increased internal demand.

The asymmetric exchange rate policy, devaluating in bad years but not revaluating in good, coupled with the efforts to keep up a high level of investment and with the fast spread of export earnings throughout the economy, made the Icelandic model inflationary. The rest of the income earners — building workers, service workers, farmers etc — all tried to link their incomes to those of the fishermen, or at least to inflation. The traditional Icelandic model was, therefore, characterized by almost complete indexation regulated by law, and by regular and rough labour disputes in order to keep the relative wage levels.

The results of the Icelandic model were a destabilizing devaluation cycle and high inflation. It was also, however, able to assure a rapid income growth and full employment.

2.2 Finland — the spirit of national self-assertion

There are several parallel features between the Finnish and the Icelandic models. If Iceland has been an economy based on fish, Finland's economy has been based on wood. As in the case of Iceland a major element in the Finnish model has been to guarantee the profitability of the forest industry, i.e. through devaluations. In both countries the rate of investment was kept at a high level despite inflationary tendencies and in disregard of the business cycle. A particular common feature was also that both countries had a substantial part of their foreign trade on a bilateral basis with the Soviet Union. Politically, Finland and Iceland stand out from the other three Nordic countries by having a split and relatively weak labour movement.

There are, however, two noteworthy differences in relation to Iceland. First, Finland, besides promoting the old dominating export industry, vigorously pursued a policy of increased processing and of diversification both on a national and on a firm level. Both through the creation of new firms in new branches, and through the efforts of the old firms producing pulp and paper to take full advantage of their forward and backward linkages, the industrial base of Finland was rapidly broadened. When, for example, Iceland continued to pay for its Soviet imports by its traditional export commodity — fish — Finland's main exports to the Soviet Union consisted of non-traditional manufactured goods, such as ships.[2]

Secondly, in contrast to Iceland, Finland put more stress on keeping down inflation than keeping employment up. The rather widespread system of indexation was outlawed in the middle of the 1960s, and incomes policies through central agreements between the employers, the trade unions, the state and the farmers were established in 1968. If Iceland can be said to have searched for growth and stability by allowing inflation, Finland strived for transformation and a stronger position on the world market even at the expense of stability. Unemployment in Finland was kept down less as a result of conscious employment policies than as a consequence of mass emigration to Sweden.

In the traditional Finnish model the state assumed a large responsibility for the economic transformation. Many of the new and capital intensive manufacturing firms were established by the state (metal industry, chemical industry, oil refineries, nuclear power etc.) and through the regulation of the credit market private firms also were supplied with loans on relatively favourable terms. The former president, Urho Kekkonen, was an active supporter of state intervention in order to create a broader and regionally more evenly spread industrial base. In a book published in 1952, *Has our Country the Patience to Prosper?*, he cherished the idea that the trade unions could be lured into moderating their wage demands if a larger share of savings and investments was undertaken by the state.

A special feature of the Finnish model has traditionally been the conviction that the activities and obligations of the state should be strictly adapted to the capacity of the economy. Thus there was little room for a Keynesian-type stabilization policy, and the development of the welfare system has been less pronounced than in the other Nordic countries. Foreign credit and foreign investments also played a minor role in the rapid economic transformation.

2.3 *Norway — how to make full advantage of an export enclave*

The main exporting sectors of the Norwegian economy used to be energy-intensive melting and chemical industries as well as shipping. Both of these sectors were highly international in character. Investment capital was raised on the international capital market, and the inputs came to a large extent from abroad. Norway's own contribution was mainly cheap energy and old shipping traditions. These exporting sectors thus functioned as relatively isolated enclaves. Fluctuations in their incomes only marginally affected the rest of the economy. Despite its exceptionally high share of exports in the total production, large parts of Norway's economy were in fact insulated from the vagaries of the world economy.

Two other important prerequisites for the Norwegian model were the strong and united labour movement and the traditionally strong and nationalistic bureaucracy. In no other Nordic country was economic planning used to such an extent as in Norway.

In order to achieve both growth and stability a lot of policy instruments were used:

1. The development of the heavy industry was promoted through a close co-operation between the state and foreign firms.
2. The credit market was regulated in order to guarantee industrial loans at low interest rates. The role of the state-owned banks was substantial in directing the loans.
3. Ambitious regional policies in order to preserve economic activity in the districts were introduced in the early 1950s.
4. Fiscal policies were mildly counter-cyclical.
5. The state left wage settlements for the central labour market organizations, but as in Sweden, this non-interference was conditional. The state was pledged to maintain full employment under the condition that wage increases did not cause inflation over and above that imported through rising international prices. The value of the crown was to be fixed.

The result of the Norwegian model clearly was stable growth. Although the variations in the export incomes were not lower than in other countries, the variations in the GNP-growth rates were much smaller. At the same time as the economy underwent a rapid transformation and a welfare state was established, unemployment and inflation were kept at low levels.

2.4 *Sweden — class compromise turned into 'volvoism'*

Besides typical Nordic goods, such as metal and forest products, Sweden was a large exporter of investment goods and some typical 'fordist' products, such as cars and household equipment. This strong and relatively diversified export sector certainly contributed to the success of the Swedish economy, which very early turned the country into a mature fordist society, although with many particular features.

Complementary to the strong and concentrated capitalist class there was a very strong and well-organized labour movement and a traditionally powerful state. When these forces could come to terms with each other in the form of an 'historical class compromise', the conditions for a long-term consistent policy were better than in other countries. However, a break-up of this compromise could lead to damaging conflicts.

In contrast to the other Nordic countries there existed in Sweden an explicit economic policy doctrine, worked out by the labour union economists Gösta Rehn and Rudolf Meidner in the late 1940s. The three main elements of this model were:

1. A generally restrictive, anti-inflationary, economic policy, coupled with countercyclical measures in order to guarantee stability (especially investment funds).
2. A solidaric wage policy, without government interference, according to the principles of equal pay for equal work and a gradual diminishing of wage differentials. An intended effect of this policy was to give extra profits in the most productive firms, and to shake out the least efficient.
3. An active labour market policy, ensuring a fast adaptation of supply to demand.[3]

Two other elements, which were an expression of social democratic efforts to create a 'people's home', can be added to this list:

4. A general welfare system covering all citizens.
5. A high level of government saving.

In the 1950s and 1960s this programme was surprisingly well adhered to. Because of international inflation and different rates of productivity growth between the 'open' and the 'sheltered' sectors a certain rate of inflation was, however, accepted. This was explicitly recognized, and the model accordingly modified during the 1960s, when both unions and employers agreed upon the analysis made in the so-called EFO report.[4]

The model was suited for a rapid fordist transformation.[5] The solidaric wage policy and the welfare state tended to make demand more homogeneous, and together with the labour market policy this promoted a rapid concentration in production. Small-scale production for local and special needs was crowded out. In comparison with the other Nordic countries the Swedish model thus tended to eliminate the small bourgeoisie as a politically important group.

2.5 *Denmark — social–liberal demand side economics*

In the 1950s Denmark's main exporting sector was still agricultural products. Because of chronic balance-of-payments problems the economic policy often had to be restrictive, and the rate of interest was kept higher than in the other Nordic countries. Economic growth was relatively slow and unemployment high.

In the 1960s, with the liberalization of trade in manufactured goods, the situation changed. Firms which earlier had mainly catered for the home market now turned into exporters of often very specialized 'niche'-products. In only ten years public expenditure rose from 25 to 40 percent of GNP. The housing sector boomed. The overall growth rate increased considerably and unemployment was almost eliminated by 1970. Real wages grew faster than in the other Nordic countries.

In comparison with the other countries the state in Denmark, despite the rapid expansion of the public sector, was averse to selective economic policies. The credit market was kept free, and foreign loans encouraged. The continuing deficit on current account and the inflationary pressures, however, prompted the government to try to regulate wages. When the incomes policies failed at the end of the 1960s, the bourgeois government resorted to restrictive policies by increasing the tax-burden from 33 to 44 percent in three years (1969–71).[6] Even before the international recession the Danish economy was in difficulties. At the same time as the parliament was brought down by a tax-payers revolt, unemployment started to rise alarmingly.

The social and political base of the Danish model, which gave fordist consumption without assuring a corresponding fordist production, was an alliance between the Social Democrats and the Liberal bourgeois parties. Because of the importance of small-scale industry and the agricultural sector, there was little interest in any possibilities for selective support to industry or for active labour market policies. Neither was there any tradition for direct state enterprise in order to supplement the production of the private firms, as in the cases of Finland and Norway.

Of the five Nordic models the Danish one was at the same time the most elusive and the one that most resembled a text-book economy. Denmark was a social–liberal welfare state, trying to ensure social security through income transfers and public consumption, but without interfering directly in the economy except by incomes policies.

TABLE 1

The central features of the Nordic economic-policy models in the golden age

	Main export sectors	Class-compromise	Business cycle	Role of the state	Monetary policies	Public sector growth
I	Fishing industry	Bourgeois dominance. Labour movement split.	Very strong fluctuations.	Profitability guarantee to the fisheries.	Low interest rates. Generous monetary policies. Devaluations.	Relatively slow.
F	Forest industry. Diversification i.a. through trade with USSR and Sweden.	Labour movement split. Centre-left governments.	Strong fluctuations, reinforced by economic policies.	Active participation in the diversification of the economy.	Low interest rates. Devaluations.	Relatively slow. Small transfers.
N	Energy-intensive production of raw materials and semi-finished goods. Shipping.	Strong labour movement. Class-compromise consolidated by intervention.	Strong automatic stabilizers. Macro-economic planning.	Active direct participation. Stress on full employment and regional policies.	Low interest rates 'Credit-socialism'. Fixed e.r.	Medium rate of growth.
S	Diversified industrial structure.	Strong labour movement. Class-compromise consolidated by self-imposed discipline of the labour market parties.	Diversified exports and economic policies assure stability.	Indirect influence, but selective labour market policies.	Low interest rates. High public saving. Fixed e.r.	Very rapid growth, as a part of the national product.
D	Agrarian exports. Shift to niche-type manufacturing industries.	Rather strong labour movement. Continued strength of agrarian interests. Government compromises.	Difficulties for the agrarian sector. Medium fluctuations.	Liberalism, but general welfare policies.	High interest rates. Integration in international credit markets. Fixed e.r.	Very rapid growth, as a consequence of 'something for everyone' compromises.

I = Iceland; F = Finland; N = Norway; S = Sweden; D = Denmark.

3. The Nordic models in the 'Phase of Blurred Objectives'
In the terminology of Angus Maddison the period from 1973 onwards is called the 'Phase of Blurred Objectives'. This label characterizes the situation in the Nordic countries quite well. External shocks and internal pressures increased the uncertainty, and when it became more evident that the problems were also structural, the traditional modes of thinking and reacting were called into question. The most important miscalculation from the Nordic point of view was the length of the recession and the slow rate of growth of the world economy that followed it. They were prepared to manage shorter recessions — all in their own way — but not to deal with a longer phase of uncertain economic development.

However, as we have seen, the economic policy models of the Nordic countries were quite different. Also the degree of fordist maturity varied considerably. It is, therefore, no surprise that they reacted differently both after the first depression (1974–6) and after the second (1980–3). What we are interested in is to what extent the national models were modified. Were the economic policy patterns retained or changed as a consequence of the new conditions? In this section a countrywide summary of our findings concerning the different adaptations will be presented.

3.1 *Iceland — from hyperinflation to neoliberalism with a vengeance*
The Icelandic case is clearest in the sense that this model was adhered to throughout the 1970s and the early 1980s. But since 1983 there has been a very conscious effort to replace it with strict neoliberal and monetarist policies.

In the early 1970s export prices for fish rose considerably. Real wages also grew — more than 15 percent yearly for the fishermen. This, of course, spilled over into rapid domestic inflation. The increase in oil prices at first implied increasing exports to the Soviet Union, the principal supplier of oil to Iceland, but because of the inelastic supply of fish and wool, Iceland had to give up the bilateral trade arrangements and was forced to pay for its oil imports in convertible currency. Increasing costs and tighter world markets plunged the fishing industry into a profitability crisis. The response was traditional: large devaluations. From 1975 to 1979 the crown was devalued by 30 percent as a yearly average.

The mechanism of an income guarantee to fishing, and general indexation resulted in an accelerated inflation. Credit policies were expansive with very low or negative real interest rates. Although fiscal policies were contractive, GDP-growth was relatively high and unemployment non-existent. Wages, however, tended to lag behind the rapid increases in prices, despite heavy striking activities in order to preserve the indexation-safeguard.

In the early 1980s the problems seem to have grown out of hand. Inflation rates were more than 50 percent, and on the increase. The permanent devaluations and the growing international interest rates made the burdens of the international debt very heavy. At the end of 1983 foreign loans corresponded to 58 percent of GDP. In 1982 production started to fall. The Icelandic model was rejected by the bourgeois parties, which also increased their support in the 1983 elections.

The programme of the new government has three main elements:

1. The curbing of inflation through strict monetary policies and high interest rates, as well as through prohibition of wage-indexation and strikes.
2. Privatization of the economy through cuts in state expenditures and taxes, and through the selling out of state firms.
3. Internationalization of the economy through 'free zone-type' support to foreign firms interested in using cheap energy or other Icelandic resources.

Inflation was reduced from 81 percent in 1983 to 29 percent in 1984, but at the same time the social and regional conflicts grew in intensity. The government was forced to rescind the ban on strikes. it is still too early to say whether a definite model shift will come about or not. The outcome depends on whether the two bourgeois parties are able to replace their traditional support from the primary sectors and regional districts with support from the urban tertiary and secondary sectors.[7]

3.2 Finland — two types of foreign trade and consensus

The reactions of the Finnish economy to the swings in the world economy in the 1970s followed the traditional pattern. However, there was an interesting new element which followed from the drastic increase in the price of oil. Since most of the oil was imported from the Soviet Union in exchange for industrial products, there was a massive increase of Finnish exports to the East at the time when markets in the West languished. Thus the boom years and inflation lasted longer in Finland. (Another reason for this was the countercyclical policies of the two other neighbouring countries, Sweden and Norway.)

When it became obvious that Finland could not escape the effects of the world crisis, an emergency-government was formed in 1975 in accordance with the personal wishes of the president. It included the parties of the Centre and the Left, as well as the People's Democratic League, which included the Communists. (The League had already participated in the government 1966–71.)

The economic policy from 1976 to 1978 aimed at restoring the 'international competitiveness'. Fiscal and monetary policies were restrictive, and the Finnish mark was devalued in 1977 and 1978. The ten-year devaluation-cycle was repeated once more! Relative unit labour costs in common currency fell from 140 dollars in 1976 to 110 dollars in 1978. The price was high. Unemployment jumped from 2 percent in 1976 to

8 percent in 1978. Production did not grow between 1975 and 1978. Real wages were cut.

The severity of this horse-cure was probably a surprise even for the policy-makers, since they did not believe that the upturn of the world economy would be so painfully slow. However, the cure did improve the trade balance,[8] and when the world economy recovered Finnish economic policy also became expansive. In 1979 and 1980 the GDP-growth was exceptionally high, and unemployment was somewhat reduced.

The new rise in oil prices (1979–80) again considerably expanded Finnish exports to the Soviet Union at a time when the western markets were contracting. The timing was even more perfect than after the first oil crisis. Thus almost sheer luck is one explanation for the so-called Finnish miracle of the 1980s.

The 1980s have been characterized by an unusual stability. Economic growth has been faster than in the other Nordic countries, and there have been no major disputes concerning the economic policy. Consensus in foreign policy seems to have been supplemented with consensus in the economic field. There seems to be a general agreement to maintain 'international competitiveness' and to keep the tax burden at a certain level of GDP (35–36 percent). In this sense the Finnish model has not only been maintained, it has even been strengthened.

There have, however, been some minor modifications in the Finnish model worth mentioning. One is that the credit market has been liberalized and the real interest rates gone up, at the same time as the traditionally large government saving has been almost eliminated. It is also possible to observe a somewhat more active countercyclical fiscal policy than in earlier years. This may, however, be the result of the unproblematic balance-of-payments situation, rather than of a definite change in the Finnish model. The real test will come only with a new world economic recession.

3.3 Norway — oil as the new export enclave

When the world economic crisis occurred in 1974 investments in the Norwegian oil industry had just begun. Today more than a third of Norway's export incomes come from oil and gas, and 10–20 percent of the central government's revenues stems from taxes paid by the petroleum sector. Thus Norway has developed another export enclave, but a much larger and probably more vulnerable one.

The Social Democratic party had great difficulty in maintaining its position at the beginning of the 1970s. The traditional alliance between workers and farmers had been eroded, and the successful populistic campaign against joining the EC dealt a heavy blow to the party. It became necessary to pursue an expansive and reformist strategy throughout the economic crisis in order to regain the position of the Social Democrats.

The government's choice was a stronger emphasis on countercyclical policies than usual in the Norwegian model. Borrowing abroad was expanded considerably in order to finance the build-up of the new petroleum industry. These bridging policies succeeded in keeping a high rate of economic growth throughout the 1970s, and there was no increase in unemployment. In 1977–8 policies were tightened up. Fiscal policies became more restrictive, real interest rates became positive, and the crown, that had been revalued, was devalued. These measures improved the trade balance, but imposed a cut in private consumption. When the oil price rose again in 1979 the problems of the trade balance and the huge foreign debt were eliminated at a stroke, and there were no further external pressures for restrictive economic policies.

In the 1981 elections the bourgeois parties took a victory by riding on a critique against the constraints on private consumption. This victory can also be seen as an expression of deeper social changes in the Norwegian electorate.

The bourgeois government has been confronted with a policy dilemma which it has not been able to solve definitely. Instead of a foreign debt problem, Norway for the first time has got a balance-of-payments surplus problem. If an expansionary policy is followed there may be inflation and ordinary industry is hurt through a loss in competitiveness. If, on the other hand, the oil money is invested abroad, there is the risk that home industry may lose out as a consequence of lack of government support. Has the new export enclave become a young cuckoo in the Norwegian nest?

On the whole the government has tried to support industry through anti-inflationary policies. High interest rates have become a new feature of the Norwegian economy. Contractive policies have also been extended to the government sector. Mainland production has grown slowly and open unemployment has increased by Norwegian standards.

In contrast to the traditional model there is an effort to create a new layer of private financiers. The role of the state in the Norwegian model will, however, remain central, since it absorbs a major part of the petroleum incomes. The prospects for the 1980s are slow economic growth both in petroleum production and in manufacturing production. It is therefore likely that Norway will have to adapt to a slower increase in total incomes than before. Yet, it is too early to speak of the demise of the old Norwegian model.

3.4 *Sweden — polarization or 'neovolvoism'*
The term 'the Phase of Blurred Objectives' following a 'Golden Age' is most appropriate in describing the Swedish case. In the 1973 elections the seats in the Riksdag were divided evenly between the two blocks. Important decisions had to be made by lottery. In 1976 the first bourgeois government since the early 1930s was formed.

In accordance with the traditional model a countercyclical economic policy was pursued from 1974 to 1976. The crown was mildly revalued, and the efficacy of the labour market policy was such that open unemployment was even reduced.

When it was realized that the world economic depression was more protracted than expected, the newly acceded bourgeois government was put in an awkward corner. It could hardly start by showing that the Social Democrats had always been right in claiming that only they were able to guarantee full employment. The economic policy that was followed by the government was quite expansive by Swedish standards. Certainly a devaluation in 1977 decreased real wages and curtailed private demand, but fiscal policies were exceptionally expansive and the industries hit by the crisis were subsidized on a large scale. Labour market policies were even intensified, and thus open unemployment was kept low despite a declining industrial production. The public surplus, which used to be some 4 percent of GDP, was turned into a steadily increasing deficit — 4 percent in 1980, and almost 7 percent in 1982.

This policy mix included elements and accents that differed from the traditional Swedish model. It was more Keynesian and defensive than the Rehn-Meidner model. Before the elections in 1982, which brought the Social Democrats back to the government, the bourgeois parties had, however, stepped back from Keynesianism towards a more neoliberal policy. The support to industry was reduced, public employment fell, and in labour market policies a shift towards support in cash to the unemployed was seen. At the same time fiscal and monetary policies became more restrictive.

The imbalances in the Swedish economy, which the Social Democrats inherited, were met with a dramatic devaluation in 1982. (The bourgeois government had already devalued by 10 percent one year earlier.) Relying on the trade unions to accept a further decline in the real wages in order to restore full employment, the government hoped to avoid strong inflationary pressures. In terms of industrial production the strategy has been successful. Sweden has almost regained its lost market shares, the profit-share in manufacturing is the highest since the 1950s, and industrial growth has been so fast that the lag between Sweden and OECD as a whole, which had increased since 1975, has now been overcome.

In the 1980s the Swedish model has been challenged but as yet it has changed only marginally. Wage-earner 'moderation has been maintained as well as 'full' employment (at least by international standards). Stabilization policy has been abandoned at the same time as income equalization policy has languished. The system of public supply of capital has completely collapsed.[9]

The future of the Swedish model is uncertain. In the economic policy debate a clear polarization has taken place. On the one hand the employers federation (SAF), the Conservative party, and a majority of the academic economists are advocating a radical change towards neoliberalism, whereas those on the left among the Social Democrats, with a large support in the workers union (LO), argue that it is now necessary to take the 'third step', to complement political and social democracy with economic democracy. The struggle over the wage-earners' funds has led to a deep polarization.

Since both the capital owners and the labour movement are strong and well organized, an all-out conflict between them could be very hurtful. Recognizing this, and remembering the traditionally strong state and the ability to construct long-run class compromises in the Swedish society, one may ask whether the end-result will not turn out to be a 'neofordist' solution, call it 'neovolvoism'. Such a solution would imply a rationalization and also decentralization of the public services, further moves in a corporativist direction, and a fusing of the functions of the private and public sectors. In discussing any such developments one has to remember that those employed in the public service sector now constitute a larger share of the population than those employed in the manufacturing sector.[10]

3.5 Denmark — crowding out the welfare state?

As mentioned earlier the Danish economy was already in a problematic position before the outbreak of the world crisis. The government tried to carry through a bridging policy by countercyclical fiscal measures in 1975-6. Credit policy was, however, straightened up and real interest rates increased. This was in accordance with the traditional Danish model.

When world depression lingered on, and the imbalances on current account and in the public finances grew bigger, the policies changed towards enhancing international competitiveness. From 1977 until 1982 private consumption was squeezed through strict incomes policies and gradual devaluations. Fiscal policies, however, were still moderately expansive. Despite these efforts the deficit on current account remained at a high level. The growing budget deficit kept interest rates high, and attracted foreign capital to Denmark. Despite the rather substantial decrease in relative unit labour costs (by some 25 percent between 1978 and 1982) private investments continued to fall. Unemployment kept on increasing, although the public sector expanded its demand for labour. The public debt grew from 0 to 50 percent of GDP from 1975 to 1982.

In 1982 unemployment, inflation and the public deficit in relation to GDP were all about 10 percent. The deficit on current account was 4 percent of GDP. That year the Social Democrats freely handed over government power to four bourgeois parties. Also the Social Democrats were convinced that cuts in public expenditures had to be made, but they preferred to let the bourgeois parties carry through the dirty work.

The period since 1982 has been characterized by a Danish version of monetarism: 'Schlüterism'. The main elements of this policy have been cuts in public expenditure and tight monetary policies. The declared aim is to create larger income and wealth differences in order to make the economy more dynamic.

The Social Democrats have not been able to put forward an alternative to this bourgeois offensive. The trade unions are demanding a reduction of the working week to thirty-five hours in order to diminish unemployment. There is no group advocating a return to the growth model of the 1960s. The 'Scandinavian' elements of the Danish model are eroded in favour of Anglo-Saxon style supply side economics. Among investors there are those who believe that Denmark will become the Nordic miracle of the 1980s. They can refer to the fact that Danish industry, although small, is specialized in advanced products and has increased its market shares throughout this decennium. In 1984 and 1985 private investments have in fact been buoyant, and private sector employment has increased markedly.

4. Concluding remarks

The immediate responses of the Nordic countries to the external pressures emanating in the 1970s were quite varied. This was no surprise since their economic-policy models were also quite different. Denmark, Norway and Sweden tried to bridge over the 1974–5 world recession, Finland tried to improve its international competitiveness, and Iceland resorted to contractive fiscal and wage policies in order to curb inflation.

The prolonged recession and the slow recovery were unexpected by all governments, and the uncertainty concerning the traditional policy routines increased. The problems were gradually perceived as structural rather than cyclical, and demands for more radical deviations from the 'Golden Age' style of thinking developed.

However, it would be wrong to forget the internal pressures that had gradually been developing inside the Nordic countries. As they matured as fordist societies the growth models of the 1950s and 1960s were undermined. In Sweden and Denmark the quantitative demand for housing was becoming saturated. Already in the 1960s industrial production started to grow slower than productivity in Sweden, and during the 1970s this also became the trend in Denmark and Norway. In terms of fordist consumption Finland was the least developed country, and this may be one explanation for the relatively rapid growth of Finnish industrial production in the 1970s and 1980s.

The formation of fordist welfare states also undermined the traditional labour–agrarian political base for the 'historical projects', and new popular protest movements developed. It is possible to speak of three types of political reactions: a 'red wave' of demands concerning economic democracy, job security and shorter working hours, a 'blue wave' demanding

TABLE 2
New features in the Nordic economic-policy models in the 1980s

	Main export sectors	Class-compromise	Business cycle	Role of the state	Monetary policies	Public sector growth
I	Dramatic drops in fish catch.	Right-dominated coalition from 1983.	Stagflation with strong fluctuations.	Attempted neoliberal austerity.	Market interest system. Lavish borrowing abroad.	Zero growth.
F	Stable export growth due to stabilizing effect of trade with USSR.	Strengthened class-compromise. 'Consensus policies'.	Stable growth.	More indirect influence. Discreet Keynesian elements.	Higher interest rates. Liberalization of credit market.	Slow growth. Expenditure ceiling.
N	Oil sector dominating export enclave.	Tendencies towards polarization. Right-dominated coalition from 1981.	Somewhat stronger fluctuations, due to the oil sector.	Changes in neo-liberal direction.	Higher interest rates. Capital exports. Liberalization of credit market.	Moderate growth.
S	Rapid increase of importance of largest firms. Recovery of lost market shares.	Polarization. Tensions between privately and publicly employed.	Stagnation followed by recovery since 1983.	Neoliberal challenge detained. 'neovolvoism' (?)	High interest rates. Public dis-saving. Devaluations.	Expenditure restraint.
D	Promising increases in manufacturing exports.	Right-dominated coalition from 1982. Polarization.	Stagnation followed by recovery since 1982.	Strong neoliberal tendencies.	High interest rates. Frequent, small depreciations.	Reductions of government spending.

I = Iceland; F = Finland; N = Norway; S = Sweden; D = Denmark.

tax reductions, less government regulation and more room for individualistic solutions, and a 'green wave' rejecting the fordist norms of production and consumption, and searching for a way of life that would be more independent of the state institutions and the large corporations. These different waves have appeared in different forms in different phases in the Nordic countries, and they have all contributed to the gradual erosion of the postwar projects and class-compromises. At the moment the neo-liberal tendencies are so strong that politics are becoming more polarized in all countries, with the possible exception of Finland. The project members Pekka Kosonen and Jukka Pekkarinen have used the term 'finlandization' of the economic-policy models of Denmark and Sweden (to a lesser extent Norway), and correspondingly 'scandinavization' of the Finnish model.

As can be seen from Table 2 some changes have occurred in all the Nordic economic-policy models. The most evident case is Denmark, where efforts to increase the international competitiveness through neoliberal austerity policies have replaced the social–liberal Keynesianism of the 1960s. In Iceland an attempt to make a radical change is also being made, but it is too early to judge whether it will in fact succeed. The developments in Finland differ from those in the 1960s and 1970s, but this may well be an accident, stemming from propitious external conditions. The growth of the oil sector has made Norway more vulnerable, but despite a right-dominated coalition the traditional Norwegian model has hardly been challenged.

The situation in Sweden is still characterized by a certain deadlock. Changes in the model have already occurred and strong pressures are still building up. Whether the outcome will be a more neoliberal regulation model of the Danish type or a Finnish-style corporational model, with the trade unions as junior partners, or if there will develop a genuine Swedish 'neovolvoism' — a new historic compromise between labour, capital and the state — is an open question.

Notes

1. Two other summaries were being prepared at the same time as this one. Lars Mjøset, Oslo, has written an extensive summary in English, which was presented at Cornell University, 30 April 1985, and at Harvard University, 7 May 1985. Pekka Kosonen and Jukka Pekkarinen have published a Finnish summary in *Tiede ja Edistys* 2, 1985. We have been able to use each others' preliminary drafts in writing the final versions.

2. In Iceland domestic processing of fish even tended to decline since exports to the US market of unprocessed fish grew rapidly. According to the Icelandic member of the project, the tariff agreement with EFTA in 1970 'destroyed the most basic conditions for further transformation of the industry oriented towards the domestic market'. Birger Björn Sigursjónsson, 'National Sovereignty and Economic Policy. The Case of Iceland', *The Scandinavian Economic History Review*, 1985.

3. Despite this intention in fact most of the ambitious Swedish labour market policy-measures were demand-oriented.

4. The EFO-model is presented in English in G. Edgren, K. O. Faxén and C. E. Odhner, *Wage Formation and the Economy*. London: 1973. A corresponding analysis had earlier been made for Norway by Odd Aukrust.

5. Labour productivity growth in the manufacturing sector was very fast in Sweden. In the four large Nordic countries the average yearly productivity growth in manufacturing 1958–1973 was:

Denmark 4.7
Finland 5.2
Norway   3.7
Sweden   6.8

based on tables published in *Economic Growth in a Nordic Perspective*, Helsinki: 1984.

6. This drastic increase was partly the unintended result of a reform of the taxation system.

7. According to the OECD *Economic Outlook*, June 1985, the consumer price index is expected to increase by nearly 30 percent in 1985. The current account deficit has not been improved, and the interest costs of foreign borrowing amount to over 6 percent of GNP. The krona was devalued after the last wage agreement.

8. The deficit of the trade balance was 8.3 percent of GDP in 1975, which changed into a surplus of 2.3 percent in 1978. This was achieved through a reduction of imports (in real terms) by 15 percent and an increase in exports by 36 percent.

9. A detailed survey of Swedish developments has been written in English by the project member Lennart Erixon: *What's Wrong with the Swedish Model? An Analysis of its Effects and Changed Conditions 1974–85*. Stockholm: The Swedish Institute of Social Research, June 1985.

10. A recent indication of a possible 'neovolvoist' evolution was the buying of a substantial amount of shares in S-E-Banken (the centre of Swedish big private capital) by LO (the trade union federation). The journal *Affärsvärlden* speculates that the selling was not for economic needs, and that is was arranged by the interest group behind Volvo(!). *Affärsvärlden*, 7 August 1985.

References

Aglietta, M. (1982) 'World Capitalism in the Eighties', *New Left Review*, 136.

Andersson, J. O. (1984a) 'From a Mixed Capitalist to a Dual Socialist Society' in *Nordic Views and Values*. Stockholm: The Nordic Council.

Andersson, J. O. (1984b) 'Den svenska modellens kris', *Finsk Tidskrift*, 9: 484–94.

Boyer, R. and J. Mistral (1983) *Accumulation, Inflation, Crises*. (First edn 1978). Paris: Presses Universitaire de France.

Economic Growth in a Nordic Perspective (1984) Helsinki. (A joint publication of five Nordic research institutions.)

Erixon L. (1985) *What's Wrong with the Swedish Model? An Analysis of its Effects and Changed Conditions 1974–85*. Stockholm: The Swedish Institute for Social Research, June.

Kosonen P. and J. Pekkarinen (1985) 'Norden dagen efter' — pohjoismaisten mallien murros', *Tiede & Edistys*, 2.

Maddison A. (1982) *Phases of Capitalist Development*. Oxford: Oxford University Press.

Mjøset L. (ed.) (1986) *Norden dagen derpå. De nordiske-økonomisk-politiske modellene og deres problemer på 70- og 80-tallet*. Oslo.

Mjøset L. (1985) *Nordic Economic Policies in the 1970s and 1980s. A Summary of the Findings of the Nordic Economic Policy Project*. University of Oslo: Department of Sociology, August.

Nordisk Tidskrift för Politisk Ekonomi (1984) Nos 15/16, contained the following articles: Knud Erik Skouby, 'Den danske modellen'; Pekka Kosonen, Tapio Lovio and Jukka Pekkarinen, 'Den finska modellen: förändringar och förvittring eller kontinuitet och allmängiltighet?'; Birgir Björn Sigurjonsson, 'Den isländska modellen'; Ådne Cappelen, Jan Fagerberg and Lars Mjøset, 'Den norske modellen'; Lennart Erixon, 'Den svenska modellen i motgång. En analys av dess effekter och förändrade förutsättningar under perioden 1974–84'.

Sigurjónsson B. B. (1985) 'National Sovereignty and Economic Policy. The Case of Iceland', *The Scandinavian Economic History Review.*

8

The monetarist experiments in the United States and the United Kingdom: policy responses to stagflation

Paul F. Whiteley

During the 1970s all western advanced industrial countries experienced a period of stagflation, or a combination of inflation and unemployment. Arguably this has produced significant electoral changes in several countries. Perhaps the most pronounced political changes took place in the United States and Great Britain when the Republican administration of Ronald Reagan was elected in 1980, and the Conservative government of Margaret Thatcher came into office in 1979. Perceptions of economic performance played an important role in both elections (Fiorina, 1981; Whiteley, 1984).

Both these new governments sought to revise trends in social and economic policy which had been developing for many years, and which the two leaders saw as the underlying cause of stagflation. They had been given their opportunities to make these changes by electorates willing to punish existing orthodoxies for their perceived failures to manage the economy properly.

One unusual feature of these governments was that they were both programmatic governments, committed to relatively well defined strategies for promoting economic recovery. This is unusual for conservatives who have generally avoided detailed ideological programmes. However, they came to power during a resurgence of the ideas of laissez-faire liberalism, a set of nineteenth-century ideas co-opted by modern conservatives (Bosanquet, 1983).

The purpose of this chapter is to evaluate the economic policies of the Reagan and Thatcher governments with particular reference to monetarism, which is a key component of new right ideology. Monetarism represents both a political analysis of how the economy works, and a technical analysis which specifies causal relationships between certain key macroeconomic variables. It was the cornerstone of the policy programmes of both governments since it promised to slay the dragon of inflation, one of the key factors which explained rising electoral support for the new right in the first place. Both governments regarded the conquest of inflation as a necessary condition for promoting economic growth.

An examination of the monetarist 'experiments' in Britain and the United

States throws important light on the question of how much control policy-makers exercise over the economy in an advanced industrial society. The existing literature stresses the limited influence which government can exert over economic outcomes (Wildavsky, 1980; Rose, 1980; Schmidt, 1982). It is argued that control over policy outcomes is limited for a variety of reasons: objectives are often unclear or in conflict with each other; there is often no well-defined theory to explain how objectives can be attained; decision-makers face great uncertainties and a pervasive shortage of information; policy instruments which are capable of achieving objectives are often not available; and finally there are fundamental problems of collective action which make policy-making very difficult when many actors are involved (Scharpf, 1983; Keman and Lehner, 1984; Paloheimo, 1984).

One of the most interesting features of the monetarist experiments is that many of these problems appear at first sight not to apply. With regard to policy objectives monetarism provides a fairly coherent analysis of how objectives can be attained; moreover, there is no goal conflict since over-riding importance is given to the control of inflation by monetary means. Other goals, such as the maintenance of full employment are regarded as being of lesser importance because theory purports to demonstrate that they cannot be controlled. Secondly, although policy-makers face un-certainties about timing there is no problem monitoring the progress of a policy, since fairly good quantitative indicators of the money supply and inflation are available on a regular basis. Thirdly, the problems of collective action associated with a policy area such as industrial relations, which contains many actors, are avoided, because it is argued that a small elite of technocrats either in the Treasury or in the Federal Reserve can control the money supply. Thus powerful interest groups do not have to agree to get the policy implemented. There are some differences between Britain and the United States which derive from the Constitutional independence of the Federal Reserve, but as we shall argue below these are not significant. Thus politicians have adequate policy instruments to pursue their objectives.

Overall, therefore, one might conclude that the influence of government action on policy outcomes in the area of monetary policy should be quite strong. If governments can control the money supply, and this is a necessary and sufficient condition for controlling inflation, then governments can control inflation. This chapter focuses specifically on these two issues. After an initial discussion of monetarist theory and the policy goals of the Reagan and Thatcher administrations, there is a section which discusses the feasibility of government controlling the money supply in an advanced industrial country in the light of the US and UK experience. This is followed by a more technical section which examines whether or not control of the money supply enables governments to control inflation.

The first section uses evidence from the first administrations of the Reagan and Thatcher governments up to 1984, and the second section uses data on the US and UK economies for more than a century from the early 1870s to 1975.

We begin by examining the main tenets of monetarism.

Monetarist theory

There have been a number of reviews of monetarism by both sympathizers and opponents of the theories (Modigliani, 1977; Purvis, 1980; Desai, 1981; Kaldor, 1982), and some of the discussions are distinctly polemical. David Laidler, a British economist, has pointed out that: 'like beauty, "monetarism" tends to lie in the eye of the beholder' (Laidler, 1981: 1).

In a concise summary Laidler reduces monetarism to three core propositions. Firstly there is the quantity theory of money, which has a long historical pedigree and in its simplest form can be written as follows:

$$M = kPY \qquad (1)$$

M is the quantity of money; k is the ratio of money stock to income, or the reciprocal of the velocity of circulation of the quantity of money; P is an index of the general level of prices; and Y is national income in real terms.

Essentially the quantity theory of money relates the volume and turnover of money in the economy to the total volume of economic activity in current prices. It can be interpreted as a theory of the demand for money, so that greater economic activity stimulates an increase in the demand for money; or it can be interpreted as a causal theory of national income in money terms. In the former case the money supply is the dependent variable in an estimating equation, and in the latter case it is an independent variable. In the second interpretation increases in the supply of money will increase nominal income in society after an appropriate lag, and it is this interpretation which most distinguished monetarists from Keynesians who discount the quantity of money as an important direct causal influence on national income. By contrast, Keynesians emphasize the importance of consumption expenditure by individuals or by the government in determining money incomes. Similarly, they are somewhat sceptical about the stability of the demand for money equation over time.

The second core proposition of monetarism is the idea that in the long run the quantity of money does not influence the real economy, or employment and productivity. As Ball puts it 'Money is said in the long run to determine money things' (1982: 48). Monetarists would argue that there is no long run Phillips curve, or trade-off between employment and inflation, because the real economy is determined by technological and institutional forces not directly influenced by monetary policy. In Friedman's terminology there is a 'natural' rate of unemployment (1968). If governments try to reduce the actual rate below this level by deficit spending this will merely boost inflationary expectations leading to accelerating price rises and no extra jobs in the long run. Since changes in the money supply causes changes in nominal incomes, but not in real incomes then any increases in the quantity of money in excess of that required to support real growth will produce inflation. This is why monetarists believe that Keynesian stabilization policies are damaging; they do nothing for real growth, but rather stimulate inflation.

The third feature of monetarism is the preference for fixed rules or pre-announced rates of growth in the quantity of money. It is argued that if economic actors can be induced to believe that the government is firmly committed to reducing the rate of growth in the money supply over a period of years, then this will dampen inflationary expectations, which in turn will mean that the government can bring down the rate of inflation more rapidly than otherwise (Friedman, 1968; Bryant, 1983; Lindberg, 1985).

These three propositions are the theoretical core of monetarism, although other writers might add other points as well. They provided the ideological background to the monetarist experiments.

Policy goals and monetarism in the US and UK
The monetarist stance of the Thatcher and Reagan governments represented the culmination of a trend apparent throughout the 1970s of attaching increasing importance to monetary aggregates in macroeconomic management. In 1975 the United States Congress had urged the Federal Reserve to adopt annual targets for monetary growth, and this was reinforced by the Full Employment and Balanced Growth Act of 1978 (CEA Report, 1982: 67). Among other things this act required the Federal Reserve to set out target ranges for the growth of the money supply. It was a measure with bi-partisan support, being co-sponsored by Hubert Humphrey, the 1968 Democratic Presidential nominee.

In Britain an emphasis on monetary targeting first arose from the financial crisis of 1976. The crisis involved the Labour government borrowing reserves of currency from the International Monetary Fund. The IMF imposed the conditions that the government accept monetary targets as part of a package of measures aimed at controlling inflation and sustaining the international value of sterling (Keegan and Pennant-Rea, 1979: 144–7).

This shift towards monetarism in both countries had come about for several reasons. Firstly, monetarist ideas had gained ground in the economics profession after the failure of Keynesian remedies to deal with the problem of inflation in the mid-1970s. Secondly, early econometric evidence purported to demonstrate that a stable demand for money function existed in both countries (Meltzer, 1963; Kavanagh and Walters, 1966). A stable demand for money function implied that the quantity of money in the economy could be reliably controlled by manipulating the arguments of this demand function, notably the rate of interest.

A third factor which gave prominence to monetary policy was the instability caused by the breakdown of the Bretton-Woods system of fixed exchange rates in 1971 and the OPEC oil price rise of 1973. The Bretton-Woods system tied western currencies to the dollar which in turn was linked to the value of gold. The system put limits on the abilities of central banks to create money, since excessive monetary creation tended to produce balance-of-payments problems. These resulted from currency speculation which either anticipated inflation from such a policy, or a devaluation of the currency. Thus the system of fixed exchanges acted as a constraint on monetary expansion. Some writers stressed the link between the demise of the Bretton-Woods system and the acceleration of inflation in the 1970s (Whitman, 1975). It was felt that new methods of monetary control would be required to take the place of fixed exchange rates. Similarly, the OPEC oil price rise created huge Petrocurrency funds, which needed to be recycled, giving many countries the opportunity to borrow their way out of recession. Such borrowing could be highly inflationary.

However, despite the earlier emphasis on monetarist policies the Reagan and Thatcher administrations represented a significant departure from the previous policies. Both gave considerably more prominence to monetary policy than their predecessors, the Thatcher government more so than the Reagan administration. The Thatcher government gave monetary policy primacy over every other aspect of economic policy. It introduced the Medium Term Financial Strategy which set out targets for the money supply and public expenditure over a four-year period (HMSO, 1980). The central feature of this strategy was a commitment to gradually reducing monetary growth over time. This was in line with the ideas of Milton Friedman (1968), who regarded this as the best method of squeezing inflationary expectations out of the system. The policy was to be accompanied by drastic cuts in public expenditure designed principally to reduce government borrowing. Since government borrowing was financed either by creating new money, or raising interest rates to attract funds, it was thought that lower borrowing would mean a tighter monetary policy without penal rates of interest.

The Reagan economic strategy also made a commitment to a declining rate of monetary growth, although since monetary policy is conducted by the nominally independent Federal Reserve Board, no target figures were given for long-term future monetary growth (Economic Report, 1982). In this respect the Reagan and Thatcher governments had much in common.

However, there were important differences between the two governments. The Reagan economic strategy differed from the Thatcher policies in three important respects. First, it very strongly emphasized the importance of tax cuts in stimulating growth — this had become known as supply side economics. In its strongest form this asserts that tax reductions will not produce increased budget deficits because they will stimulate the economy sufficiently to raise national income enough to increase revenues. Stein (1984: 237) describes this as the 'economics of joy', a rejection of traditional Republican policies of austerity. These ideas developed from the work of supply side economists like Arthur Laffer, and from Congressional advocates like Congressman Jack Kemp and Senator William Roth. Supply side economics conveniently allowed the Republicans to pursue traditional goals such as increased defence spending and tax cuts without having to advocate electorally damaging cuts in domestic programmes. The Thatcher government did make modest tax cuts shortly after achieving office in 1979, but it was the last time that this occurred during the Conservative government and the rhetoric surrounding supply side economics in the United States was seldom heard in Britain.

A second feature of the Reagan approach to macroeconomic policy concerned the costs of disinflation in terms of higher unemployment. It was argued that these costs would be small and temporary. This view derived partly from supply side economics — the argument that tax cuts would stimulate the economy sufficiently to offset the deflationary effects of monetary restraint. But it was also influenced by the so-called rational-expectations school of economics. In this view, individuals have an accurate macroeconomic model in their minds which tells them how the economy works and governs their expectations about future inflation. It is argued that when the government announces its determination to stop inflation this immediately affects their expectations, making workers, for example, bargain for lower wage increases. This rapidly reduces inflationary wage demands without incurring the costs of adjustment associated with unemployment. These ideas have been described by one economist as the 'economics of Dr Pangloss' (Buiter, 1980). However, they provide a convenient doctrine to policy-makers seeking to reduce inflation without what was perceived as electorally damaging unemployment.

By contrast the Thatcher strategy sought to deal with the unemployment costs of disinflation by arguing that the government had little or no control over unemployment. The benefits of reduced inflation were stressed in terms of long-term growth, and the government worked to distance itself from short-term employment consequences of the policy. This was clearly an alternative strategy to the Reagan approach, although both ran considerable political risks, in terms of long-run credibility.

The third, and perhaps most significant difference between the Reagan and Thatcher governments concerned fiscal policy. Both governments advocated a reduction of public expenditure, but the Thatcher administration gave this a very high priority because, as we pointed out earlier, it saw this as a precondition for controlling the money supply. By contrast the Reagan administration gave it a much lower priority, partly because of a bigger emphasis on deregulation than the Thatcher government, but also because supply side theories appeared to sanction a relaxed attitude to the problem of budget deficits. As a consequence, the Reagan administration broadly implemented the tax reductions proposed in the Kemp-Roth Tax Bill, which called for a 30 percent reduction in marginal tax rates over a period of three years. This, coupled with an unprecedented peacetime increase in defence spending, was to have a major impact on subsequent developments.

The policy outcomes from 1979 to 1984

In evaluating the policy outcomes of the two governments it is useful to examine performance in relation to the policy instruments on the one hand i.e. the money supply and budget deficits, and in relation to the target variables on the other i.e. growth and inflation.

Tables 1 and 2 contain information on the behaviour of the money supply, measured by M3, the broad definition of money which includes types of bank credit. They also include information on budget deficits over the period 1980 to 1984 in the US and UK.

In the case of the US it can be seen that the money supply grew at approximately a constant rate throughout the entire period, averaging just over 10 percent. The money supply in constant prices is also included since this measures how accommodating the administration was in dealing with inflation. A completely non-accommodating monetary policy would permit no increase in the money supply in constant prices at all, and so this is a rough guide as to how determined the administration was in reducing the growth of the money supply.

It is clear from Table 1 that the Reagan administration made no progress at all in reducing the money supply in nominal terms, but had a modest influence in reducing the rate of growth in real terms. Clearly outcomes were rather different from the original plan to progressively reduce the increase in the money supply each successive year. However, the most dramatic difference between policy objectives and outcomes for the Reagan administration related to the budget deficit. The plans set out by the office of Management and Budgeting soon after the inauguration in 1981 called for a small budget surplus by 1984. In the event, the budget deficit exploded, and would have been even higher had not corrective action been taken in 1982 (Heclo and Penner, 1983: 33–35).

In the case of Britain the newly elected government set out monetary targets over a five-year period in the first Government Expenditure White Paper (HMSO, 1980). It can be seen that the money supply grew consistently faster than government plans, with a particularly marked discrepancy between plans and performance in 1980–1 and 1982–3. The Public Sector Borrowing Requirement or Budget deficit remained

TABLE 1

Increases in the money supply, and planned and actual increases in the budget deficit in the US 1980–4

Fiscal year	Money supply increases (M3)	Money supply constant prices	Budget deficit ($bn) Planned	Actual	As % GNP
1980	10.3	16.91	−60	−74	2.81
1981	12.5	12.05	−55	−79	2.67
1982	10.0	9.06	−45	−128	4.17
1983	10.1	8.63	−23	−208	6.29
1984	10.2	8.44	+ 1	−185	5.05

Sources: Money Supply: *Annual Report* of Council of Economic Advisers (1985: 303); Planned Deficit: Office of Management and Budgeting (1981: 11); Actual Deficit: *Economic Indicators* (1985: 32).

TABLE 2

Planned and actual increases in the money supply (M3) and the public sector borrowing requirement 1980–1 to 1983–4

Financial year	Money supply (M3) Planned in current prices	Actual	Actual in constant prices	PSBR as % of GDP Planned	Actual
1980–1	7–11	16.4	4.4	3.75	4.58
1981–2	6–10	14.0	4.3	3.0	4.08
1982–3	5–9	13.6	9.4	2.25	1.74
1983–4	4–8	8.1	2.8	1.50	3.79

Sources: Planned figures from HMSO (1980); Actual M3 calculated from HMSO (1985b); Actual PSBR calculated from HMSO (1984a) and HMSO (1984b).

consistently above target except for 1982–3, so that by the end of the period the gap between plans and performance was particularly wide. Once again the money supply figures in constant prices showed that the counter inflation policy was a long way from being non-accommodating, but it was tighter than the policy in the US.

An important point to stress is that these policy instruments cannot be judged in isolation from the behaviour of the real economy. A given deficit may be 'loose' or 'tight' depending on capacity utilization, or the extent to which the economy approaches full employment. Tables 3 and 4 give information about the performance of the real economy during these years.

On all of the indicators in Tables 3 and 4 the US economy performed better than the UK economy. Both countries experienced a recession with a low point occurring in 1981 in the UK, and 1982 in the US. However, in Britain unemployment rose to record heights, and remained there. In

TABLE 3
US economic performance 1979–84

	Gross national product	Consumer price index	Unemployment rate	Industrial production	Investment (gross private)
1979	100.3	88.1	5.8	103.7	105.3
1980	100.0	100.0	7.0	100.0	100.0
1981	102.5	110.4	7.5	102.7	120.5
1982	100.3	117.1	9.5	94.3	103.2
1983	104.0	120.9	9.5	100.4	117.3
1984	111.2	126.1	7.4	111.2	158.5

Source: *Economic Indicators* February (1985).

TABLE 4
Britain's economic performance 1979–84

	Gross domestic product	Index retail prices	Unemployment (millions)	Manufacturing output	Investment (GDCF)
1979	103.0	84.8	1.24	107.0	105.5
1980	100.0	100.0	1.51	100.0	100.0
1981	98.3	119.9	2.56	96.4	91.5
1982	100.3	121.5	2.94	98.1	97.6
1983	103.2	127.1	3.10	101.3	101.7
1984	104.8	132.9	3.09	101.1	103.2

Source: HMSO (1984b).

the US unemployment rose, but fell to nearly pre-recession levels by 1984. In the UK, manufacturing output fell by more than 10 percent in two years, whereas in the US it rebounded from a low point in 1982 to reach levels well above those of 1979 by the end of the period. No such rebound occurred in the UK.

These figures broadly indicate that Britain experienced a depression rather than a recession, and the effects of this were felt up to 1984 and beyond. The experience of the US was very different.

There are many structural and cultural differences between the UK and US economies which might be used to account for such outcomes. However, we will concentrate on the macroeconomic policies of the two governments. As we have seen monetary policy was rather tighter in the UK than in the US, but the differences between the two countries were not very large. The key difference between the two governments was the fiscal stance. The US budget deficit increased rapidly, fuelled by large tax cuts and increases in defence spending. By contrast the UK budget deficit declined, despite rising defence spending and an increase in social security expenditure of about 25 percent in real terms (HMSO, 1985b). The latter was largely a product of the rapidly rising unemployment. Essentially US fiscal policy stimulated the economy by what might be described as 'Warfare Keynesianism'. By contrast UK fiscal policy squeezed the economy, even though the Conservatives did not achieve their planned reductions in expenditure. Buiter and Miller (1981, 1983) in their analysis of the Thatcher government's economic performance concluded that the fiscal squeeze imposed by this government made the recession much deeper than it otherwise would have been.

In fact the fiscal squeeze in the UK was greater than the figures in Table 2 would suggest, since the fiscal stance has to be judged in relation to capacity utilization. In 1984 the UK had a budget deficit of some 3.8 percent of GDP with an unemployment rate just over 13 percent. By contrast the US had a budget deficit of 5.1 percent of GNP with an unemployment rate of 7.4 percent. Total output was much further below capacity in the UK than in the US, which would in more normal times have called for a larger budget deficit.

The primary focus of this paper in monetary policy, and the relationship between the money supply and inflation. It can be seen that these relationships appear to be rather confusing. The money supply in nominal terms grew faster in Britain than in the United States in each year except 1984. At the same time inflation was more rapid in the former country compared with the latter. However, the money supply in constant prices grew more slowly in Britain than in the United States. By this criteria UK monetary policy was tighter than that of the US. Obviously it is impossible to assess the relationship between monetary policy and inflation in these countries over such a short period of time. There is a need to look at a longer period in order to assess the links. Before doing this, however, it is important to examine the effectiveness of monetary control. We have seen that monetary targets were exceeded by a considerable margin in both countries. It appears to be very difficult for governments to control the money supply in line with plans. We examine reasons for this next.

Can the money supply be controlled?

In their theoretical models monetarists typically assume that the central bank can fairly easily control the money supply either directly by acting on the cash base or indirectly by acting on interest rates. However, even for the moment assuming that a strong and stable relationship exists between the money supply and inflation, the government would find it very difficult to control inflation by monetary means. This is because of what has become known as 'Goodhart's Law' after Charles Goodhart, the chief economist at the Bank of England who first suggested it. It states:

'any observed statistical regularity will tend to collapse once pressure is placed upon it for control purposes!' (Goodhart, 1981: 116). This is true for a number of reasons.

The first reason concerns the measurement of the quantity of money. In both Britain and the United States it varies from M1, a narrow definition of money consisting of notes and coins in circulation and short-term deposits in Banks, to M3 which, as we pointed out earlier, is a broader measure including interest bearing deposits in banks (Bain, 1982: 17–20). In Britain PSL1 and PSL2 (private sector liquidity) are even broader measures which attempt to capture the notion of liquidity and which include various additional measures of credit. If a government attempts to control, say M1 then the financial community would circumvent it by using credit as a money substitute. If it used M3 then financial markets would use forms of credit not included in the definition of M3. It cannot really control PSL1 or PSL2 because they are so broadly based. Thus in an advanced industrial society with a sophisticated financial system it is difficult if not impossible to precisely define money, and as a consequence even more difficult to control it. There are many money substitutes which can be used to get round government restrictions (Balogh, 1982). Moreover, as credit cards become increasingly used to settle day-to-day transactions, this task becomes even harder, since within defined limits credit card users create their own money. They can spend more than their current incomes, and thereby create money in a way which cannot be done in a purely cash economy.

A second factor which helps to explain Goodhart's Law concerns the reactions of banks to government monetary policy. In 1971 and 1972 the Conservative government in Britain was trying to bring about faster economic growth by accelerating monetary growth and pursuing reflationary fiscal policies. By mid-1973 there were clear signs of overheating in the economy and so the authorities sharply increased interest rates. This had the effect of reducing the rate of growth of M1, but M3 continued to surge ahead despite the increased costs of borrowing. This was because banks were competing aggressively for business and were willing to allow their 'blue-chip' customers to borrow at a lower rate than the current market rate of interest. Theoretically, if individuals or companies can borrow at a lower rate in one market than they can receive interest payments in another their demand for loans should be infinite. Thus M3 continued to grow because companies increased their borrowing in order to make arbitrage profits (Goodhart, 1984: 103). This frustrated the government's attempts to control the money supply at that time. Clearly, even when the supply of money can be precisely defined, problems arise from the behaviour of institutions which can create credit, when governments attempt to control the quantity of money.

A third factor relates to interest rates. As we mentioned earlier monetarists generally assume that the demand for money is a stable function of the rate of interest. This means that governments can control the demand for money by raising interest rates. However, as we show, the demand for money is not a stable function of interest rates in either Britain or the United States, a fact which further helps to explain 'Goodhart's Law'. The events of 1980–1 in the UK illustrate this point rather well. At that time companies were forced to undertake 'distress' borrowing, even though interest rates were at penal levels, merely in order to stay in business. This meant that at a certain point interest rates became an ineffective policy instrument for controlling the creation of credit.

An additional factor which can frustrate government attempts to constrain money demand is the international financial system and the policies of other governments. Since the collapse of the Bretton Woods system of exchange controls in 1971–2 international currencies have been floating against each other with varying degrees of flexibility. Large amounts of short-term cash and credit exist such as the Petrocurrency funds and the huge Eurodollar market; such funds seek to maximize their earnings by moving around the world to different financial centres. This has created ever increasing currency instability as speculative movements trigger subsequent speculative action. The Keynesian analysis of the influence of expectations on the demand for money has become ever more relevant (Keynes, 1936: 147–64). The dollar, pound or mark can change values in a short period of time in ways quite unrelated to the underlying strengths or weaknesses of the US, UK or German economies. This means that the domestic supply of money is influenced by international currency speculation which may have little to do with current government policies. To the extent that this is true then governments cannot control the money supply. Some of the EEC member countries, notably France and West Germany, have been partly insulated from this by their membership of the European Monetary System, or the currency 'snake', but Britain has not joined this system of partially pegged exchange rates. Thus to the extent that UK or US monetary variables are influenced by global inflation, it is clearly impossible for one government to pursue an independent monetary policy.

We next examine the relationship between the money supply and inflation.

Does the money supply cause inflation?

We pointed out earlier that one of the key propositions of monetarism was that the money supply does not directly influence real income, and thus increases in the quantity of money above that warranted by exogenously determined rates of growth of the real economy will produce inflation.

The most comprehensive and definitive statement of monetarist theory was provided by Friedman and Schwartz (1982) in a book consisting of more than 600 pages of painstaking theoretical and empirical analysis. The latter was based on US and British data over a 100-year period. They concluded:

> Our data are consistent with the theoretical expectation that the cumulative effect of a 1 percentage point change in monetary growth will be a 1 percentage point change in the same direction in the rate of nominal income growth. (p.7)

and

> The results are consistent with a simple quantity theory that regards price change as determined primarily by monetary change and output by independent other factors. (p.8)

Thus is if the money supply determines nominal income, and the growth in output is determined exogenously, this implies that excessive growth in the money supply causes inflation.

However, in a technically complex and empirically sophisticated analysis of the UK data, Hendry and Ericsson (1983) have systematically attacked Friedman and Schwartz's conclusion. They have argued:

> A number of assertions in Friedman and Schwartz (1982) concerning the empirical validity of their money demand equation have been tested using their data series for the United Kingdom and were found to be without empirical support. (1983: 82)

They criticize Friedman and Schwartz for not following contemporary econometric practice, and for adjusting the data in arbitrary ways to make the results conform more readily with theoretical preconceptions.

Friedman and Schwartz's basic model is very simple and can be summarized by Figure 1. They argue that the demand for money in constant prices is a stable function of two basic variables: real national income and the differential yield on nominal asset which is a function of the short-term rate of interest (Friedman and Schwartz, 1982: 280–7). In addition they include two dummy variables as controls in their demand for money equation: the first measures the impact of the great depression and the war years, and the second measures monetary expansion caused by the removal of wartime controls on currencies. The demand for money is a positive function of real income since increases in real income require increased stocks of money to finance them. It is a negative function of the rate of interest since interest foregone is the price of holding money. The demand for money is equated with the supply of money which is assumed to be exogenously determined by government and this causes inflation. It is important to note that if the money supply was measured in current rather than constant prices then the rate of inflation would be included as an independent variable influencing the demand for money without any lags. The authors would not accept that past inflation causally influences the current quality of money, although they would accept that it is

FIGURE 1
Friedman and Schwartz's theoretical model

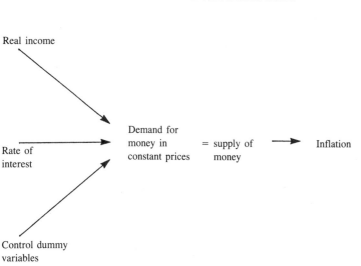

contemporaneously correlated with it. This interpretation has implications for our later analysis of their model.

In the light of Hendry and Ericsson's theoretical critique it is interesting to examine the relationship between the money supply, national income and inflation in the United States and in Britain using Friedman and Schwartz's data which consists of annual observations for more than a century (1982: 30–7). This is done using the Box-Jenkins transfer function modelling procedure which is a generalization of the intervention modelling strategy (Box and Jenkins, 1976). The Box-Jenkins method allows one to determine whether or not one series 'Granger-Causes' another. The idea of Granger causation provides a rigorous theoretical definition of causation applied to time series analysis (Granger, 1969; Freeman, 1983). Briefly, one series X_t is said to cause another series Y_t if after extracting all the information from the past behaviour of Y_t the use of X_t as predictor reduces the error variance of Y_t. In other words X_t causes Y_t if it explains variance in Y_t after the past behaviour of Y_t has been taken into account. The Box-Jenkins approach is ideally suited to investigating Granger causality.

The starting point of this analysis was Friedman and Schwartz's basic model set out in Figure 2. This was evaluated in the light of the various diagnostic tests involved in transfer function estimation, in order to determine which variables Granger-Caused with other variables.[1]

FIGURE 2
The causal links between the money supply, interest rates,
real income and inflation in the
United States 1870–1975

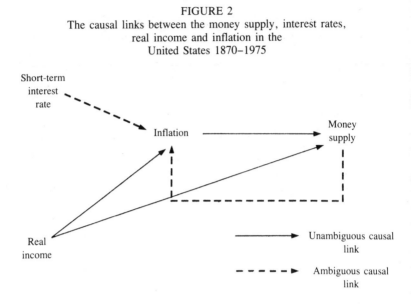

The United States models
Table 5 contains the transfer function models of the demand for money and inflation in the United States. The model in this table differs from the model adduced by Friedman and Schwartz in a number of key respects. Firstly, the demand for money function depends on the current and lagged values of inflation. Thus inflation Granger-Causes the money supply, and is not just contemporaneously associated with it, as is implied in Figure 1. This complicates the entire theory and has serious implications for counter inflation policy since it implies that one of the preconditions for a reduction in inflation via monetary policy is a reduction in inflation!

However, an even more fundamental point is that in terms of Granger causality inflation causes the money supply, but the causal influence of the money supply on inflation is ambiguous. This is because there is a lag in the former relationship, but no lag in the latter. Lags provide unambiguous evidence of causation, so that the absence of a lag makes it hard to decide the actual causal link.

An additional problem for a monetarist interpretation of the data involves the strengths of the relationship between the money supply and inflation. The combined effect of inflation on the money supply in the first equation is 0.50 (i.e. 0.28 plus 0.22) after one year. In the second equation the effect of the money supply on inflation is 0.37. Thus inflation has a larger influence on the money supply than the money supply has on inflation.

TABLE 5
Friedman and Schwartz's models of the money supply and
inflation in the United States 1870–1975

Money supply (M_t)

$$\nabla \ln \nabla M_t = + \frac{\overset{(4.9)}{(2.87}\ \overset{(1.1)}{-\ 0.19B^2)}}{\underset{(5.0)}{(1 + 0.67B^1)}}\ \nabla \ln \nabla RINC_t + \underset{(3.2)}{(0.28}\ +\ \underset{(2.6)}{0.22B)}\ \nabla \ln \nabla INF_t$$

$$-\ \underset{(0.89)}{0.05}\ \nabla \ln \nabla INT_t + a_t \underset{(6.1)}{(1 - 0.53B)}$$

RMS = 0.109;   URMS = 0.154; $F(^m_{n\text{-}k}) = 68.59$;   Q = 21., 20d.f.

Inflation (INF_t)

$$\nabla \ln \nabla INF_t = \underset{(4.0)}{0.37}\ \nabla \ln \nabla M_t + \underset{(2.4)}{0.47}\ \nabla \ln \nabla INT_t + \underset{(2.0)}{1.07}\ \nabla \ln \nabla RINC_{t-7}$$

$$+\ \frac{a_t}{\underset{(5.8)}{1 + 0.52B^1}}$$

RMS = 0.155;   URMS = 0.18   Q = 27, 20d.f.

Note: RMS = Residual Mean Square Statistic; URMS = RMS of Univariate model.

One commonly stated explanation of this relationship is that neo-Keynesian governments are willing to accommodate inflation by expanding the money supply in order to avoid recession (Buchanan and Wagner, 1977). For this reason inflation produces an increase in the money supply which produces more inflation still. However, this idea cannot explain the present evidence, for the simple reason that for about 70 percent of our estimation period Keynesianism did not exist. Before the Second World War governments generally expressed an official ideology of balancing the budget in line with classical economic theories. This was certainly true in Britain, and was also true in the United States prior to the New Deal. Thus the influence of inflation on the money supply is not a Keynesian phenomenon.

Most probably, this relationship derives from the weakness of government control over the economy in an advanced industrial society. The institutions and mechanisms for creating credit are not under the control of the government, for reasons discussed earlier, and so inflation stimulates the money supply because it is profitable for banks to create credit in inflationary times. Short of full nationalization of the banking system together with tight control over foreign trade, it is hard to see how government can prevent this.

A third important difference between the estimates in Table 5 and the Friedman and Schwartz model concerns the causal influence of real income. Real income has a causal influence on inflation as well as on the money supply. The link between real income and inflation involves rather a long lag, but it does operate independently of the money supply. The most plausible interpretation of this relationship is that it is linked to the business cycle. Thus growth in real incomes institutionalizes expectations which stimulate inflation in the downswing phase of the business cycle. Those expectations continue even after real growth has slowed down, thereby generating inflation. Again this complicates counter-inflation policy.

A fourth complication is that the short-term rate of interest is a significant predictor of inflation, but not a significant predictor of the money supply. However, the causal relationships in both models are ambiguous due to the absence of lags. Most probably the first of these relationships is an effect of inflation rather than a cause, since interest rates have to maintain a premium above inflation if lenders are to receive a real rate of return. However, the absence of a relationship between interest rates and the money supply is potentially the most devastating for monetarist counter-inflation policy. If interest rates, which can be manipulated by the government, cannot be used to restrain the growth of the money supply then it is hard to see how the money supply can be controlled. This evidence goes a long way towards explaining the increases in the money supply in the US of above 10 percent during the early 1980s, when interest rates were at a historically high level.

Finally, a fifth complication for monetarist counter-inflation policy concerns the stability of the demand for money equation. Friedman and Schwartz assert that the demand for money equation is stable over time. As we mentioned earlier this is an important requirement of monetarist counter-inflation policy. However, a parameter stability test applied to the demand for money equation shows that the model parameters have significantly shifted over time. Thus Friedman and Schwartz are quite wrong in asserting that the demand for money equation is stable. The instability can be inferred from the Chow test, the F test appearing below the money supply equation in Table 5. It is highly statistically significant which shows that the model parameters shifted in the second half of the estimation period in comparison with the first half. Clearly, if the demand for money equation shifted over time it cannot easily be used to control the quantity of money.

Taken as a whole this evidence suggests that the quantity of money in the economy is largely demand-determined. Changes in real income and in inflation call forth additional supplies of money to finance them. This interpretation accords with the analysis by Kaldor (1982), and others. In his view there is a crucial difference between a commodity money economy typically based on a gold standard, and a credit money economy. In the former case money has an independent supply function based on its costs of production, in the latter it comes into existence by the action of banks, financial institutions and credit card users. Central banks can influence the rate of interest but they cannot control the quantity of money which is largely determined by the growth of nominal incomes. Thurow (1983) makes a similar point.

The United Kingdom models
The UK models of the money supply and inflation appear in Table 6, and they tell a similar story to the US models. Inflation has a bigger causal influence on the money supply than the money supply has on inflation. Real income exerts a stronger influence on inflation than it does on the money supply. Also the demand for money equation is unstable, since the Chow test is statistically significant.

The major difference between the UK and US models concerns the role of short-term interest rates. In the UK the rate of interest has a significant influence on the money supply, although again the causal influences are ambiguous because of the absence of lags. In the inflation equation the interest rate does not have a statistically significant effect at any lag. This accords more closely with monetarist theoretical arguments than in the US, but the other differences mentioned above do not make monetarist counter-inflation policy any more feasible in the UK.

TABLE 6
Friedman and Schwartz's models of the money supply and inflation
in Britain 1872–1975

Money Supply (M_t)

$$\nabla \ln \nabla M_t = + (0.22\ B^2 + 0.18\ B^4)\ \nabla \ln \nabla RINC_t + 0.93\ \nabla \ln \nabla INF_{t-1}$$
$$\quad\quad\quad (4.1)\quad\quad (2.0)\quad\quad\quad\quad\quad\quad (6.1)$$

$$\quad - 0.35\ \ \nabla \ln \nabla INT_t + a_t\ (1- 0.43\ B^2)$$
$$\quad (2.7)\quad\quad\quad\quad\quad (4.4)$$

$$RMS = 0.16\ ,\quad URMS = 0.47\quad F(\tfrac{m}{n\text{-}k}) = 8.59\quad Q = 28.0,\ 20\text{d.f.}$$

Inflation

$$\nabla \ln \nabla INF_t = 0.09\ \ \nabla \ln \nabla M_{t-1} + (0.30\ B^2 + 0.57\ B^3)\ \nabla \ln \ \nabla RINC_t$$
$$\quad\quad\quad (3.0)\quad\quad\quad\quad (9.7)\quad\quad (18.3)$$

$$\quad + a_t\ (1\ -\ 0.57\ B^2)$$
$$\quad (5.9)$$

$$RMS = 0.04\ ,\quad URMS = 0.21\quad Q = 21,\ 20\text{d.f.}$$

In explaining the difference between the US and the UK with regard to interest rates it is important to remember that for most of the estimation period the UK had a more developed financial system than the US. Not merely did London act as a financial centre for the Empire and other European economies, but there were few restrictions on the development of credit-creating institutions in the UK in comparison with the US. It seems plausible that the influence of interest rates on the money supply operates primarily through credit rather than through the cash base. Thus a more developed and sophisticated credit economy will be more responsive to changes in interest rates than a less developed financial system. This could explain the differences.

Overall the UK evidence further supports the analysis that the quantity of money in the economy is largely demand-determined, and that the relationships between the macroeconomic variables preclude an effective monetarist counter-inflation policy.

Discussion
The evidence relating to the US and UK economies both in recent years and in the longer term suggests that monetary policy is rather ineffective in controlling inflation. Both the Reagan and Thatcher governments embarked on monetarist experiments, although the Thatcher government placed a much greater emphasis on monetarism than the Reagan administration. Neither succeeded in controlling the money supply in line with initial plans, but this did not greatly affect the political position of the Reagan government since it achieved a reduction in inflation by stimulating a fiscally induced boom in the US economy, which paved the way for a resounding election victory in 1984. The rapid economic growth accompanying the burgeoning budget deficit reduced inflationary pressure, and made the issue less politically salient.

By contrast, the Thatcher government initiated a fiscal squeeze which drastically affected the real economy, and which ultimately reduced both the growth in the money supply and inflation. This of course presents a puzzle: if the UK recession was so bad why did the Conservatives win such a clear-cut victory in the General Election of 1983? The answer to this puzzle lies in two classes of factors. The first involves the importance of non-economic issues in the 1983 election, and the second involves a disjunction between the voters' perceptions of economic performance, and the actual economic performance.

To consider the first, the main non-economic issue influencing the election of 1983 was the Falklands War. Victory in the war in 1982 gave the Conservatives an immediate boost to their popularity which was sustained until the general election. According to one estimate the 'Falklands factor' added 6 percent to the Conservative vote in that election, raising it from 38 percent to 44 percent of the popular vote (Norpoth, 1986).

Another non-economic issue was the disarray of Labour, the main opposition party. The party split in 1981, and was beset by internecine conflict from that time up to the election. Thus the main alternative party to the Conservatives, lacked credibility (Whiteley, 1983).

The second major influence on the election campaign relates to the impact of the economy on electoral behaviour. It is clear that voter perceptions of economic performance have a major influence on electoral support (Whiteley, 1984). However, it is also clear that actual economic performance has a much less significant impact on the vote than perceptions of performance in both the US and Britain (Norpoth and Yantek, 1983; Whiteley, 1986). In other words, there is a disjunction between perceptions and actual performance. The precise nature of this disjunction has yet to be fully explored, but for our purposes it means that the Conservatives did not pay a significant electoral 'price' for the rapid increase in unemployment. They succeeded in convincing many voters that governments could do very little about the problem, and therefore even if their own record was poor, the opposition party record would be no better. This diffused the electoral threat of the issue to the Conservative government.

Conclusions

Our central concern in this chapter has been to examine the extent to which governments can control their economies by means of monetary policy. We have discovered that both the Thatcher and Reagan administrations were unable to control the money supply in line with their objectives, and furthermore even if they had been able to do this, it would not have strongly influenced the rate of inflation.

There are of course institutional differences between Britain and the United States in terms of the mechanisms of monetary control. In the US the Federal Reserve controls monetary policy, and it is nominally independent of the Executive. However, most specialists in this area do not attach great importance to the formal Constitutional position (Beck, 1982; Woolley, 1984). The Federal Reserve does not generally pursue a monetary policy which is diametrically opposed to the wishes of an incumbent President. Thus the institutional differences do not amount to much. In any case the institutional differences between the US, with its separation of powers, and the UK with its highly centralized executive, did not produce very large differences in performance, with regard to monetary control. The really large difference between the two countries was in the fiscal policies of the governments. The US fiscal stance was very loose, whereas the UK fiscal stance was very tight. Thus differences in real outcomes reflect differences in fiscal policy rather than monetary policy.

In conclusion, this analysis attests to the importance of fiscal policy, rather than monetary policy in macroeconomic management. It appears to be very difficult for governments to control the money supply in an advanced industrial society, and even if they could this policy would not be sufficient to control inflation. This is the lesson that the Monetarist 'experiments' in the two countries teaches.

Note

1. Granger causation implies two things. First, the independent variable X_t should significantly reduce the error of variance in the dependent variable Y_t in comparison with a univariate ARIMA model of the latter. Second, it implies that X_t influences Y_t with a lag; in the absence of such a lag the causal links are ambiguous.

References

Bain, A. D. (1982) *The Control of the Money Supply*. Harmondsworth, Middlesex: Penguin.

Ball, R. J. (1982) *Money and Employment*. London: Macmillan.

Balogh, T. (1982) *The Irrelevance of Conventional Economics*. London: Weidenfeld and Nicolson.

Beck, N. (1982) 'Presidential Influence on the Federal Reserve in the 1970s', *American Journal of Political Science*, 26: 415–45.

Bosanquet, N. (1983) *After the New Right*. London: Heinemann.

Box, G. E. P. and G. M. Jenkins (1976) *Time Series Analysis, Forecasting and Control*. San Francisco: Holden-Day.

Bryant, R. C. (1983) *Controlling Money: The Federal Reserve and Its Critics*. Washington: The Brookings Institution.

Buchanan, J. M. and R. E. Wagner (1977) *Democracy in Deficit: The Political Legacy of Lord Keynes*. New York: Academic Press.

Buiter, W. H. (1980) 'The Macroeconomics of Dr Pangloss. A Critical Survey of the New Classical Macroeconomics', *Economic Journal*, 9: 34–50.

Buiter, W. H. and M. Miller (1981) 'The Thatcher Experiment; The First Two Years', pp. 315–79 in *Brookings Papers on Economic Activity*, 2. Washington: The Brookings Institution.

Buiter, W. H. and M. Miller (1983) 'Changing the Rules: Economic Consequences of the Thatcher Regime', pp. 305–65 in *Brookings Papers on Economic Activity*, 2. Washington: The Brookings Institution.

Council of Economic Advisers (1982) *Annual Report*. Washington: US Government.

Council of Economic Advisers (1985) *Annual Report*. Washington: US Government.

Desai, M. (1981) *Testing Monetarism*. London: Frances Pinter.

Economic Indicators (1985) (February). Washington: US Government.

Economic Report of the President (1982) Washington: US Government.

Fiorina, M. P. (1981) *Retrospective Voting in American National Elections*. New Haven: Yale University Press.

Freeman, J. (1983) 'Granger Causality and Time Series Analysis of Political Relationships', *American Journal of Political Science*, 27: 325–58.

Friedman, M. (1968) 'The Role of Monetary Policy', *American Economic Review*, 63(1): 1–17.

Friedman, M. and A. Schwartz (1982) *Monetary Trends in the United States and the United Kingdom*. Chicago/London: University of Chicago Press.

Goodhart, C. A. (1981) 'Problems of Monetary Management: The UK Experience', in A. S. Courakis (ed.) *Inflation, Depression and Economic Policy in the West*. London: Mansell.

Goodhart, C. A. (1984) *Monetary Theory and Practice*. London: Macmillan.

Granger, C. W. J. (1969) 'Investigating Causal Relations by Econometric Models and Cross Spectoral Methods', *Econometrica*, 37: 424–35.

Heclo, M. and R. G. Penner (1983) 'Fiscal and Political Strategy in the Reagan Administration', in F. Greenstein (ed.) *The Reagan Presidency*. Baltimore/London: The Johns Hopkins University Press.

Hendry, D. F. and N. R. Ericsson (1983) 'Assertion without Empirical Basis: An Econometric Appraisal of Friedman and Schwartz's "Monetary Trends in . . . the United Kingdom"', in Bank of England Panel of Academic Consultants, panel paper No. 22. London: Bank of England.

HMSO (1980) *The Government's Expenditure Plans 1980–81 to 1983–84*, Cmnd 7841. London: HMSO.

HMSO (1984a) *Monthly Digest of Statistics*, 467 (November). London: HMSO.

HMSO (1984b) *Economic Trends Annual Supplement 1984*. London: HMSO.

HMSO (1985a) *The Government's Expenditure Plans 1985–86 to 1987–88*. Cmnd 9428, Vol. II. London: HMSO.

HMSO (1985b) *Economic Trends*, 375 (January). London: HMSO.

Kaldor, N. (1982) *The Scourge of Monetarism*. Oxford: Oxford University Press.

Kavanagh, N. J. and A. A. Walters (1966) 'Demand for Money in the UK 1877–1961: Some Preliminary Findings', *Bulletin of the Oxford University Institute of Economics and Statistics*: 93–116.

Keegan, W. and R. Pennant-Rea (1979) *Who Runs the Economy?* London: Maurice Temple Smith.

Keman, H. and F. Lehner (1984) 'Economic Crisis and Political Management: An Introduction to the Problems of Politico-economic Interdependence', *European Journal of Political Research*, 12: 121–30.

Keynes, J. M. (1936) *The General Theory of Employment, Interest and Money*. London: Macmillan.

Laidler, D. (1981) 'Monetarism: An Interpretation and an Assessment', *Economic Journal*, 91: 1–28.

Lindberg, L. N. (1985) 'Models of the Inflation-disinflation Process', pp. 25–50 in L. N. Lindberg and C. S. Maier (eds) *The Politics of Inflation and Economic Stagnation*. Washington: The Brookings Institution.

Meltzer, A. M. (1963) 'The Demand for Money: The Evidence from Time Series', *Journal of Political Economy*, 71: 219–46.

Modigliani, F. (1977) 'The Monetarist Controversy, or Should We Forsake Stabilization Policies?', *American Economic Review*, 67: 1–19.

Niehans, J. (1981) 'The Appreciation of Sterling — Causes, Effects and Policies', SSRC Money Study Group Discussion Paper. New York: SSRC.

Norpoth, H. (1986) 'War and Government Popularity in Britain'. SUNY: Stony Brook, Mimeo.

Norpoth, H. and T. Yantek (1983) 'Macro Economic Conditions and Fluctuations of Presidential Popularity: The Question of Lagged Effects', *American Journal of Political Science*, 27: 785–807.

Office of Management and Budgeting (1981) *Fiscal Year 1982 Budget Revisions*, March. Washington: US Government.

Paloheimo, H. (1984) 'Distributive Struggle and Economic Development in the 1970s in Developed Capitalist Countries', *European Journal of Political Research*, 12: 171–90.

Purvis, D. D. (1980) 'Monetarism — a Review', *Canadian Journal of Economics*, 1: 96–121.

Rose, R. (1980) *Do Parties Make a Difference?* London: Macmillan.

Scharpf, F. W. (1983) 'Economic and Institutional Constraints of Full Employment Strategies:

Sweden, Austria, and West Germany, 1973–1982', pp. 257–90 in J. H. Goldthorpe (ed.) *Order and Conflict in Contemporary Capitalism.* Oxford: Clarendon Press.

Schmidt, M. G. (1982) 'The Role of Parties in Shaping Macroeconomic Policy', pp. 97–176 in F. Castles (ed.) *The Impact of Parties.* London/Beverly Hills: Sage.

Stein, H. (1984) *Presidential Economics.* New York: Simon and Schuster.

Thurow, L. (1983) *Dangerous Currents: The State of Economics.* Oxford: Oxford University Press.

Whiteley, P. (1983) *The Labour Party in Crisis.* London: Methuen.

Whiteley, P. (1984) 'Perceptions of Economic Performance and Voting Behavior in the 1983 General Election in Britain', *Political Behavior,* 6: 395–410.

Whiteley, P. (1986) 'Macroeconomic Performance and Government Popularity in Britain — The Short Run Dynamics', *European Journal of Political Research,* 14: 45–61.

Whitman, M. V. (1975) 'Global Monetarism and the Monetary Approach to the Balance of Payments', pp. 491–551 in *Brookings Papers on Economic Activity,* 3. Washington: The Brookings Institution.

Wildavsky, A. (1980) *Speaking Truth to Power.* Boston: Little Brown.

Woolley, J. T. (1984) *Monetary Politics.* Cambridge: Cambridge University Press.

9

Coping with crisis:
divergent strategies and outcomes

Hans Keman and Paul F. Whiteley

Introduction

What can be learnt from the various contributions to this book with respect to the explanation of the nature and magnitude of the present economic crisis? Economic stagnation and its ill-effects in terms of high rates of unemployment and inflation are not natural disasters and thus not inevitable consequences of the course of capitalist development. At the same time it does not appear helpful to follow the elegant but relatively technocratic analyses of many economists. Their work is certainly useful in helping to map out the various causes and consequences of the present crisis (as has been elaborated in Chapter 1 by Heikki Paloheimo), but their freely given advice to governments has not yet had the desired effects (see also Lindberg and Maier, 1985). Finally we have seen that the relationship between policy formation, i.e. making choices, selecting instruments and developing feasible strategies to cope with this crisis is not straightforward. It implies outcomes which are often not compatible with the preferences of powerful socio-economic actors or of the voting public (Whiteley, 1986).

It also appears that the economy does not always respond to the policy instruments used, even if the relevant political and societal actors have decided to co-operate with a given strategy. The persistent pattern of stagflation (i.e. high unemployment and inflation) has, for instance, led Niskanen (1986) to argue that political economists should learn from the 1980s that no 'school', be it monetarist, supply-sider or Keynesian, has developed an adequate diagnosis of the problems, let alone a suitable therapy. For example, budget-deficits, which are considered by most Keynesians to be the appropriate policy instrument to manage the business cycle, have produced some degree of recovery in only some countries; monetarists, on the other hand, should be able to account for the fact that a high growth rate of the money supply in many of the countries under review here did not result in an increase of inflation. Indeed, in some of these countries there was even a decrease in the rate of inflation; finally, supply-siders ought to explain why considerable cuts in the levels of taxation have not produced a concurrent growth of economic activity.

According to Niskanen several factors may account for the poor record of prescriptive macroeconomic theory:

1. The fact that the public economy is difficult to control and continues to induce unintended budget deficits.
2. Public incentives to get the private economy going again seem to be less effective than is often assumed.
3. Policy co-ordination appears to be much more difficult to achieve than is often expected.

It is precisely at this point when perhaps economists must remain silent that political scientists may step in. The relationship between economic analysis and the political responses is much more complex and less straightforward than many economists think. Therefore we focused explicitly in this book on the relationship between politics and the economy, with a special emphasis on the institutional aspects of policy-making, and on the political factors that underlie the relationship between strategy and performance. All contributors shared the belief that the present economic crisis cannot be adequately understood either as a consequence of inevitable natural forces, or as the result of political mismanagement. Political factors and social and economic structures are therefore included in the analysis. In addition, we focused on the relationship between government, the public, office-holders, interest groups and the state, in order to research the relationship between political and institutional variables. We try to understand the significance of these factors for the explanation of economic performance within capitalist democracies.

In Part II we focused mainly on the relationship between political actors and institutions which lead to the choice of a particular economic strategy. One particular point of interest was whether the existing approach of the 'Logic of Collective Action' (cf. Olson, 1982) should be complemented with a 'Logic of Accommodation' (cf. Crouch, 1985). We hold the view that this may not only improve our knowledge of the relationship between policy choice and implementation, but also why this relationship appears to be so hazardous and prone to induce failure.

In Part III we have concentrated on the relationship between different strategies and economic performance. The fact that this relationship is relatively weak has received, in our opinion, too little attention in much of the political and economic literature. This is mainly due to the neglect of 'contextual' variables, i.e. those factors which may appear unrelated to the policy-making process, but which nevertheless influence it in the final analysis. In particular, the interaction between internal and external factors needs to be emphasized, together with the complex relationship between social structure and events (see for this Keman and Lehner, 1984). If the relationships between policy choice, strategies and outcomes are not viewed from such a perspective, then analysts are unlikely to be able to give an adequate account of economic policy in advanced capitalist societies.

We shall therefore conclude this chapter by pointing out what remains to be done and which avenues for further research need to be explored.

Two logics of political behaviour
In much recent literature one finds typologies of interest group behaviour which can be applied to the political processes of capitalist democracies (e.g. Goldthorpe, 1984; Katzenstein, 1985; Lindberg and Maier, 1985; Braun and Keman, 1986). To a large extent these typologies are over-lapping, since they all described the degree and mode of state intervention in advanced industrial countries, with special reference to the role of interest groups. According to this literature there are three dominant forms of capitalism: 'Liberalism' in the Anglo-Saxon countries, 'Statism' in countries like France and Japan, and 'Corporatism' in the smaller European countries and the Federal Republic of Germany (see Katzenstein, 1985: 20ff.).

Lindberg and Maier have linked these types to three different forms of interest representation which are consistently associated with certain models of economic policy. The first type is often associated with a strategy of relying on market mechanisms; the second is associated with pluralist forms of interest-intermediation; and the third can best be labelled as neocorporatist. Unlike Katzenstein, both Lindberg and Maier and Braun and Keman view this typology as a continuum rather than as distinct categories. All three types, and the related forms of interest group behaviour, can occur in every type of capitalist democracy, but with varying degrees of probability. In fact, Lindberg and Maier see a develop-ment from market-oriented policy strategies toward more neocorporatist approaches. Braun and Keman stress the role of structural and historical conditions which enhance the neocorporatist behaviour of the relevant political and societal actors, but which also leave room for developments in an opposite direction if certain conditions are absent. At this point we think Katzenstein's analysis to be helpful, since it spells out in great detail where and why such conditions are likely to prevail. These conditions are:
1. The existence of an ideology of social partnership.
2. A centralized and concentrated system of interest groups.
3. A voluntary and informal co-ordination of policy-making.

The development and existence of these conditions mark in principle a movement from conflict to co-operation in economic policy-making, or a shift from the problems of the 'logic of collective action' to the 'logic of accommodation'. This relationship and its influence on policy-making are comprehensively researched and discussed in Part II.

Roland Czada explicitly compares both these 'logics' by comparing Katzenstein's ideas with those of Olson. The main focus in on the policies of industrial adjustment as a response to the 'oil-shock'. He thinks it necessary to modify the views held by both authors in the light of his empirical analysis. In those countries that are neither wholly pluralist nor liberal–corporatist, it appears that bureaucratic and electoral politics do matter with respect to strategies and implementation.

Czada's analysis is, by and large, supported by Franz Lehner, who criticizes Olson for stressing the negative effects of interest intermediation between powerful producer groups in capitalist society. Lehner shows that, contrary to Olson, in Japan and Switzerland there has been no decline in economic performance. He explains this by pointing to the degree of 'inclusion' of interest groups in Switzerland and the degree of policy 'integration' in Japan. If such a process can be repeated elsewhere or extended where it exists, it may very well lead to favourable policy outcomes. According to Lehner, these conditions do not exist in the US and the UK. Hence in these countries the prospects for an effective management of the economy are slim.

Esping-Andersen and Armingeon provided us with a detailed analyses of the possibilities of corporatist policy-making. However, they both examine the limitations of this form of state intervention in capitalist society. Armingeon argues that the value of corporatist policy-making is largely symbolic rather than substantive. Esping-Andersen develops the point that the trade-off between full employment and Welfare Statism is in the final analysis incompatible with capitalism. Hence, although corporatism appears to be able to weather economic stagnation, its 'logic of accommodation' is also constrained by the 'logic of capitalism'.

The observations of Armingeon and Esping-Andersen point to important features of the relationship between the choice of a strategy, and its implementation; institutional factors appear to be equi-functional, but apparently stagflation is detrimental to the success of corporatist modes of state intervention. This is because, on the one hand, there is a fading away of the 'symbolic' value of corporatism, and on the other, because positive sum-games are simply not feasible any more. It is therefore clear why most of the smaller European, corporatist countries show such a poor performance during the 1980s, after the second 'oil-shock'.

These findings may oblige us to rethink much of the existing literature on corporatism, in particular the impact of institutional structures on the behaviour of interest groups. The declining efficacy of corporatism may for instance have to do with the increased independence of the actors within the corporatist structures, as Olson argues (1985:79). However, we think that a more likely explanation is the duration and extent of the crisis, which inhibits the continuation of certain forms of bargaining and leads to zero-sum conflicts instead of the positive-sum conflicts of the 1960s and early 1970s (Keman et al., 1985; Crouch, 1985). It should be noted therefore that the institutional focus, as advocated by Katzenstein, Lindberg and others (e.g. Scharpf, 1984; Goldthorpe, 1984) runs the danger of exaggerating the positive effects of institutional arrangements and appears to underestimate the constraining conditions of other political and economic factors. This concerns not only the bureaucratic style or lack of co-ordinated policy-making as Czada and Lehner suggest, but also more structural constaints such as the growing rate of international economic interdependence (Krasner, 1983; Keohane, 1984).

Yet, it goes almost without saying, that societal actors and the related 'logics' are crucial units of analysis in any study of economic policy. It is vital, however, to ensure that the behaviour of interest groups is always analysed within a context. This means, inter alia, that actions should be explained not only from a rational choice perspective, or an institutional viewpoint, but also in relation to the interaction of these two factors within specific social and political contexts. It will be clear therefore that both the 'logic of accommodation', and the 'logic of collective action' do not constitute sufficient or exclusive categories for explaining the relationship between the choice of a policy strategy and the eventual outcomes. It will also be clear that the behaviour of interest groups is important to an understanding of the relationship between strategy and performance. However, such an understanding does not yet tell us why different strategies may lead to dissimilar economic performances. It is this puzzling relationship that has been closely scrutinized in Part III of this book.

Economic performance: variations in outcomes

The interaction between policy strategies and outcomes is one of the most complex and under-researched relationships in political economy. This is particularly noticeable in the case of post-1973 developments; the endurance and severity of stagflation has surpassed the expectations of even the most pessimistic commentators. As is clear by now, the relationship between strategies and outcomes, or to put it more precisely, the correspondence between policy intentions and economic performance, is on average rather low. This is partly a consequence of processes of policy-formation. The apparent slowness of processes of implementation and the varying impacts of existing policy instruments are additional explanations of the low degree of correspondence in almost every capitalist democracy. Finally, institutional factors of the type discussed in the previous section are also important. However, these are not yet a sufficient explanation for the obvious mismanagement of the economy.

Keman and van Dijk showed that it is precisely those policy strategies which are closest in content to the conventional wisdom of prescriptive macroeconomics that perform the worst. The strategies that appear to be more or less incoherently organized or are characterized by an inactive interventionist stance perform much better, whatever period of time is considered. The explanation of this paradox depends by and large on the context in which the strategies were selected and implemented. The success of a strategy of state intervention is less dependent on 'fine tuning' with appropriate policy instruments. Instead the relevant institutional factors and the contextual variables are the main significant determinants of outcomes. These observations also imply that certain strategies are more able to accommodate diverse goals than other ones. Thus the correspondence between strategies and outcomes does not seem to be determined only by prescriptive economic theory and the adequacy of policy instruments, but also by the knowledge and abilities of the actors involved and the institutional and environmental context. More often than not a strategy of 'muddling through' emerges which contradicts much conventional wisdom. Yet, in actual fact, such an outcome is easier to understand than the other more apprarently efficient outcomes, since this reflects the political reality of a given society, whereas the latter is the product of abstract and often simplistic theory.

Whiteley illustrates the above points succinctly in his discussion of Reaganomics and Thatcherism. He stresses the fact that the development of these strategies was understandable at that particular time, given the specific economic and political situations in the UK and US. These strategies could be pursued, because the relevant actors, including the voting public, were more or less convinced of the fact that something had to be done in the face of evident policy failure. Whether or not monetarism and supply-side economics were theoretically the best alternative strategies available was irrelevant. The relative success of Reaganomics cannot therefore be attributed to its monetarist stance or the adequacy of the instruments employed. On the contrary, according to Whiteley the record of the Reagan administration can best be explained by favourable international economic circumstances, and by the stimulus provided by the huge budget deficits, which were of course contrary to the original policy intentions. A similar point can be made about the Thatcher strategy. The Falklands War and the divided opposition parties were the main reasons why the Thatcherite economic strategy was not punished by the electorate, in spite of the poor economic record.

Another weakness of many analyses is that the effectiveness of policy instruments is very often assumed, and is hardly ever questioned. But this can never be taken for granted in practice. This fact has serious consequences, since strategies formulated in general terms and based on prescriptive macroeconomic theory will seldom be applicable and almost always lead to failure. This appears to be the case with Thatcherism in England, and may explain its poor record.

We conclude therefore that apart from the institutional environment in which policies are shaped, we also need to develop more knowledge of the relationship between domestic and international economic forces that shape the correspondence between policy strategies and economic outcomes in a country.

Andersson and also Keman and van Dijk have tried to capture the complex interaction between internal and external factors. Andersson, for example, states in his analysis that there is no 'Nordic' model of economic policy-making, and that each Scandinavian country has developed a strategy in its own right. This is the result of specific internal social and economic factors, and also certain external economic constraints. His analysis supports our view that general prescriptive models of economic policy either do not work or must be substantially modified before putting them into practice. In other words, although most of the Nordic countries have great ideological and cultural similarities, the relationship between strategy and performance is still quite divergent. These differences do not only show up in cross-sectional terms but also over time. Like Whiteley, Andersson emphasizes the fact that the effectiveness of response to the crisis depended on perceptions of the nature and magnitude of the crisis by both the policy-makers and the public. This fact has also contributed to the weak relationship between policy strategies and economic outcomes in the Scandinavian countries.

In summary we can say that Part III has not only contributed to a deeper understanding of the weak relationship between strategies and outcomes in most advanced capitalist societies, but also it points the direction in which political-economic research should go in the future.

Learning to cope with crisis: further avenues for research
The most conspicuous result of this book is to show that the various strategies of state intervention developed to cope with the crisis are strongly influenced by specific domestic political and social factors, which must also be understood in an historical context. In addition, these strategies can be accounted for in terms of several intervening variables, particularly the 'logics of collective action and accommodation' on the one hand, and international pressures and economic interdependence on the other. Many other factors have also been discussed and this only reinforces our view that strategies of economic policy are multi-faceted in almost all countries under review in this book. This observation is strongly related to the way in which various political and societal actors interact over time, and this in turn depends on the way in which the relationship between state and society is institutionalized. In other words, the structure of the state and society and the relationship between them is important for an understanding of the interaction between political management and economic life. In periods of crisis it can be expected that different forms of state intervention will establish a new societal equilibrium that, more often than not, is jeopardized by the occurrence of market failures. However, strategies for coping with crisis induce divergent rather than convergent economic performances. The reason for this is that policy strategies do not lead to desired outcomes. As we have already noted, it appears that the relationship between strategies and economic outcomes is rather weak. This is not only the result of external factors, but also the way in which the institutions of the state and society are structured. This can prevent certain

actors and agencies from co-operating with each other. Similarly the conflicting and contradictory behaviour of political parties and interest groups may frustrate certain implementation processes. Although by now we know something about these complex and disturbing influences, we do not know enough yet. It is one of the major challenges ahead to gain a deeper knowledge of these processes.

The first avenue for further investigation is to analyse the interactions between the logics of collective action and of accommodation. These are not separate categories, but more or less different sides of the same coin, concerned with the various ways in which actors try to influence decision-making and implementation processes. It is our view that the way the relationship between state and society is structured influences the way in which rational self-interested action can be reconciled with the common goal of economic recovery. A second avenue for further research concerns the extent to which the feasibility of a strategy of state intervention can be improved by way of domestic 'symbolic' politics and the way this relates to policy-making. Little research has been done in this area, but as some of the contributions show (e.g. Esping-Andersen), it could be a fruitful direction for further work.

In general, we surmise three different, but related, aspects of the relationship between strategies of state intervention and economic performance in advanced capitalist society. Firstly, there is the question whether or not a strategy is contingent upon what is both publicly as well as theoretically perceived to be necessary. In many analyses it has been shown that unpopular or contested strategies are in fact less effective than the less disputed ones. This may explain the fact that decisions based on rational arguments often have such a sub-optimal outcome (see also Offe, 1984; Dean, 1984);

Secondly, strategies need to be formulated with an eye to problems of implementation. It appears vital therefore to find out under what conditions the two logics of interest group behaviour discussed previously improve performance. This should help to prevent policy strategies failing because of a fragmented implementation process and inadequate policy instruments.

Finally, we must know more about the extent to which certain instruments make a strategy of state intervention feasible. This is particularly important with respect to the use of fiscal and monetary means to control the economy (see Whiteley in this book). Too often the effectiveness of these instruments is taken for granted. Effectiveness clearly also depends on the extent to which they are accompanied by societal co-operation as well as by favourable external conditions.

All contributions to this book, particularly those in Part III, have addressed these matters, but it is clear that a more detailed analysis is needed in this area. It is particularly important to be able to combine economic insights with political knowledge, and to find out in more detail the options open and the constraints on economic policy-formation in periods of crisis.

The quest for options and constraints in order to cope with crisis must also entail examining the 'environment' in which these strategies originate. Earlier on, we already pointed to the effects of public opinion and the likely influence of ideology of shaping certain strategies and on implementation. These are all aspects of the policy environment. The diagnosis of the causes and solutions to consequences of economic crisis is developed best if we approach it by considering several 'concentric circles' of factors which indirectly influence the relationship between policy strategies and economic outcomes. Only in this way can these complex problems be researched more fully. To this end the following two points need to be examined:

First, the interaction between internal and external factors, which influences the development of strategies and eventually impacts policy-outcomes. This interaction not only explains cross-national variations in economic policies, but also why some lead to positive, and others to negative outcomes. As has become clear in the various contributions, the degree of opennesss of the economy is an important aspect of this interaction; it not only shapes the economic policy-formation, but in turn it also affects the behaviour of the different political and societal actors, which in turn influences performance.

Second, the relationship between social and economic structures and certain specific events, like the oil shocks of the 1970s, is important in explaining outcomes. Thus countries like the UK which has been self-sufficient in oil during the 1980s will react differently to further oil shocks than, say, Germany where the economy is heavily dependent on imported oil. The impact of such structural factors and of shocks has, we think, received too little attention, when this can seriously impair the economic performance of a country.

Though a difficult task to undertake, we need to investigate these 'contextual' or environmental factors more fully. This should help us to understand better why there are so many multi-faceted strategies of state-intervention and why these lead to such divergent outcomes. In fact one may wonder why any degree of correspondence exists between these two. We take the view, therefore, that this book has at least contributed to give a better insight into what we know and do not know. This knowledge shows what remains to be done and in what ways the complex relationships between policy-making, implementation and economic performance could be further analysed. Until then, coping with economic crisis in advanced capitalist society will inevitably be inefficient and will induce much unwanted conflict and will probably fail to provide fundamental solutions.

References

Braun, D. and H. Keman (1986) 'Politikstrategien und Konfliktregulierung in den Niederlanden', *Politische Vierteljahresschrift*, 27(1): 78–100.

Crouch, C. (1985) 'Conditions for Trade Union Wage Restraint', pp. 105–39 in Lindberg and Maier (eds) *The Politics of Inflation and Economic Stagnation*.

Dean, J. (1984) 'Interest Groups and Political X-inefficiency', *European Journal of Political Research*, 12(2): 191–212.

Goldthorpe, J. H. (ed.) (1984) *Order and Conflict in Contemporary Capitalism*. Oxford: Clarendon Press.

Katzenstein, P. J. (1985) *Small States in World Markets. Industrial Policy in Europe*. Ithaca/London: Cornell University Press.

Keman H. and F. L. Lehner (1984) 'Economic Crisis and Political Management: An Introduction to the Problems of Political-Economic Interdependence', *European Journal of Political Research*, 12(2): 121–30.

Keman, H., J. Woldendorp and D. Braun (1985) *Het Neo-Korporatisme als nieuwe politieke strategie krisisbeheersing met beleid en (door) overleg*. Amsterdam: C. T. Press.

Keohane, R. O. (1984) *After Hegemony. Cooperation and Discord in the World Political Economy*. Princeton (New Jersey): Princeton University Press.

Krasner, S. D. (ed.) (1983) *International Regimes*. Ithaca/London: Cornell University Press.

Lindberg, L. N. and C. S. Maier (eds) (1985) *The Politics of Inflation and Economic Stagnation*. Washington (DC): The Brookings Institution.

Niskanen, W. (1986) 'Reagans economische erfenis', *Intermediair*, 22(50): 47–57.

Offe, C. (1984) *Contradictions of the Welfare State*. London: Hutchinson.

Olson, M. (1982) *The Rise and Decline of Nations*. New Haven: Yale University Press.

Olson, M. (1985) 'An Appreciation of the Tests and Criticisms', *Scandinavian Political Studies*, 9(1): 65–80.

Scharpf, F. W. (1984) 'Strategy Choice, Economic Feasibility and Institutional Constraints as Determinants of Full Employment Policy during the Recession', pp. 67–113 in K. Gerlach, W. Peters and W. Sengenberger (eds) *Public Policies to Combat Unemployment in a Period of Economic Stagflation. An International Comparison*. Frankfurt/New York: Campus.

Whiteley, P. (1986) *Political Control of the Macro-Economy. The Political Economy of Public Policy Making*. London/Beverly Hills: Sage.

Index

Notes on contributors

Jan Otto Andersson (1943), Reader in Economics, Abo Akademi Turku, Finland.

Klaus Armingeon (1954), Lecturer in Political Sociology, University of Heidelberg, West Germany.

Roland Czada (1952), Lecturer in Political Science, University of Konstanz, West Germany.

Tibert van Dijk (1958), Assistant, University of Amsterdam, Netherlands.

Gøsta Esping-Andersen (1947), Professor of Political Science, European University Institute, Florence.

Hans Keman (1948), Senior Lecturer in Political Science, University of Leiden, Netherlands.

Franz Lehner (1946), Professor of Political Science, Ruhr-University Bochum, West Germany.

Heikki Paloheimo (1946), Lecturer in Political Science, University of Turku, Finland.

Paul Whiteley (1946), Lecturer in Political Science, University of Bristol, England.